MASTERING MACHINE LEARNING

A Comprehensive Guide to Success

RICK SPAIR

CONTENTS **PAGE**

CONTENTS **PAGE**

CONTENTS **PAGE**

CONTENTS **PAGE**

CONTENTS **PAGE**

Chapter 1: Introduction to Machine Learning

1.1 Understanding the Basics of Machine Learning

Machine Learning (ML) is a branch of artificial intelligence (AI) that focuses on developing algorithms and models capable of learning from data and making predictions or decisions without explicit programming. It enables computers to automatically learn and improve from experience, making it a powerful tool for solving complex problems and extracting valuable insights from large datasets.

To grasp the basics of machine learning, it's essential to understand its core components and terminology:

1.1.1 Data: Machine learning relies on data as its primary input. Data can be in various forms, such as structured data (tables, databases), unstructured data (text, images), or even audio and video recordings. The quality, quantity, and relevance of data directly impact the performance and accuracy of machine learning models.

1.1.2 Features: In machine learning, features are the measurable properties or characteristics of the data. These features are used to represent and describe the patterns and relationships in the data. Selecting informative and relevant features is crucial for effective model training and prediction.

1.1.3 Labels or Targets: In supervised learning, which is one of the main types of machine learning, data is labeled with corresponding outcomes or target variables. These labels serve as the ground truth for training the model to make predictions or classifications on unseen data.

1.1.4 Model: A machine learning model is a mathematical representation of the relationship between the input features and the target variable. It learns patterns, rules, or functions from the training data to make predictions or decisions. The model is typically represented by a set of parameters that are adjusted during the training process.

1.1.5 Training: Training a machine learning model involves presenting it with a labeled dataset and iteratively adjusting its internal parameters to minimize the difference between its predictions and the true labels. This process is accomplished using various optimization algorithms, such as gradient descent.

1.1.6 Testing and Evaluation: After training the model, it is essential to evaluate its performance on unseen data. This is done by measuring its accuracy, precision, recall, F1-score, or other relevant evaluation metrics. Testing the model helps assess its generalization ability and identify potential issues like overfitting (when the model performs well on training data but poorly on new data).

1.1.7 Prediction or Inference: Once a model is trained and evaluated, it can be deployed to make predictions or decisions on new, unseen data. The trained model takes the input features and generates an output, which could be a classification, regression, or any other form of prediction or decision.

1.1.8 Types of Machine Learning: Machine learning can be categorized into different types based on the learning approach and availability of labeled data. The main types are supervised learning, unsupervised learning, and reinforcement learning. Supervised learning involves training models using labeled data, unsupervised learning focuses on discovering patterns and structures in unlabeled data, and reinforcement learning revolves around learning optimal decision-making through interactions with an environment.

Understanding these fundamental concepts and terms sets the stage for diving deeper into the different types of machine learning algorithms, techniques, and applications. In the subsequent chapters, we will explore supervised learning algorithms such as linear regression, logistic regression, decision trees, and more. We will also delve into unsupervised learning techniques like clustering and dimensionality reduction. Furthermore, we will cover reinforcement learning and its applications in areas such as robotics and game playing.

Machine learning has the potential to revolutionize various industries and domains. By harnessing the power of data and algorithms, it enables intelligent decision-making, automation, and the discovery of valuable insights. In the upcoming chapters, we will explore these concepts in greater detail, providing tips, recommendations, and strategies for success in machine learning. Stay tuned for Chapter 2: Data Collection and Preparation, where we will delve into the process of collecting and preparing data for machine learning tasks.

1.2 Importance and Applications of Machine Learning

Machine Learning (ML) has become increasingly important and impactful across various industries and fields. Its ability to analyze vast amounts of data, identify patterns, and make accurate predictions or decisions has led to numerous applications that have transformed businesses and improved people's lives. Let's explore the importance and diverse applications of machine learning.

1.2.1 Importance of Machine Learning

1.2.1.1 Data-driven Insights: In today's data-driven world, organizations collect massive amounts of data. Machine learning algorithms excel at extracting meaningful insights from this data, enabling businesses to make data-driven decisions, identify trends, and gain a competitive edge.

1.2.1.2 Automation and Efficiency: Machine learning automates repetitive and time-consuming tasks, freeing up human resources for more complex and creative endeavors. It improves efficiency by streamlining processes, reducing errors, and optimizing resource allocation.

1.2.1.3 Personalization: Machine learning enables personalized experiences by analyzing individual preferences, behavior, and historical data. This personalization is seen in recommender systems, targeted advertising, personalized medicine, and more.

1.2.1.4 Scalability: Machine learning models can scale effortlessly to process and analyze large datasets, allowing organizations to handle growing data volumes efficiently. This scalability is crucial for managing the exponential growth of data in various industries.

1.2.1.5 Adaptive Systems: Machine learning algorithms can adapt and improve over time by continuously learning from new data. This adaptability makes them well-suited for dynamic environments, where models need to adjust to changing patterns and trends.

1.2.2 Applications of Machine Learning

1.2.2.1 Healthcare: Machine learning has revolutionized healthcare by enabling accurate disease diagnosis, predicting patient outcomes, optimizing treatment plans, and improving drug discovery. ML models analyze medical images, genomic data, electronic health records, and wearable device data to provide personalized healthcare solutions.

1.2.2.2 Finance and Banking: Machine learning is widely used in fraud detection, credit risk assessment, algorithmic trading, and personalized financial recommendations. ML algorithms identify fraudulent transactions, assess creditworthiness, and predict market trends, helping financial institutions make informed decisions.

1.2.2.3 E-commerce and Marketing: Machine learning powers recommender systems in e-commerce platforms, suggesting products based on user preferences and historical data. ML algorithms analyze customer behavior, segment markets, and optimize pricing strategies to improve customer engagement and increase sales.

1.2.2.4 Natural Language Processing (NLP): Machine learning plays a crucial role in NLP applications such as sentiment analysis, language translation, chatbots, and voice recognition. ML models process and understand human language, enabling communication and interaction between humans and machines.

1.2.2.5 Transportation and Logistics: Machine learning is transforming the transportation industry through applications like autonomous vehicles, route optimization, demand forecasting, and predictive maintenance. ML algorithms analyze traffic patterns, predict travel times, and optimize logistics operations.

1.2.2.6 Manufacturing and Industry: Machine learning enhances manufacturing processes by detecting anomalies, optimizing production lines, and predicting equipment failures. ML models analyze sensor data, monitor quality control, and enable predictive maintenance to minimize downtime and improve efficiency.

1.2.2.7 Energy and Utilities: Machine learning helps optimize energy consumption, predict energy demand, and improve grid management. ML algorithms analyze smart meter data, predict equipment failure, and optimize energy distribution, contributing to sustainable energy management.

1.2.2.8 Environmental Monitoring: Machine learning aids in environmental monitoring and conservation efforts. ML models analyze sensor data, satellite imagery, and climate data to predict natural disasters, monitor air and water quality, and protect biodiversity.

These are just a few examples of the wide-ranging applications of machine learning. Virtually every industry can benefit from ML by leveraging the power of data and intelligent algorithms to solve complex problems and drive innovation.

Understanding the importance and applications of machine learning sets the stage for delving into specific ML techniques, algorithms, and strategies. In the upcoming chapters, we will explore supervised and unsupervised learning algorithms, data preprocessing techniques, model evaluation strategies, and practical tips for achieving success in machine learning projects. Stay tuned for Chapter 2: Data Collection and Preparation, where we will dive into the process of collecting and preparing data for machine learning tasks.

1.3 Types of Machine Learning Algorithms

Machine Learning (ML) encompasses a wide range of algorithms and techniques that enable computers to learn from data and make predictions or decisions without explicit programming. These algorithms can be classified into three main types: supervised learning, unsupervised learning, and reinforcement learning. Understanding these types and their associated algorithms is fundamental to developing a strong foundation in machine learning.

1.3.1 Supervised Learning

Supervised learning is the most common and well-studied type of machine learning. It involves training models on labeled data, where the input data is paired with corresponding output labels or target variables. The goal is to learn a mapping function that can accurately predict the labels for new, unseen data. Here are some popular algorithms in supervised learning:

1.3.1.1 Linear Regression: Linear regression is a regression algorithm that models the relationship between the input features and the continuous output variable. It assumes a linear relationship and estimates the coefficients that best fit the data.

1.3.1.2 Logistic Regression: Logistic regression is a classification algorithm used when the target variable is binary or categorical. It models the probability of an instance belonging to a particular class using a logistic function.

1.3.1.3 Decision Trees: Decision trees are versatile algorithms that recursively split the data based on features to create a tree-like model. They are commonly used for classification tasks and can handle both numerical and categorical data.

1.3.1.4 Random Forests: Random forests are an ensemble learning method that combines multiple decision trees. They create a diverse set of trees and aggregate their predictions to make more accurate and robust predictions.

1.3.1.5 Support Vector Machines (SVM): SVM is a powerful algorithm for both classification and regression tasks. It finds a hyperplane that maximally separates the data points of different classes or predicts continuous values.

1.3.1.6 Naive Bayes Classifiers: Naive Bayes classifiers are probabilistic algorithms that use Bayes' theorem with the assumption of feature independence. They are particularly useful for text classification and spam filtering.

1.3.1.7 Neural Networks: Neural networks, specifically deep learning models, have gained immense popularity in recent years. They consist of interconnected layers of artificial neurons and can learn complex patterns and relationships in the data. Convolutional Neural Networks (CNNs) are commonly used for image classification, while Recurrent Neural Networks (RNNs) are suitable for sequential data like language processing.

1.3.2 Unsupervised Learning

Unsupervised learning involves training models on unlabeled data, where the algorithm aims to discover patterns, structures, or relationships within the data. It is particularly useful when the desired outputs or target variables are unknown or not available. Some common algorithms in unsupervised learning include:

1.3.2.1 Clustering Algorithms: Clustering algorithms group similar instances together based on their features. K-means clustering, Hierarchical clustering, and DBSCAN (Density-Based Spatial Clustering of Applications with Noise) are popular clustering algorithms.

1.3.2.2 Dimensionality Reduction Techniques: Dimensionality reduction techniques aim to reduce the number of features while preserving the important information in the data. Principal Component Analysis (PCA) and t-distributed Stochastic Neighbor Embedding (t-SNE) are widely used for dimensionality reduction.

1.3.2.3 Association Rule Learning: Association rule learning discovers interesting relationships or associations between variables in large datasets. The Apriori algorithm and FP-growth algorithm are commonly used for association rule mining, often applied in market basket analysis and recommendation systems.

1.3.3 Reinforcement Learning

Reinforcement learning (RL) is a unique type of machine learning that focuses on training agents to make sequential decisions in an environment to maximize cumulative rewards. The agent interacts with the environment, receives feedback in the form of rewards or penalties, and learns optimal policies through trial and error. Key algorithms in reinforcement learning include:

1.3.3.1 Q-Learning: Q-Learning is a popular model-free reinforcement learning algorithm. It uses a value function called the Q-function to estimate the expected future rewards for taking specific actions in a given state.

1.3.3.2 Deep Q-Networks (DQN): DQN combines deep neural networks with Q-Learning, allowing the agent to handle high-dimensional state spaces. DQN has been successful in achieving superhuman performance in various games.

1.3.3.3 Policy Gradient Methods: Policy gradient methods directly optimize the policy function, which defines the agent's action selection strategy. They use techniques such as the REINFORCE algorithm and Proximal Policy Optimization (PPO) to find optimal policies.

These are just a few examples of the algorithms in each category, and there are many more specialized algorithms and variations within each type. Understanding the characteristics and appropriate use cases of these algorithms is crucial for selecting the right approach for a given machine learning task.

By comprehending the types of machine learning algorithms and their underlying principles, you are equipped to explore their practical implementation and further advance your knowledge in machine learning. In the upcoming chapters, we will delve into topics such as data collection and preparation, exploratory data analysis, model evaluation, deployment, and various advanced machine learning techniques. Stay tuned for Chapter 2: Data Collection and Preparation, where we will discuss strategies for collecting and preparing data for machine learning tasks.

1.4 Setting Up Your Machine Learning Environment

To start your journey in machine learning, it is essential to set up an environment that provides the necessary tools and resources for development. Creating a suitable machine learning environment allows you to efficiently work with data, implement algorithms, and experiment with various techniques. Here are the key components to consider when setting up your machine learning environment:

1.4.1 Programming Language

The choice of programming language is crucial in machine learning. Python is the most widely used language in the ML community due to its simplicity, vast ecosystem of libraries, and strong community support. Python offers powerful libraries such as NumPy, Pandas, and scikit-learn that provide efficient data manipulation, scientific computing, and machine learning capabilities. Other popular languages for machine learning include R and Julia, which have their own strengths and ecosystems.

1.4.2 Integrated Development Environment (IDE)

An Integrated Development Environment (IDE) provides a comprehensive development environment that includes a code editor, debugging tools, and other features to enhance productivity. Some popular IDEs for machine learning include:

PyCharm: PyCharm is a powerful IDE specifically designed for Python development. It offers features like code completion, debugging, and integration with version control systems.

Jupyter Notebook/JupyterLab: Jupyter Notebook is a web-based interactive environment that allows you to create and share documents containing live code, equations, visualizations, and explanatory text. JupyterLab is an enhanced version of Jupyter Notebook with a more flexible and feature-rich interface.

Visual Studio Code: Visual Studio Code is a lightweight, cross-platform IDE that supports various programming languages. It offers an extensive collection of extensions for Python and machine learning.

1.4.3 Libraries and Frameworks

Machine learning libraries and frameworks provide pre-built implementations of algorithms, tools for data preprocessing, model evaluation, and more. They simplify the development process and enable you to focus on the core ML tasks. Here are some essential libraries and frameworks:

scikit-learn: scikit-learn is a popular open-source machine learning library for Python. It provides a comprehensive set of algorithms for classification, regression, clustering, dimensionality reduction, and model evaluation.

TensorFlow: TensorFlow is an open-source framework developed by Google for deep learning. It provides a flexible ecosystem for building and deploying machine learning models, especially neural networks.

PyTorch: PyTorch is another popular deep learning framework known for its dynamic computation graph and ease of use. It has gained significant traction in the research community and offers extensive support for neural network models.

Keras: Keras is a high-level neural network library that runs on top of TensorFlow or other backend frameworks. It provides a user-friendly API for quickly prototyping and building deep learning models.

1.4.4 Data Visualization Tools

Data visualization is crucial for understanding patterns, relationships, and insights in your data. There are several libraries that facilitate data visualization in Python:

Matplotlib: Matplotlib is a powerful plotting library for creating static, animated, and interactive visualizations in Python. It provides a wide range of plots and customization options.

Seaborn: Seaborn is a statistical data visualization library that is built on top of Matplotlib. It simplifies the process of creating attractive and informative statistical graphics.

Plotly: Plotly is a versatile library that enables interactive and web-based visualizations. It offers a wide range of chart types and can be integrated with Jupyter Notebook and web applications.

1.4.5 Hardware Considerations

Depending on the scale and complexity of your machine learning tasks, you may need to consider hardware requirements:

Central Processing Unit (CPU): Most machine learning tasks can be performed on CPUs, but complex deep learning models may benefit from CPUs with multiple cores and high clock speeds.

Graphics Processing Unit (GPU): GPUs excel in parallel processing, making them highly efficient for training deep neural networks. NVIDIA GPUs, particularly those with CUDA support, are commonly used in machine learning.

Tensor Processing Unit (TPU): TPUs are specialized hardware accelerators developed by Google specifically for deep learning workloads. They provide even faster performance for certain types of models.

1.4.6 Additional Tools and Packages

Depending on your specific needs, you might want to explore additional tools and packages that can enhance your machine learning environment:

Version Control Systems: Version control systems like Git are essential for managing code repositories, tracking changes, and collaborating with others.

Data Management: Consider tools like SQL databases or NoSQL databases (e.g., MongoDB) for efficient storage and retrieval of large datasets.

Cloud Services: Cloud platforms such as Amazon Web Services (AWS), Google Cloud Platform (GCP), and Microsoft Azure provide machine learning services, infrastructure, and scalable computing resources.

It is important to note that while setting up your machine learning environment, you should also have a solid understanding of the fundamental mathematical concepts that underpin machine learning, such as linear algebra, calculus, and probability theory.

By creating a well-configured machine learning environment, you can streamline your development process, leverage powerful libraries and frameworks, and effectively work with data to build and train machine learning models. This sets the stage for success in your machine learning endeavors.

In the upcoming chapters, we will dive deeper into the practical aspects of machine learning, including data collection and preparation, exploratory data analysis, model evaluation, deployment, and advanced techniques. Stay tuned for Chapter 2: Data Collection and Preparation, where we will discuss strategies for collecting and preparing data for machine learning tasks.

Chapter 2: Data Collection and Preparation

2.1 Data Collection

Data collection is a crucial step in any machine learning project. The quality, quantity, and relevance of the data directly impact the performance and effectiveness of your machine learning models. Here are some key considerations for data collection:

2.1.1 Identify Data Sources: Determine the sources from which you can obtain relevant data for your machine learning task. These sources may include databases, public repositories, APIs, online platforms, or even data collected through sensors or IoT devices. Ensure that the data you collect aligns with the problem you are trying to solve.

2.1.2 Data Access and Permissions: Understand the legal and ethical considerations surrounding the data you plan to collect. Ensure that you have the necessary permissions, licenses, or agreements to access and use the data for your machine learning project. Respect privacy regulations and take measures to anonymize or protect sensitive information if required.

2.1.3 Data Diversity: Aim for diversity in your data to ensure that your machine learning model can generalize well. Collect data that represents different scenarios, demographics, or variations present in the target population. A diverse dataset helps to avoid biases and improves the robustness of your models.

2.1.4 Data Size: Consider the size of the dataset you need to train your models effectively. In some cases, larger datasets may be required to capture the complexity and variability of the problem. However, it's important to strike a balance between data size and computational resources, as larger datasets may require more processing power and time.

2.1.5 Data Annotation: Depending on the nature of your machine learning task, you may need to annotate or label the data. Annotation involves adding meaningful tags, labels, or annotations to the data to provide ground truth for supervised learning tasks. Manual annotation can be time-consuming and expensive, so explore options for leveraging existing annotated datasets or consider semi-supervised or active learning techniques to optimize the annotation process.

2.2 Data Preprocessing

Once you have collected your data, the next step is to preprocess and prepare it for machine learning. Data preprocessing involves cleaning, transforming, and organizing the data to ensure it is in a suitable format for training and testing machine learning models. Here are some key steps in data preprocessing:

2.2.1 Data Cleaning: Clean the data by handling missing values, outliers, and noisy entries. Missing values can be imputed or dropped depending on the extent of missingness and the impact on the overall dataset. Outliers can be treated by either removing them or transforming them to reduce their influence on the model.

2.2.2 Feature Selection: Select the relevant features or variables that are most informative for your machine learning task. Feature selection helps to reduce dimensionality, remove irrelevant or redundant features, and improve model performance. Techniques such as statistical tests, correlation analysis, or domain knowledge can guide the feature selection process.

2.2.3 Feature Encoding: Encode categorical variables into numerical representations that machine learning algorithms can process. Common encoding techniques include one-hot encoding, label encoding, and ordinal encoding. Choose the appropriate encoding method based on the nature of the categorical variables and the requirements of your machine learning algorithms.

2.2.4 Feature Scaling: Scale the numerical features to a similar range to prevent any particular feature from dominating the learning process. Standardization (mean normalization and variance scaling) and normalization (min-max scaling) are common scaling techniques. The choice of scaling method depends on the characteristics of your data and the requirements of your machine learning algorithms.

2.2.5 Data Transformation: Transform the data to adhere to assumptions of certain algorithms or to make it more amenable to learning. Common transformations include logarithmic transformation, power transformation, and normalization. Data transformation can help address issues like skewness, heteroscedasticity, or non-linearity in the data.

2.2.6 Data Splitting: Split the data into training, validation, and test sets. The training set is used to train the model, the validation set is used to fine-tune hyperparameters and make model selection decisions, and the test set is used to evaluate the final model's performance on unseen data. Ensure that the data split is representative and avoids introducing bias or leakage.

2.3 Data Augmentation

Data augmentation techniques can be employed to artificially increase the diversity and size of your dataset. This is particularly useful when the collected data is limited or imbalanced. Data augmentation involves applying various transformations or perturbations to the existing data to create additional training examples. Some common data augmentation techniques include:

2.3.1 Image Data Augmentation: For image-based tasks, techniques such as rotation, flipping, cropping, scaling, zooming, and adding noise can be applied to augment the dataset.

2.3.2 Text Data Augmentation: Text data augmentation techniques include word replacement, synonym substitution, sentence shuffling, and back-translation, which involves translating the text into another language and then translating it back.

2.3.3 Time-Series Data Augmentation: Time-series data augmentation can involve perturbing the time axis by adding random noise, scaling, shifting, or applying smoothing filters.

Data augmentation enhances the robustness and generalization capabilities of machine learning models by providing additional variations in the training data. It is important to apply data augmentation techniques wisely and avoid creating unrealistic or biased samples.

In this chapter, we have covered the crucial steps of data collection, preprocessing, and augmentation. These steps lay the foundation for building effective machine learning models. In the next chapter, we will dive into exploratory data analysis, which involves gaining insights and understanding the characteristics of the dataset. Stay tuned for Chapter 3: Exploratory Data Analysis, where we will explore techniques for understanding and visualizing the data.

2.1 Identifying Relevant Data Sources

Data collection is a critical step in the machine learning process. To build effective models, it is essential to identify and gather relevant data from various sources. Here are some key considerations for identifying data sources:

2.1.1 Internal Data Sources

Start by exploring internal data sources within your organization. These may include:

Databases: Look for structured data stored in databases within your organization's infrastructure. Examples include customer relationship management (CRM) systems, enterprise resource planning (ERP) systems, and transactional databases.

Log Files: Log files generated by various systems, such as web servers, applications, or sensors, often contain valuable information that can be used for analysis.

Data Warehouses: If your organization has a data warehouse, it can serve as a centralized repository of integrated data from multiple sources. Extracting relevant data from the data warehouse can provide a comprehensive view for analysis.

APIs: Check if your organization provides APIs (Application Programming Interfaces) that expose data for consumption. These APIs can be a valuable source of structured or semi-structured data.

By exploring internal data sources, you can leverage existing data assets and ensure that you have access to the data that is directly related to your organization's domain and operations.

2.1.2 Publicly Available Data Sources

There is a vast amount of publicly available data that can be valuable for machine learning projects. Some popular sources include:

Government Datasets: Governments often release datasets on various topics, ranging from demographics and economic indicators to public health and environmental data. Websites like data.gov (for the United States) and data.gov.uk (for the United Kingdom) provide access to a wide range of public datasets.

Open Data Platforms: Platforms like Kaggle, UCI Machine Learning Repository, and Google Public Datasets provide access to diverse datasets contributed by researchers, organizations, and the data science community.

Social Media APIs: Social media platforms like Twitter, Facebook, and Instagram offer APIs that allow access to public posts, user profiles, and social connections. This data can be valuable for sentiment analysis, social network analysis, and user behavior modeling.

Research Publications: Many research papers make their datasets publicly available for replication and further analysis. Explore repositories like arXiv, IEEE Xplore, or ACM Digital Library to find research datasets related to your domain.

Publicly available data sources provide a rich variety of data across different domains, enabling you to explore and experiment with diverse datasets that may align with your machine learning objectives.

2.1.3 Data Marketplaces and Commercial Data Providers

In some cases, you may need to acquire specialized or proprietary datasets from commercial data providers or data marketplaces. These sources offer access to a wide range of curated datasets with specific domains or industries in mind.

Examples include financial data providers, market research firms, and data aggregators.

It is important to carefully evaluate the terms, licensing agreements, and costs associated with obtaining data from commercial sources. Ensure that the data provider has the necessary permissions and rights to distribute the data.

2.1.4 Data Collection through Surveys or Experiments

In certain scenarios, you may need to collect data through surveys or experiments. This approach allows you to collect data tailored to your specific research question or problem. Surveys can be conducted online or offline, while experiments involve controlled interventions or treatments to gather data on the effect of certain factors.

When collecting data through surveys or experiments, ensure that proper ethical considerations and privacy regulations are followed. Obtain informed consent from participants and ensure the security and confidentiality of the collected data.

2.1.5 Data Scraping and Web APIs

Web scraping involves extracting data from websites and web pages. It can be a valuable method for collecting data that is not available through traditional data sources. However, when scraping data from websites, be mindful of legal and ethical considerations, respect website terms of service, and ensure that you are not violating any intellectual property rights.

Some websites provide APIs that allow programmatic access to their data. These web APIs can be a more reliable and efficient way to access data compared to web scraping. Familiarize yourself with the documentation and terms of the APIs to ensure compliance with usage guidelines.

Remember to validate the quality, reliability, and relevance of the data obtained from any source before proceeding with data preprocessing and model building.

By identifying relevant data sources, you can gather diverse and comprehensive datasets to power your machine learning projects. In the next section, we will discuss data preprocessing techniques, including data cleaning, feature selection, encoding, scaling, and splitting. Stay tuned for Chapter 2.2: Data Preprocessing, where we will explore strategies for preparing your data for machine learning tasks.

2.2 Data Cleaning and Preprocessing Techniques

Data cleaning and preprocessing are essential steps in preparing your data for machine learning tasks. The quality, accuracy, and relevance of the data significantly impact the performance and reliability of your models. In this chapter, we will explore various techniques for data cleaning and preprocessing.

2.2.1 Handling Missing Values

Missing values are a common issue in real-world datasets. It is crucial to address missing values appropriately before training your models. Here are some techniques for handling missing values:

Removal: In cases where the missing values are negligible or occur randomly, you may choose to remove the corresponding instances or features from the dataset. However, this approach should be used cautiously as it may result in a loss of valuable information.

Imputation: Imputation involves filling in the missing values with estimated values. Simple imputation techniques include replacing missing values with the mean, median, mode, or a constant value. More sophisticated imputation methods, such as regression imputation or multiple imputation, can be employed based on the nature of the data and the characteristics of the missing values.

Advanced Techniques: Advanced imputation techniques, such as k-nearest neighbors imputation or matrix completion methods, can be utilized when the missingness has a specific pattern or correlation with other variables in the dataset.

2.2.2 Handling Outliers

Outliers are data points that deviate significantly from the overall pattern of the dataset. They can adversely affect the performance and robustness of machine learning models. Consider the following approaches to handle outliers:

Removal: Outliers can be removed from the dataset if they are the result of errors or noise. However, removing outliers should be done judiciously, considering the impact on the overall data distribution and the potential loss of valuable information.

Transformation: Outliers can be transformed using mathematical operations such as truncation, winsorization, or logarithmic transformation to reduce their impact without completely discarding them.

Capping and Flooring: Outliers can be replaced with a predefined maximum or minimum value to limit their influence on the model. This approach is suitable when the outliers are likely to be caused by measurement errors or data entry mistakes.

Robust Models: Robust machine learning models, such as support vector machines (SVMs) or decision trees, are naturally less sensitive to outliers. Consider using these models if outliers are prevalent in your dataset.

2.2.3 Encoding Categorical Variables

Machine learning algorithms typically work with numerical data. Therefore, categorical variables need to be encoded into numerical representations. Here are some common techniques for encoding categorical variables:

One-Hot Encoding: One-hot encoding creates binary columns for each category in the variable. Each column represents whether a particular category is present or not in the original data.

Label Encoding: Label encoding assigns a unique numeric label to each category in the variable. This encoding is suitable for ordinal variables where the order of categories matters.

Ordinal Encoding: Ordinal encoding maps categories to numerical values based on their order or rank. This encoding preserves the ordinal relationship between the categories.

Target Encoding: Target encoding replaces each category with the mean or median of the target variable within that category. This encoding is useful for classification tasks and can capture the relationship between the categorical variable and the target variable.

The choice of encoding technique depends on the nature of the categorical variable, the number of categories, and the requirements of the machine learning algorithm.

2.2.4 Feature Scaling

Feature scaling ensures that all features in the dataset have a similar scale, preventing any particular feature from dominating the learning process. Here are two common feature scaling techniques:

Standardization: Standardization, also known as Z-score normalization, scales the data to have zero mean and unit variance. It transforms the data such that it follows a standard normal distribution.

Normalization: Normalization, also called min-max scaling, scales the data to a specific range, usually between 0 and 1. It preserves the relative relationships between the data points.

The choice of feature scaling technique depends on the distribution of the features and the requirements of the machine learning algorithm. Some algorithms, such as neural networks, benefit from standardized inputs, while others, like decision trees, are insensitive to feature scaling.

2.2.5 Data Splitting

Before building machine learning models, it is crucial to split the data into training, validation, and test sets. The typical split ratios are 70% for training, 15% for validation, and 15% for testing. The training set is used to train the model, the validation set is used for hyperparameter tuning and model selection, and the test set is used to evaluate the final model's performance on unseen data.

It is important to ensure that the data split is representative, preserves the distribution of the original data, and avoids introducing bias or leakage.

By applying appropriate data cleaning and preprocessing techniques, you can ensure that your data is in a suitable form for machine learning. These techniques set the foundation for building robust and reliable models. In the next chapter, we will explore exploratory data analysis techniques to gain insights and understand the characteristics of the data.

2.3 Dealing with Missing Data

Missing data is a common issue in datasets, and handling it appropriately is crucial for accurate and reliable machine learning models. Missing data can occur for various reasons, such as data entry errors, incomplete surveys, or system malfunctions. In this chapter, we will explore techniques for dealing with missing data effectively.

2.3.1 Understanding Types of Missing Data

Before addressing missing data, it is important to understand the types of missingness:

Missing Completely at Random (MCAR): The missingness is completely random and unrelated to any other variable. In this case, the missing data does not introduce bias into the analysis.

Missing at Random (MAR): The missingness is related to other observed variables but not to the missing values themselves. The missingness can be predicted using the available data.

Missing Not at Random (MNAR): The missingness is related to the missing values themselves, and the missingness cannot be predicted using the available data. MNAR missing data can introduce biases into the analysis.

2.3.2 Deletion Techniques

Deletion techniques involve removing instances or variables with missing data from the dataset. While deletion can be a simple solution, it should be used judiciously, as it can lead to a loss of valuable information. There are three common deletion techniques:

Listwise Deletion (Complete Case Analysis): In this approach, instances with any missing values are removed entirely from the dataset. This can lead to a reduction in the sample size and potential bias if the missingness is related to the outcome.

Pairwise Deletion: Pairwise deletion involves using available data for each analysis separately. Missing values are ignored on a case-by-case basis. This approach maximizes the use of available data but can lead to biased results if the missingness is related to the variables being analyzed.

Variable Deletion: In this technique, variables with a high percentage of missing values are removed from the dataset. This approach can be used when the missingness in a variable is excessive and cannot be reliably imputed.

Deletion techniques should be used with caution, as they can introduce biases and reduce the representativeness of the dataset.

2.3.3 Imputation Techniques

Imputation techniques involve estimating missing values based on the available data. Imputation allows for the retention of valuable information and reduces the potential biases introduced by deletion. Here are some commonly used imputation techniques:

Mean/Median/Mode Imputation: Missing values are replaced with the mean, median, or mode of the respective variable. This technique assumes that the missing values are missing at random (MAR) and does not consider relationships between variables.

Regression Imputation: A regression model is built using the variables with complete data to predict missing values. The predicted values are used to impute the missing values. This technique considers the relationships between variables and is suitable when variables are correlated.

Multiple Imputation: Multiple imputation involves creating multiple plausible imputations to account for the uncertainty in the imputation process. Multiple imputation considers the variability in the missing values and allows for valid statistical inference.

K-Nearest Neighbors (KNN) Imputation: KNN imputation involves finding the K nearest instances based on other variables and using their values to impute missing values. This technique considers the similarity between instances and is suitable for both numerical and categorical variables.

The choice of imputation technique depends on the type of missing data, the characteristics of the dataset, and the assumptions made about the missingness.

2.3.4 Advanced Techniques

Advanced techniques, such as expectation-maximization (EM) algorithms, probabilistic modeling, or data augmentation methods, can be used to address missing data. These techniques involve more complex statistical modeling and are particularly useful when missingness patterns are complex or when the assumptions of simpler techniques are violated.

It is important to consider the assumptions, limitations, and potential biases introduced by the chosen imputation technique. Multiple imputation and sensitivity analyses can be employed to assess the impact of missing data on the results and to quantify the uncertainty introduced by imputation.

By appropriately addressing missing data, you can ensure that your machine learning models are trained on complete and representative datasets. In the next chapter, we will explore exploratory data analysis techniques to gain insights and understand the characteristics of the data. Stay tuned for Chapter 3: Exploratory Data Analysis.

2.4 Handling Imbalanced Data

Imbalanced data occurs when the classes or categories in a classification problem are not represented equally. This can pose challenges for machine learning algorithms, as they tend to be biased towards the majority class, leading to poor performance on the minority class. In this chapter, we will explore techniques for handling imbalanced data effectively.

2.4.1 Understanding Imbalanced Data

Imbalanced data commonly occurs in real-world scenarios, such as fraud detection, disease diagnosis, or rare event prediction. Typically, the majority class is referred to as the negative class (e.g., non-fraudulent transactions), and the minority class is referred to as the positive class (e.g., fraudulent transactions).

It is important to understand the impact of imbalanced data on model training. When the classes are imbalanced, accuracy alone is not a reliable metric for evaluating model performance. Additional metrics such as precision, recall, F1-score, and area under the ROC curve (AUC-ROC) provide a more comprehensive assessment.

2.4.2 Resampling Techniques

Resampling techniques are commonly employed to address imbalanced data. They involve manipulating the training data by either oversampling the minority class or undersampling the majority class to achieve a more balanced distribution. Here are two common resampling techniques:

Oversampling: Oversampling involves increasing the number of instances in the minority class. This can be done by duplicating existing instances or generating synthetic instances using techniques like SMOTE (Synthetic Minority Over-sampling Technique). Oversampling helps the model learn from the minority class and improves its representation.

Undersampling: Undersampling involves reducing the number of instances in the majority class. This can be done randomly or with more sophisticated techniques like Cluster Centroids or Tomek Links. Undersampling helps reduce the dominance of the majority class and ensures a more balanced representation.

Resampling techniques can be applied before model training or within the training process using techniques like Adaptive Synthetic Sampling (ADASYN) or Balanced Bagging. It is important to strike a balance between oversampling and undersampling to avoid overfitting or loss of information.

2.4.3 Class Weighting

Class weighting is a technique that assigns different weights to the classes during model training to account for the class imbalance. By assigning higher weights to the minority class, the model gives more importance to its correct classification. Most machine learning algorithms provide options for incorporating class weights, either directly or through hyperparameter tuning.

2.4.4 Ensemble Methods

Ensemble methods combine multiple models to improve predictive performance. They can be effective in handling imbalanced data by leveraging the diversity of models. Two popular ensemble methods for imbalanced data are:

Bagging: Bagging involves training multiple models on different subsets of the imbalanced data using bootstrapping. The predictions from each model are then aggregated to make the final prediction. Bagging helps reduce the impact of imbalanced classes and improve model generalization.

Boosting: Boosting iteratively trains models, giving more emphasis to misclassified instances. Boosting algorithms like AdaBoost, Gradient Boosting, or XGBoost can be effective in handling imbalanced data by focusing on the minority class during training.

2.4.5 Performance Evaluation Metrics

When evaluating models on imbalanced data, it is important to consider metrics beyond accuracy. Here are some key metrics to assess model performance:

Precision: Precision measures the proportion of correctly predicted positive instances out of all instances predicted as positive. It provides an indication of the model's ability to avoid false positives.

Recall (Sensitivity): Recall measures the proportion of correctly predicted positive instances out of all actual positive instances. It indicates the model's ability to identify the positive instances (sensitivity).

F1-score: The F1-score is the harmonic mean of precision and recall. It provides a balanced measure of a model's performance, considering both precision and recall.

Area Under the ROC Curve (AUC-ROC): AUC-ROC measures the model's ability to rank positive instances higher than negative instances. It provides an overall assessment of the model's performance across various classification thresholds.

It is essential to choose the evaluation metric based on the specific requirements of the problem and the relative importance of false positives and false negatives.

By applying appropriate techniques for handling imbalanced data and selecting suitable evaluation metrics, you can improve the performance and reliability of machine learning models on imbalanced datasets. In the next chapter, we will explore exploratory data analysis techniques to gain insights and understand the characteristics of the data.

Chapter 3: Exploratory Data Analysis (EDA)

3.1 Introduction to Exploratory Data Analysis

Exploratory Data Analysis (EDA) is a crucial step in the machine learning process. It involves examining and understanding the characteristics of the dataset to gain insights, discover patterns, identify anomalies, and make informed decisions about data preprocessing and modeling strategies. In this chapter, we will explore various techniques for conducting EDA effectively.

3.2 Descriptive Statistics

Descriptive statistics provide summary measures that help in understanding the basic properties and distribution of the variables in the dataset. Some commonly used descriptive statistics include:

Measures of Central Tendency: These include the mean, median, and mode, which provide information about the typical or central value of a variable.

Measures of Dispersion: These include the range, variance, and standard deviation, which provide information about the spread or variability of the values in a variable.

Quantiles: Quantiles, such as quartiles or percentiles, divide the data into equal-sized groups and help understand the distribution of the variable.

Descriptive statistics can be calculated for individual variables or across multiple variables to gain a comprehensive understanding of the dataset.

3.3 Data Visualization

Data visualization is a powerful technique for understanding the relationships, patterns, and trends within the dataset. By visualizing the data, you can uncover hidden insights and communicate findings effectively. Here are some common visualization techniques:

Histograms: Histograms provide a graphical representation of the distribution of a variable. They display the frequency or count of values falling within specific intervals or bins.

Box Plots: Box plots summarize the distribution of a variable using quartiles, median, and outliers. They provide information about the central tendency, spread, and skewness of the data.

Scatter Plots: Scatter plots visualize the relationship between two variables. They help identify correlations, clusters, or patterns in the data.

Heatmaps: Heatmaps display data in a grid format, with colors representing the magnitude or intensity of the values. They are useful for visualizing correlations or relationships between multiple variables.

Bar Plots: Bar plots represent categorical variables, displaying the frequency or proportion of each category. They are useful for comparing categories or displaying distributions.

Line Plots: Line plots display the trend or pattern of a variable over time or any ordered variable. They help identify trends, seasonality, or changes over a period.

These are just a few examples of data visualization techniques. Choose the appropriate visualization based on the type of data and the insights you want to extract.

3.4 Correlation Analysis

Correlation analysis helps identify the relationships between variables in the dataset. Understanding correlations can assist in feature selection, identifying important predictors, and avoiding multicollinearity. Here are some techniques for correlation analysis:

Correlation Matrix: A correlation matrix displays the pairwise correlations between variables. It helps identify strong positive or negative relationships between variables.

Scatter Plots: Scatter plots can visually display the correlation between two continuous variables. A positive correlation is indicated by points clustering in an upward direction, while a negative correlation is indicated by points clustering in a downward direction.

Heatmaps: Heatmaps can be used to visualize the correlation matrix, making it easier to identify strong or weak correlations.

Statistical Tests: Statistical tests, such as the Pearson correlation coefficient, Spearman rank correlation, or Kendall's tau, can quantify the strength and significance of correlations between variables.

Correlation analysis provides insights into the dependencies and interactions among variables, which can guide feature engineering and model selection.

3.5 Handling Outliers and Anomalies

Outliers and anomalies are data points that deviate significantly from the overall pattern of the dataset. They can impact the performance and reliability of machine learning models. Here are some techniques for handling outliers and anomalies:

Visual Inspection: Visualize the data using box plots, scatter plots, or histograms to identify potential outliers or anomalies. Visual inspection can help identify extreme values or unusual patterns.

Statistical Methods: Statistical methods, such as z-score, modified z-score, or the interquartile range (IQR), can be used to identify and remove outliers based on their deviation from the mean or median.

Robust Models: Robust models, such as support vector machines (SVMs) or decision trees, are naturally less sensitive to outliers. Consider using these models if outliers are prevalent in your dataset.

Winsorization: Winsorization replaces extreme values with values at a specified percentile. This approach helps limit the impact of outliers without removing them entirely.

It is important to analyze outliers carefully, as they may contain valuable information or represent genuine phenomena. The decision to handle outliers depends on the specific context and problem domain.

3.6 Dimensionality Reduction

Dimensionality reduction techniques help reduce the number of variables while preserving as much information as possible. This is particularly useful when dealing with high-dimensional datasets. Here are two common techniques for dimensionality reduction:

Principal Component Analysis (PCA): PCA transforms the original variables into a new set of orthogonal variables called principal components. These components capture the maximum variance in the data and allow for dimensionality reduction.

Feature Selection: Feature selection techniques identify the most relevant subset of variables based on their importance or contribution to the model's performance. This can be done using statistical tests, feature importance rankings, or regularization methods.

Dimensionality reduction can simplify the modeling process, reduce computational complexity, and help mitigate the curse of dimensionality.

By conducting thorough exploratory data analysis, you gain insights into the dataset's characteristics, identify data quality issues, and make informed decisions about data preprocessing and modeling strategies. In the next chapter, we will delve into the techniques for feature engineering, which involve creating new features from existing ones to improve model performance.

3.1 Visualizing and Summarizing Data

Visualizing and summarizing data is a fundamental step in exploratory data analysis (EDA). It helps in understanding the structure, patterns, and distributions within the dataset. In this chapter, we will explore various techniques for visualizing and summarizing data effectively.

3.1.1 Descriptive Statistics

Descriptive statistics provide summary measures that describe the basic properties and characteristics of the variables in the dataset. Some commonly used descriptive statistics include:

Measures of Central Tendency: These measures, such as the mean, median, and mode, provide insights into the typical or central values of the variables.

Measures of Dispersion: Measures such as the range, variance, and standard deviation indicate the spread or variability of the values in the variables.

Quantiles: Quantiles, such as quartiles or percentiles, divide the data into equal-sized groups and help understand the distribution of the variables.

Descriptive statistics can be calculated for individual variables or across multiple variables to gain a comprehensive understanding of the dataset.

3.1.2 Data Visualization

Data visualization techniques provide visual representations of the data, making it easier to identify patterns, trends, and relationships. Visualizations help in gaining insights and communicating findings effectively. Here are some common visualization techniques:

Histograms: Histograms display the distribution of a numerical variable by grouping data into bins and representing the frequency or count of values in each bin.

Box Plots: Box plots summarize the distribution of a numerical variable using quartiles, median, and outliers. They provide information about the central tendency, spread, and skewness of the data.

Scatter Plots: Scatter plots visualize the relationship between two numerical variables. They help identify correlations, clusters, or patterns in the data.

Bar Plots: Bar plots represent categorical variables by displaying the frequency or proportion of each category. They are useful for comparing categories or displaying distributions.

Line Plots: Line plots display the trend or pattern of a variable over time or any ordered variable. They help identify trends, seasonality, or changes over a period.

Heatmaps: Heatmaps use color-coded cells in a grid format to represent the magnitude or intensity of values. They are useful for visualizing correlations or relationships between multiple variables.

Data visualization techniques should be chosen based on the type of data and the insights you want to extract.

3.1.3 Cross-Tabulation and Pivot Tables

Cross-tabulation, also known as contingency tables, provides a way to analyze the relationship between two categorical variables. It shows the distribution of one variable across the levels of another variable. Cross-tabulation is useful for identifying associations or dependencies between variables.

Pivot tables are similar to cross-tabulation but provide more flexibility. They allow you to summarize and analyze data by grouping and aggregating values based on multiple variables. Pivot tables enable you to calculate various summary statistics, such as means, sums, counts, or percentages, across different dimensions.

3.1.4 Summary Tables

Summary tables provide aggregated information about the dataset. They can include various statistics and metrics such as means, medians, standard deviations, counts, or percentages for different variables or groups of variables. Summary tables offer a concise overview of the data and facilitate comparisons and summarization.

3.1.5 Interactive Visualizations

Interactive visualizations enable users to interact with the data, explore different aspects, and gain deeper insights. These visualizations often allow for zooming, panning, filtering, and highlighting specific data points or subsets. Interactive visualizations can be created using libraries like D3.js, Plotly, or Tableau, which provide dynamic and engaging ways to explore and present data.

By effectively visualizing and summarizing data, you can uncover patterns, detect outliers or anomalies, and gain a better understanding of the dataset. These insights inform subsequent data preprocessing steps and guide the selection of appropriate machine learning models. In the next chapter, we will delve into techniques for feature engineering, which involve creating new features from existing ones to improve model performance.

3.2 Identifying Data Patterns and Correlations

Exploratory Data Analysis (EDA) involves identifying patterns, relationships, and correlations within the dataset. These insights help in understanding the underlying structure of the data and guide subsequent modeling decisions. In this chapter, we will explore techniques for identifying data patterns and correlations effectively.

3.2.1 Scatter Plots

Scatter plots are a powerful visualization tool for identifying relationships between two numerical variables. Each data point is plotted as a point on the graph, with one variable represented on the x-axis and the other on the y-axis. By observing the scatter plot, you can identify the presence of any linear or nonlinear relationships, clusters, or outliers.

If a scatter plot exhibits a clear linear trend, it suggests a strong correlation between the variables. Positive correlation is indicated by points clustering in an upward direction, while negative correlation is indicated by points clustering in a downward direction. Scatter plots help in determining the strength and direction of the relationship between variables.

3.2.2 Correlation Matrix

A correlation matrix provides a comprehensive view of the relationships between multiple numerical variables. It calculates the correlation coefficient between each pair of variables, ranging from -1 to +1. The correlation coefficient measures the strength and direction of the linear relationship between variables.

A positive correlation coefficient close to +1 indicates a strong positive relationship, while a negative correlation coefficient close to -1 indicates a strong negative relationship. A correlation coefficient close to 0 suggests a weak or no relationship. By examining the correlation matrix, you can identify variables that are highly correlated, which can help in feature selection or identifying multicollinearity.

3.2.3 Heatmaps

Heatmaps are a visual representation of a correlation matrix, where each cell is color-coded based on the correlation coefficient. Heatmaps provide a quick and intuitive way to identify patterns and relationships between variables. Strong correlations are represented by cells with intense colors, while weak correlations have lighter colors.

Heatmaps are particularly useful when dealing with a large number of variables. They help in identifying groups of variables that are positively or negatively correlated, which can guide feature selection, dimensionality reduction, or model building.

3.2.4 Line Plots and Time-Series Analysis

Line plots are commonly used to visualize the trend or pattern of a variable over time. They are especially relevant when working with time-series data, where the variable is recorded at different time points. Line plots allow you to observe trends, seasonality, or changes over time.

Time-series analysis techniques, such as decomposition, autocorrelation, or forecasting, can be applied to identify patterns and dependencies within the time-series data. These techniques help in understanding the underlying structure of the data, detecting anomalies or outliers, and making predictions.

3.2.5 Cluster Analysis

Cluster analysis is a technique used to group similar data points together based on their characteristics or features. It helps identify natural clusters or subgroups within the data. There are various clustering algorithms, such as K-means, hierarchical clustering, or DBSCAN, which can be applied depending on the nature of the data and the desired outcomes.

Cluster analysis is particularly useful when dealing with unlabeled data or when exploring similarities and differences between groups. It can assist in identifying customer segments, market segments, or patterns in unstructured data.

3.2.6 Association Rules

Association rules mining is a technique used to identify interesting relationships or associations between categorical variables. It aims to discover patterns such as "if X, then Y" or "X implies Y." Association rules can reveal interesting insights, such as items frequently purchased together in market basket analysis or symptoms associated with a particular disease.

Apriori and FP-Growth are popular algorithms used for mining association rules. They help in identifying strong associations based on measures like support, confidence, or lift.

By applying these techniques for identifying data patterns and correlations, you can gain valuable insights into the relationships and dependencies within the dataset. These insights guide feature engineering, model selection, and subsequent steps in the machine learning pipeline. In the next chapter, we will delve into techniques for feature engineering, which involve creating new features from existing ones to improve model performance.

3.3 Feature Engineering and Selection

Feature engineering is a crucial step in the machine learning pipeline. It involves transforming and creating new features from the existing ones to improve the performance of machine learning models. Feature selection, on the other hand, aims to identify the most relevant subset of features that contribute the most to the predictive power of the model. In this chapter, we will explore techniques for feature engineering and selection.

3.3.1 Feature Engineering Techniques

Feature engineering involves transforming the raw data into a format that is more suitable for machine learning algorithms. Here are some common techniques for feature engineering:

Polynomial Features: Polynomial features involve creating new features by taking combinations of the existing features with higher degrees. This can capture nonlinear relationships between variables.

Interaction Features: Interaction features are created by combining two or more features to capture the joint effects or interactions between them. This can help in representing complex relationships.

Encoding Categorical Variables: Categorical variables need to be encoded into numerical representations. Techniques like one-hot encoding, label encoding, or target encoding can be used to convert categorical variables into numeric form.

Scaling and Normalization: Scaling or normalizing features ensures that all features have a similar scale. Common scaling techniques include standardization (mean 0, standard deviation 1) or min-max scaling (scaling to a specific range, often 0 to 1).

Time-based Features: For time-series data, creating features based on time can be beneficial. These features can include day of the week, month, season, or time lags (e.g., lagged values of a variable).

Domain-Specific Features: Domain knowledge can be leveraged to create features that are relevant to the problem at hand. This involves understanding the domain and identifying features that capture important characteristics.

These are just a few examples of feature engineering techniques. The choice of technique depends on the nature of the data, the problem domain, and the specific requirements of the machine learning task.

3.3.2 Feature Selection Techniques

Feature selection aims to identify the most informative and relevant subset of features for building machine learning models. It helps in reducing the dimensionality of the data, improving model interpretability, and reducing overfitting. Here are some common feature selection techniques:

Univariate Feature Selection: Univariate feature selection involves selecting features based on their individual relationship with the target variable. Statistical tests like chi-square, ANOVA, or correlation coefficients can be used to determine the significance of each feature.

Recursive Feature Elimination (RFE): RFE recursively selects features by training the model iteratively and eliminating the least important features based on their coefficients or feature importance scores.

L1 Regularization (Lasso): L1 regularization encourages sparsity by penalizing the absolute values of the feature coefficients. This leads to automatic feature selection as irrelevant features are assigned zero coefficients.

Tree-Based Feature Importance: Tree-based models, such as decision trees or random forests, can provide feature importance scores based on the reduction in impurity achieved by each feature. Features with higher importance scores are considered more relevant.

Principal Component Analysis (PCA): PCA is a dimensionality reduction technique that transforms the features into a lower-dimensional space while preserving as much information as possible. The transformed components can be used as features for modeling.

The choice of feature selection technique depends on factors such as the dataset size, the number of features, the nature of the problem, and the interpretability requirements.

3.3.3 Iterative Process

Feature engineering and selection are often an iterative process. It involves experimenting with different transformations, creating new features, selecting subsets of features, and evaluating the impact on model performance. It is important to assess the performance of the models at each step to ensure that the engineered features or selected subset of features improve the model's predictive power.

By applying appropriate feature engineering techniques and selecting relevant features, you can improve the performance and interpretability of machine learning models. In the next chapter, we will explore techniques for model selection and evaluation, which involve choosing the best model architecture and assessing its performance.

3.4 Dimensionality Reduction Techniques

Dimensionality reduction is a crucial step in data preprocessing that aims to reduce the number of features while preserving the most important information. High-dimensional datasets can be challenging to analyze and can lead to computational inefficiency and overfitting. In this chapter, we will explore techniques for dimensionality reduction.

3.4.1 Principal Component Analysis (PCA)

Principal Component Analysis (PCA) is a popular linear dimensionality reduction technique. It identifies the directions, called principal components, along which the data varies the most. The first principal component captures the maximum variance in the data, and subsequent components capture the remaining variance in orthogonal directions.

PCA transforms the original features into a new set of uncorrelated features, called principal components. These components are linear combinations of the original features. By selecting a subset of the principal components that capture most of the variance, you can effectively reduce the dimensionality of the dataset.

PCA is particularly useful when dealing with highly correlated features and when the data lies in a lower-dimensional subspace. It is widely used in various domains, including image processing, genetics, and text analysis.

3.4.2 t-SNE (t-Distributed Stochastic Neighbor Embedding)

t-SNE is a nonlinear dimensionality reduction technique that is particularly effective in visualizing high-dimensional data. It maps the high-dimensional data points to a lower-dimensional space while preserving the local relationships between them.

t-SNE works by modeling the similarity between data points in both the high-dimensional and low-dimensional spaces. It aims to place similar data points closer together in the low-dimensional space while pushing dissimilar data points farther apart. This makes t-SNE useful for visualizing clusters or patterns in the data.

t-SNE is commonly used in tasks such as visualizing word embeddings, analyzing gene expression data, or exploring high-dimensional datasets with complex structures.

3.4.3 Linear Discriminant Analysis (LDA)

Linear Discriminant Analysis (LDA) is a dimensionality reduction technique that is primarily used for classification tasks. LDA aims to find a linear projection of the data that maximizes the separation between different classes while minimizing the within-class scatter.

LDA identifies the directions in the feature space that maximize the ratio of between-class variance to within-class variance. It transforms the data into a lower-dimensional space, where the classes are well-separated.

LDA is particularly useful when the goal is to reduce dimensionality while preserving class separability. It can improve classification performance by highlighting the most discriminative features.

3.4.4 Autoencoders

Autoencoders are a type of neural network architecture used for unsupervised learning and dimensionality reduction. They consist of an encoder network that compresses the input data into a lower-dimensional representation (latent space) and a decoder network that reconstructs the original data from the compressed representation.

During training, autoencoders learn to capture the essential features of the data in the latent space. The bottleneck layer in the middle of the network forces the network to learn a compact representation of the input.

Autoencoders can be used for dimensionality reduction by discarding the decoder part of the network and using only the encoder to obtain the reduced-dimensional representation of the data. They are especially useful for nonlinear dimensionality reduction and can capture complex relationships in the data.

3.4.5 Considerations and Trade-offs

When applying dimensionality reduction techniques, it is important to consider the trade-offs involved. Here are some considerations:

Information Loss: Dimensionality reduction inherently involves losing some information from the original data. The challenge is to strike a balance between reducing dimensionality and preserving the most important information for the specific task.

Interpretability: Some dimensionality reduction techniques, such as PCA, provide interpretable components. Others, like t-SNE, focus on visualizing patterns without explicit interpretability. Consider the requirements of your specific task when choosing a technique.

Computational Complexity: Some dimensionality reduction techniques, such as t-SNE or autoencoders, can be computationally expensive, especially for large datasets. Consider the scalability of the technique to your specific dataset size and computational resources.

By applying dimensionality reduction techniques, you can reduce the computational burden, improve model performance, and gain insights from high-dimensional data. In the next chapter, we will delve into techniques for model selection and evaluation, which involve choosing the best model architecture and assessing its performance. Stay tuned for Chapter 4: Model Selection and Evaluation.

Chapter 4: Supervised Learning Algorithms

4.1 Introduction to Supervised Learning

Supervised learning is a popular category of machine learning algorithms that learn from labeled data to make predictions or classifications. In this chapter, we will explore various supervised learning algorithms, their characteristics, and how to choose the right algorithm for your task.

4.2 Linear Regression

Linear regression is a simple yet powerful algorithm used for predicting continuous numeric values. It models the relationship between independent variables (features) and a dependent variable (target) by fitting a linear equation. The algorithm learns the coefficients of the equation to minimize the difference between predicted and actual values.

Linear regression assumes a linear relationship between the features and the target variable. It is widely used for tasks such as predicting house prices, stock market trends, or sales forecasting.

4.3 Logistic Regression

Logistic regression is a binary classification algorithm used when the target variable is categorical with two classes. It models the relationship between the features and the probability of the target belonging to a particular class using the logistic function.

Logistic regression is interpretable and provides the probability of an instance belonging to a class. It is commonly used in applications such as spam detection, disease diagnosis, or churn prediction.

4.4 Decision Trees

Decision trees are versatile algorithms that can handle both regression and classification tasks. They partition the feature space into regions based on the values of the features and make predictions based on the majority class or average value within each region.

Decision trees are intuitive and can capture non-linear relationships between features and the target variable. However, they can suffer from overfitting. Techniques like pruning, ensemble methods (discussed later), or random forests can mitigate this issue.

4.5 Naive Bayes

Naive Bayes is a probabilistic classification algorithm based on Bayes' theorem. It assumes that features are conditionally independent given the class label, which simplifies the calculation of probabilities.

Naive Bayes is computationally efficient and performs well in high-dimensional datasets. It is commonly used in text classification, sentiment analysis, or spam filtering.

4.6 Support Vector Machines (SVM)

Support Vector Machines (SVM) are powerful algorithms used for both classification and regression tasks. SVM finds a hyperplane that maximally separates the data points of different classes while maintaining the largest margin.

SVM can handle linear and non-linear relationships by using kernel functions. It is effective in tasks such as image recognition, text categorization, or gene expression analysis.

4.7 Random Forests

Random Forests are ensemble methods that combine multiple decision trees to make predictions. Each tree in the forest is trained on a random subset of features and the predictions are aggregated through voting (classification) or averaging (regression).

Random Forests are robust, handle high-dimensional data, and mitigate overfitting. They are widely used for tasks such as credit scoring, fraud detection, or image classification.

4.8 Gradient Boosting

Gradient Boosting is an ensemble method that combines weak learners (usually decision trees) in a sequential manner. Each subsequent learner is trained to correct the mistakes made by the previous learner.

Gradient Boosting is highly effective and has gained popularity in machine learning competitions. Algorithms like XGBoost, LightGBM, or AdaBoost are popular implementations of gradient boosting.

4.9 Neural Networks

Neural Networks are versatile algorithms inspired by the structure and functioning of the human brain. They consist of interconnected nodes (neurons) organized in layers. Each neuron applies an activation function to its inputs and passes the output to the next layer.

Neural Networks can handle complex relationships and learn hierarchical representations. Deep learning, a subfield of neural networks, has achieved remarkable success in image recognition, natural language processing, and speech recognition.

4.10 Choosing the Right Algorithm

Choosing the right algorithm depends on several factors:

Nature of the problem: Determine whether the problem requires regression, binary classification, or multi-class classification.

Dataset characteristics: Consider the size of the dataset, the number of features, and the presence of non-linear relationships.

Interpretability: Some algorithms provide interpretable models, while others prioritize performance.

Computational resources: Complex algorithms like neural networks or ensemble methods may require more computational resources.

Algorithm performance: Experiment with different algorithms and evaluate their performance using appropriate metrics and cross-validation techniques.

By selecting the appropriate supervised learning algorithm, you can build models that accurately predict or classify new instances. In the next chapter, we will explore techniques for model evaluation and fine-tuning to optimize the performance of machine learning models.

4.1 Linear Regression and Logistic Regression

Linear regression and logistic regression are fundamental supervised learning algorithms used for regression and binary classification tasks, respectively. In this chapter, we will explore the principles, characteristics, and applications of linear regression and logistic regression.

4.1.1 Linear Regression

Linear regression is a predictive modeling technique used for estimating the relationship between a dependent variable (target) and one or more independent variables (features). It assumes a linear relationship between the features and the target variable, following a linear equation:

$$y = \beta_0 + \beta_1 x_1 + \beta_2 x_2 + \ldots + \beta_p x_p + \varepsilon$$

where:

y is the target variable

β_0 is the y-intercept (bias term)

$\beta_1, \beta_2, \ldots, \beta_p$ are the coefficients associated with the features $x_1, x_2, \ldots, x_p$

$x_1, x_2, \ldots, x_p$ are the independent variables (features)

ε represents the error term

The goal of linear regression is to estimate the coefficients ($\beta_0, \beta_1, \beta_2, \ldots, \beta_p$) that minimize the sum of squared differences between the predicted values and the actual values. This is typically achieved using optimization techniques like Ordinary Least Squares (OLS).

Linear regression is widely used for tasks such as predicting housing prices, stock market analysis, or sales forecasting. It provides interpretable results, as the coefficients represent the impact of each feature on the target variable.

4.1.2 Logistic Regression

Logistic regression is a classification algorithm used for binary classification tasks, where the target variable has two classes (e.g., yes/no, true/false, 0/1). Unlike linear regression, logistic regression models the probability of the target variable belonging to a particular class.

Logistic regression uses the logistic function (sigmoid function) to map the linear combination of the features to a value between 0 and 1. The logistic function transforms the linear equation into the following form:

$$p = 1 / (1 + e^{(-z)})$$

where:

p is the probability of the target variable being in class 1

z is the linear combination of the features and their corresponding coefficients

The coefficients in logistic regression represent the influence of each feature on the log-odds of the target variable. The log-odds can then be converted to probabilities using the logistic function.

Logistic regression is commonly used for tasks such as spam detection, disease diagnosis, or customer churn prediction. It provides interpretable results in terms of the impact of each feature on the probability of belonging to a particular class.

4.1.3 Similarities and Differences

Linear regression and logistic regression have several similarities and differences:

Similarities:

Both are supervised learning algorithms used for modeling the relationship between features and a target variable.

They both involve estimating coefficients that represent the impact of features on the target variable.

The coefficients can be used to interpret the influence of features on the target variable.

Differences:

Linear regression is used for regression tasks, while logistic regression is used for binary classification tasks.

Linear regression models the relationship between features and a continuous target variable, whereas logistic regression models the probability of the target variable belonging to a specific class.

Linear regression uses the least squares method to estimate the coefficients, while logistic regression uses maximum likelihood estimation.

4.1.4 Model Evaluation and Fine-Tuning

To evaluate the performance of linear regression and logistic regression models, various evaluation metrics can be used, such as Mean Squared Error (MSE) for linear regression and metrics like accuracy, precision, recall, and F1-score for logistic regression. Cross-validation techniques can help assess the model's generalization performance.

Fine-tuning the models involves selecting the most appropriate features, addressing multicollinearity, handling outliers, and applying regularization techniques like Ridge regression or Lasso regression to prevent overfitting.

By understanding the principles and characteristics of linear regression and logistic regression, you can effectively apply these algorithms to regression and binary classification tasks. In the next chapter, we will explore additional supervised learning algorithms and their applications.

4.2 Decision Trees and Random Forests

Decision trees and random forests are powerful supervised learning algorithms used for both regression and classification tasks. In this chapter, we will explore the principles, characteristics, and applications of decision trees and random forests.

4.2.1 Decision Trees

Decision trees are versatile algorithms that create a flowchart-like structure to make predictions or classifications. They partition the feature space into regions based on the values of the features and make decisions at each internal node based on the feature conditions.

The process of building a decision tree involves selecting the best split point at each node to maximize the information gain or minimize the impurity measure (e.g., Gini impurity or entropy). This splitting process continues recursively until a stopping criterion is met, such as reaching a maximum depth, having a minimum number of samples in a leaf node, or other predefined conditions.

Decision trees are interpretable and can capture non-linear relationships between features and the target variable. However, they can suffer from overfitting when they become too complex and highly adapted to the training data.

4.2.2 Random Forests

Random forests are ensemble methods that combine multiple decision trees to make predictions or classifications. Each tree in the forest is trained on a random subset of the data (bootstrap samples) and a random subset of the features. The predictions from all the trees are aggregated through voting (classification) or averaging (regression).

The randomization in random forests helps in reducing overfitting and improving generalization. The ensemble nature of random forests provides robustness and stability by reducing the impact of individual trees' biases and errors.

Random forests can handle high-dimensional data, capture complex relationships, and are less sensitive to outliers compared to individual decision trees. They are widely used in various domains, including finance, healthcare, image classification, and anomaly detection.

4.2.3 Feature Importance and Interpretability

Decision trees and random forests provide feature importance measures, indicating the relative importance of each feature in making predictions or classifications. These measures can be derived from the information gain, Gini importance, or permutation importance, among others.

The feature importance can help in feature selection, identifying the most informative features, and gaining insights into the relationships between features and the target variable. It can also contribute to model interpretability by explaining the key factors influencing the predictions or classifications.

4.2.4 Hyperparameter Tuning

Both decision trees and random forests have hyperparameters that control their behavior and performance. Some important hyperparameters include the maximum depth of the tree, the minimum number of samples required to split a node, the number of trees in the forest, and the number of features considered at each split.

Hyperparameter tuning involves selecting the optimal values for these hyperparameters to achieve the best model performance. Techniques like grid search, random search, or Bayesian optimization can be used for hyperparameter optimization.

4.2.5 Advantages and Considerations

Advantages of decision trees and random forests include:

Interpretable: Decision trees provide clear decision rules, while random forests offer feature importance measures.

Nonlinear Relationships: Decision trees and random forests can capture complex nonlinear relationships between features and the target variable.

Robustness: Random forests are less sensitive to outliers and noisy data compared to individual decision trees.

Considerations when using decision trees and random forests:

Overfitting: Decision trees can overfit the training data, while random forests mitigate this issue through ensemble learning.

Computational Complexity: Random forests can be computationally expensive, especially with a large number of trees or features.

Hyperparameter Tuning: Careful selection and tuning of hyperparameters are important for optimal model performance.

4.2.6 Applications

Decision trees and random forests are applied in various domains and tasks, including:

Predictive Maintenance: Identifying potential equipment failures based on sensor data and maintenance records.

Credit Scoring: Assessing creditworthiness of borrowers based on financial and demographic features.

Disease Diagnosis: Predicting the presence of a disease based on symptoms, medical history, and diagnostic test results.

Object Recognition: Classifying objects in images based on their visual features.

By understanding the principles and characteristics of decision trees and random forests, you can effectively apply these algorithms to regression and classification tasks. In the next chapter, we will explore additional supervised learning algorithms and their applications.

4.3 Support Vector Machines (SVM)

Support Vector Machines (SVM) is a powerful supervised learning algorithm used for both classification and regression tasks. In this chapter, we will explore the principles, characteristics, and applications of Support Vector Machines.

4.3.1 Introduction to Support Vector Machines

Support Vector Machines (SVM) is a binary classification algorithm that aims to find an optimal hyperplane that separates data points of different classes while maximizing the margin between the classes. The hyperplane is defined by a subset of training instances called support vectors.

The key idea behind SVM is to transform the input data into a higher-dimensional feature space, where the data can be linearly separable. SVM seeks to find the hyperplane that maximizes the margin between the support vectors of different classes, as illustrated in the case of linearly separable data.

If the data is not linearly separable, SVM employs the kernel trick, which allows it to implicitly map the data into a higher-dimensional space without explicitly calculating the transformed features. This allows SVM to handle non-linear relationships between the features and the target variable.

4.3.2 SVM for Classification

In SVM classification, the goal is to find the hyperplane that separates the data points of different classes while maximizing the margin. The margin is the distance between the hyperplane and the nearest data points of each class. SVM aims to find the hyperplane that has the largest margin, which improves the generalization ability of the model.

SVM uses a loss function called hinge loss to encourage the model to assign the correct class label to each data point. The optimization problem is formulated as a convex optimization problem, which can be solved efficiently using optimization techniques.

SVM has a parameter called the regularization parameter (C), which controls the trade-off between maximizing the margin and minimizing the classification error. A higher value of C emphasizes accurate classification of the training data, potentially leading to overfitting, while a lower value of C allows for a wider margin at the expense of potential misclassifications.

4.3.3 SVM for Regression

SVM can also be used for regression tasks, known as Support Vector Regression (SVR). In SVR, the goal is to find a hyperplane that best fits the data while allowing a specified level of tolerance (ε) for deviations from the hyperplane.

SVR seeks to find a hyperplane that passes through a region called the epsilon-insensitive tube, which contains a subset of training instances. The tube defines an interval around the predicted values within which no penalty is incurred. Data points outside this interval contribute to the loss function and are considered errors.

Similar to SVM classification, SVR uses the kernel trick to handle non-linear relationships between the features and the target variable.

4.3.4 Advantages and Considerations

Advantages of Support Vector Machines include:

Versatility: SVM can handle both linear and non-linear relationships between features and the target variable using the kernel trick.

Robustness to Outliers: SVM is less sensitive to outliers due to the focus on support vectors, which are the most relevant data points.

Margin Maximization: SVM aims to maximize the margin between different classes, which can improve the generalization ability of the model.

Considerations when using Support Vector Machines:

Parameter Tuning: SVM has parameters such as C (regularization parameter) and the choice of kernel function. Proper tuning of these parameters is crucial for optimal performance.

Computational Complexity: SVM can be computationally expensive, especially for large datasets or non-linear kernels.

4.4 Naive Bayes Classifiers

Naive Bayes classifiers are simple yet powerful probabilistic classifiers widely used in machine learning for both binary and multi-class classification tasks. In this chapter, we will explore the principles, characteristics, and applications of Naive Bayes classifiers.

4.4.1 Introduction to Naive Bayes Classifiers

Naive Bayes classifiers are based on Bayes' theorem, which describes the probability of an event based on prior knowledge. The "naive" assumption in Naive Bayes is that features are conditionally independent given the class label. Although this assumption may not hold in real-world scenarios, Naive Bayes classifiers often perform well and are computationally efficient.

The algorithm calculates the posterior probability of each class given the features and selects the class with the highest probability as the predicted class label. Naive Bayes classifiers estimate the prior probabilities of each class and the likelihood probabilities of features given each class based on the training data.

4.4.2 Types of Naive Bayes Classifiers

There are several types of Naive Bayes classifiers, depending on the probability distribution assumption of the features:

Gaussian Naive Bayes: Assumes that features follow a Gaussian (normal) distribution. It is suitable for continuous numerical features.

Multinomial Naive Bayes: Assumes that features follow a multinomial distribution. It is commonly used for text classification tasks, where features represent word frequencies.

Bernoulli Naive Bayes: Assumes that features are binary variables (0 or 1). It is suitable for binary classification tasks, such as spam detection.

Each type of Naive Bayes classifier makes different assumptions about the underlying distribution of the features, allowing for flexibility in handling different types of data.

4.4.3 Advantages and Considerations

Advantages of Naive Bayes classifiers include:

Simplicity and Efficiency: Naive Bayes classifiers are computationally efficient and have low memory requirements. They are particularly suitable for large datasets.

Scalability: Naive Bayes classifiers can handle high-dimensional data with a large number of features.

Interpretable and Explainable: The probabilistic nature of Naive Bayes allows for easy interpretation of the results and understanding of the model's decision-making process.

Considerations when using Naive Bayes classifiers:

Independence Assumption: The assumption of feature independence may not hold in all real-world scenarios. However, Naive Bayes classifiers can still perform well even with this simplifying assumption.

Sensitivity to Feature Correlation: Naive Bayes classifiers may not perform well when features are highly correlated, as the assumption of independence is violated.

Lack of Continuous Feature Handling: Gaussian Naive Bayes assumes that features follow a Gaussian distribution, which may not be suitable for all types of continuous data.

4.4.4 Applications

Naive Bayes classifiers are widely used in various domains and applications, including:

Text Classification: Naive Bayes classifiers are commonly used for sentiment analysis, spam detection, document categorization, and language identification tasks.

Recommendation Systems: Naive Bayes classifiers can be used in collaborative filtering-based recommendation systems to predict user preferences or item recommendations.

Medical Diagnosis: Naive Bayes classifiers are applied in medical diagnosis, where the features represent symptoms or medical test results.

Fraud Detection: Naive Bayes classifiers can be used to detect fraudulent transactions or activities based on various features.

By understanding the principles and characteristics of Naive Bayes classifiers, you can effectively apply these algorithms to classification tasks. In the next chapter, we will explore additional supervised learning algorithms and their applications.

4.5 Neural Networks and Deep Learning

Neural networks and deep learning are powerful and versatile supervised learning algorithms that have revolutionized many fields of artificial intelligence. In this chapter, we will explore the principles, characteristics, and applications of neural networks and deep learning.

4.5.1 Introduction to Neural Networks

Neural networks are inspired by the structure and functioning of the human brain. They consist of interconnected nodes, called neurons, organized in layers. Each neuron receives inputs, applies an activation function, and passes the output to the next layer.

Neural networks learn from data by adjusting the weights and biases associated with the connections between neurons. The learning process, known as training, involves feeding the network with input data and comparing the predicted outputs with the true outputs to calculate an error. The error is then used to update the weights and biases through a process called backpropagation.

The number of layers and neurons in a neural network determine its architecture. Shallow neural networks with one or two hidden layers are suitable for simpler tasks, while deep neural networks with multiple hidden layers excel in handling complex patterns and relationships.

4.5.2 Deep Learning and Deep Neural Networks

Deep learning refers to the use of deep neural networks, typically with several hidden layers, to learn intricate representations of data. Deep learning algorithms have been instrumental in achieving state-of-the-art performance in various domains, including computer vision, natural language processing, and speech recognition.

Deep neural networks can automatically extract high-level features from raw data, enabling the network to learn hierarchical representations. This hierarchical representation learning allows deep learning models to capture complex patterns and relationships, making them highly effective in handling large and unstructured datasets.

Popular deep learning architectures include Convolutional Neural Networks (CNNs) for image analysis, Recurrent Neural Networks (RNNs) for sequential data, and Transformer models for natural language processing tasks.

4.5.3 Advantages and Considerations

Advantages of neural networks and deep learning include:

Flexibility: Neural networks can model complex and non-linear relationships between features and the target variable.

Representation Learning: Deep learning enables automatic feature extraction and hierarchical representation learning.

Performance: Deep learning has achieved state-of-the-art performance in various domains, surpassing traditional machine learning algorithms.

Considerations when using neural networks and deep learning:

Computational Complexity: Training deep neural networks can be computationally expensive, requiring powerful hardware and longer training times.

Large Data Requirements: Deep learning models often require large amounts of data to learn meaningful representations and generalize well.

Hyperparameter Tuning: Choosing the appropriate network architecture, activation functions, and regularization techniques is crucial for achieving optimal performance.

4.5.4 Applications

Neural networks and deep learning have demonstrated success in numerous applications, including:

Image Classification: Convolutional Neural Networks (CNNs) excel at image recognition, object detection, and semantic segmentation tasks.

Natural Language Processing: Recurrent Neural Networks (RNNs) and Transformer models are used for machine translation, sentiment analysis, and text generation.

Speech Recognition: Deep learning models such as Recurrent Neural Networks (RNNs) and Long Short-Term Memory (LSTM) networks have greatly improved speech recognition systems.

Autonomous Vehicles: Deep learning models are used for perception tasks in self-driving cars, including object detection and lane detection.

By understanding the principles and characteristics of neural networks and deep learning, you can harness the power of these algorithms for various supervised learning tasks. In the next chapter, we will explore additional supervised learning algorithms and their applications.

Chapter 5: Unsupervised Learning Algorithms

5.1 Introduction to Unsupervised Learning

Unsupervised learning is a branch of machine learning that deals with analyzing and discovering patterns in unlabeled data. Unlike supervised learning, unsupervised learning algorithms work with input data without any corresponding output labels. In this chapter, we will explore the principles, characteristics, and applications of unsupervised learning algorithms.

5.2 Clustering

Clustering is a fundamental unsupervised learning technique that involves grouping similar data points together based on their inherent patterns or similarities. The goal of clustering is to discover natural clusters or subgroups within the data without prior knowledge of their labels.

There are several clustering algorithms, including:

K-Means Clustering: It partitions the data into K clusters by minimizing the within-cluster sum of squared distances to the cluster centroids.

Hierarchical Clustering: It builds a tree-like structure (dendrogram) to represent the relationships between data points and iteratively merges or splits clusters based on a distance or linkage criterion.

Density-Based Spatial Clustering of Applications with Noise (DBSCAN): It groups dense regions of data points and identifies outliers as noise based on density connectivity.

Clustering algorithms find applications in customer segmentation, image segmentation, anomaly detection, and social network analysis.

5.3 Dimensionality Reduction

Dimensionality reduction techniques aim to reduce the number of features in a dataset while preserving its essential information. By reducing the dimensionality, these techniques help in visualizing high-dimensional data, mitigating the curse of dimensionality, and improving the performance of machine learning algorithms.

Some commonly used dimensionality reduction techniques include:

Principal Component Analysis (PCA): It transforms the features into a lower-dimensional space by finding orthogonal components that capture the maximum variance in the data.

t-Distributed Stochastic Neighbor Embedding (t-SNE): It is a non-linear technique that preserves the local relationships between data points while mapping them to a lower-dimensional space for visualization.

Autoencoders: They are neural networks that learn to reconstruct the input data by encoding it into a lower-dimensional representation (encoder) and then decoding it back to the original space (decoder).

Dimensionality reduction techniques are useful in image and text analysis, genetic analysis, and feature engineering.

5.4 Association Rule Mining

Association rule mining is a technique used to discover interesting relationships or associations among items in a dataset. It is commonly used in market basket analysis, where the goal is to find patterns in customer purchasing behavior.

Association rules consist of an antecedent (a set of items) and a consequent (another item or set of items). The rules are derived by analyzing the frequency and co-occurrence of items in the dataset.

Frequent Itemset Mining (e.g., Apriori algorithm) and FP-Growth algorithm are commonly used for association rule mining.

Association rule mining finds applications in recommendation systems, market basket analysis, and cross-selling strategies.

5.5 Anomaly Detection

Anomaly detection, also known as outlier detection, aims to identify rare or unusual data points that significantly deviate from the expected patterns. Anomalies often represent critical events, errors, or abnormalities in the data.

There are several approaches to anomaly detection, including statistical methods, clustering-based methods, and proximity-based methods.

Anomaly detection is applied in fraud detection, network intrusion detection, system monitoring, and health monitoring.

5.6 Reinforcement Learning

Reinforcement learning is a branch of machine learning where an agent learns to interact with an environment to maximize a cumulative reward signal. It is often used in scenarios where there is no labeled data, and the agent learns through trial and error.

In reinforcement learning, the agent takes actions in an environment, receives feedback in the form of rewards or penalties, and adjusts its behavior to optimize the long-term cumulative reward.

Reinforcement learning is commonly applied in robotics, game playing, autonomous vehicles, and resource management.

By understanding the principles and characteristics of unsupervised learning algorithms, you can apply these techniques to explore and gain insights from unlabeled data. In the next chapter, we will explore additional machine learning concepts and techniques.

5.1 Clustering Algorithms (K-means, DBSCAN, Hierarchical Clustering)

Clustering is an unsupervised learning technique that involves grouping similar data points together based on their inherent patterns or similarities. It is a powerful tool for exploratory data analysis, pattern recognition, and data understanding. In this chapter, we will explore the principles, characteristics, and applications of popular clustering algorithms, including K-means, DBSCAN, and hierarchical clustering.

5.1.1 K-means Clustering

K-means clustering is a widely used partitioning-based algorithm that aims to partition the data into K distinct clusters, where K is a user-specified parameter. The algorithm iteratively assigns data points to the nearest cluster centroid and updates the centroids based on the mean of the assigned data points. The process continues until convergence or a specified number of iterations.

The steps of the K-means algorithm are as follows:

Initialize K centroids randomly or using some heuristic method.

Assign each data point to the nearest centroid based on a distance metric (usually Euclidean distance).

Recalculate the centroids as the mean of the data points assigned to each cluster.

Repeat steps 2 and 3 until convergence (when the centroids no longer change significantly) or a predetermined number of iterations is reached.

K-means clustering aims to minimize the within-cluster sum of squared distances, also known as the "inertia" or "within-cluster variance." It is computationally efficient and works well for datasets with a large number of samples.

5.1.2 Density-Based Spatial Clustering of Applications with Noise (DBSCAN)

DBSCAN is a density-based clustering algorithm that groups data points into clusters based on their density. It defines clusters as dense regions separated by sparser regions, allowing for the discovery of clusters of arbitrary shape. DBSCAN does not require specifying the number of clusters as a parameter.

The key idea behind DBSCAN is to identify "core points" and expand clusters by including "reachable points" within a specified radius and minimum number of points (density threshold).

The steps of the DBSCAN algorithm are as follows:

Select a random unvisited data point.

If the point has a sufficient number of neighboring points within a specified radius, it becomes a core point and a new cluster is created.

Expand the cluster by including all reachable points within the specified radius from the core point.

Repeat steps 1-3 until all data points have been visited.

DBSCAN classifies data points into three categories: core points, which form the dense regions of clusters; reachable points, which are in the vicinity of core points; and noise points, which are not part of any cluster.

DBSCAN is effective in identifying clusters of varying densities and handling noise and outliers. It is particularly useful when the number of clusters is not known in advance and when clusters have irregular shapes.

5.1.3 Hierarchical Clustering

Hierarchical clustering is a bottom-up (agglomerative) or top-down (divisive) clustering technique that creates a tree-like structure, known as a dendrogram, to represent the relationships between data points. It does not require specifying the number of clusters beforehand.

Agglomerative hierarchical clustering starts by considering each data point as an individual cluster and then iteratively merges the closest clusters based on a distance or linkage criterion. The process continues until all data points belong to a single cluster.

Divisive hierarchical clustering, on the other hand, starts with all data points in a single cluster and recursively divides clusters into smaller clusters until each data point forms its own cluster.

The choice of distance metric (e.g., Euclidean distance, Manhattan distance) and linkage criterion (e.g., single linkage, complete linkage, average linkage) affects the clustering results.

Hierarchical clustering provides a visual representation of the clustering structure through the dendrogram, allowing users to determine the optimal number of clusters by observing the clustering at different levels of the tree.

5.1.4 Advantages and Considerations

Advantages of clustering algorithms include:

Unsupervised Learning: Clustering does not require labeled data and can identify patterns or groupings in unlabeled datasets.

Exploratory Data Analysis: Clustering provides insights into the structure and relationships within the data, aiding in data understanding and discovery of hidden patterns.

Scalability: Clustering algorithms can handle large datasets efficiently.

Considerations when using clustering algorithms:

Number of Clusters: The determination of the optimal number of clusters can be subjective and domain-specific. Evaluation metrics like silhouette score or elbow method can assist in the selection.

Feature Scaling: Preprocessing the data and scaling features to a similar range can impact the performance of clustering algorithms.

Sensitivity to Initialization: The performance of clustering algorithms, particularly K-means, can be sensitive to the initial placement of centroids. Multiple runs with different initializations may be required to improve the stability of the results.

Interpretability: The interpretation of clustering results can be challenging, especially in high-dimensional data, as the meaning of the clusters may not always be apparent.

5.1.5 Applications

Clustering algorithms find applications in various domains, including:

Customer Segmentation: Grouping customers based on similar behaviors, preferences, or purchase patterns for targeted marketing strategies.

Image Segmentation: Partitioning images into meaningful regions for object recognition or computer vision tasks.

Anomaly Detection: Identifying unusual patterns or outliers in data for fraud detection, network intrusion detection, or system monitoring.

Document Clustering: Organizing documents into clusters based on their content for information retrieval or document management.

By understanding the principles and characteristics of clustering algorithms, you can effectively apply these techniques to discover patterns and structure within unlabeled data. In the next chapter, we will explore additional concepts and techniques for evaluating and selecting machine learning models.

5.2 Dimensionality Reduction Techniques (PCA, t-SNE)

Dimensionality reduction is a crucial technique in unsupervised learning that aims to reduce the number of features in a dataset while preserving its essential information. By reducing the dimensionality, these techniques help in visualizing high-dimensional data, mitigating the curse of dimensionality, and improving the performance of machine learning algorithms. In this chapter, we will explore two popular dimensionality reduction techniques: Principal Component Analysis (PCA) and t-Distributed Stochastic Neighbor Embedding (t-SNE).

5.2.1 Principal Component Analysis (PCA)

Principal Component Analysis (PCA) is a widely used linear dimensionality reduction technique. It transforms the features into a new set of uncorrelated variables called principal components. Each principal component is a linear combination of the original features, capturing the maximum variance in the data.

The steps of PCA are as follows:

Standardize the data by subtracting the mean and scaling it to have unit variance.

Compute the covariance matrix or correlation matrix of the standardized data.

Perform an eigendecomposition on the covariance matrix to obtain the eigenvalues and eigenvectors.

Sort the eigenvalues in descending order and select the top k eigenvectors corresponding to the largest eigenvalues.

Project the data onto the selected eigenvectors to obtain the reduced-dimensional representation.

PCA provides a compact representation of the data by retaining the most important features while discarding the least informative ones. It is particularly useful for visualizing high-dimensional data and identifying the major sources of variation in the dataset.

5.2.2 t-Distributed Stochastic Neighbor Embedding (t-SNE)

t-Distributed Stochastic Neighbor Embedding (t-SNE) is a non-linear dimensionality reduction technique primarily used for visualization. It aims to preserve the local relationships between data points while mapping them to a lower-dimensional space.

The steps of t-SNE are as follows:

Compute pairwise similarities or distances between data points.

Construct a probability distribution that represents the similarities or distances between points.

Initialize the low-dimensional embeddings randomly.

Optimize the embeddings to minimize the divergence between the high-dimensional and low-dimensional probability distributions using gradient descent.

Iterate the optimization process until convergence.

t-SNE emphasizes the separation of dissimilar data points and tries to preserve the local structure of the data. It is particularly effective in visualizing clusters and revealing the inherent structure or patterns in the data.

5.2.3 Advantages and Considerations

Advantages of dimensionality reduction techniques include:

Visualization: Dimensionality reduction helps visualize high-dimensional data in a reduced-dimensional space, facilitating data exploration and interpretation.

Curse of Dimensionality: Reducing the dimensionality can mitigate the curse of dimensionality, where the performance of machine learning algorithms deteriorates with increasing dimensions.

Noise Reduction: Dimensionality reduction can remove noisy or irrelevant features, leading to improved model performance.

Considerations when using dimensionality reduction techniques:

Loss of Information: Dimensionality reduction may result in the loss of some information, especially with aggressive reduction. It is important to strike a balance between dimensionality reduction and information preservation.

Interpretability: Interpreting the reduced-dimensional representation can be challenging, especially when there is a significant loss of original feature interpretability.

Parameter Tuning: Some dimensionality reduction techniques have parameters that need to be tuned, such as the number of principal components in PCA or the perplexity in t-SNE.

5.2.4 Applications

Dimensionality reduction techniques find applications in various domains, including:

Image and Video Processing: Reducing the dimensionality of image or video data for visualization, compression, or feature extraction tasks.

Genomic Data Analysis: Dimensionality reduction is used to analyze gene expression data, identify disease subtypes, or discover biomarkers.

Natural Language Processing: Reducing the dimensionality of text data for document classification, topic modeling, or sentiment analysis.

Sensor Data Analysis: Reducing the dimensionality of sensor data for anomaly detection, predictive maintenance, or fault diagnosis.

By understanding the principles and characteristics of dimensionality reduction techniques, you can effectively apply these techniques to reduce the dimensionality of high-dimensional data and gain insights from the reduced representation.

5.3 Association Rule Learning (Apriori, FP-growth)

Association rule learning is a powerful technique used in unsupervised learning to discover interesting relationships or associations among items in a dataset. It is widely applied in market basket analysis, where the goal is to find patterns in customer purchasing behavior. In this chapter, we will explore two popular association rule learning algorithms: Apriori and FP-growth.

5.3.1 Apriori Algorithm

The Apriori algorithm is a classic algorithm for mining frequent itemsets, which are sets of items that occur together frequently in a dataset. The algorithm uses a level-wise search approach to generate frequent itemsets of different lengths, starting from frequent itemsets of length 1 and progressively expanding to longer itemsets.

The steps of the Apriori algorithm are as follows:

Scan the dataset to find frequent itemsets of length 1 by counting the occurrences of each item.

Generate candidate itemsets of length 2 by joining frequent itemsets of length 1.

Prune the candidate itemsets that contain subsets that are not frequent.

Repeat steps 2 and 3 to generate candidate itemsets of higher lengths and prune them until no more frequent itemsets can be generated.

The Apriori algorithm generates frequent itemsets by exploiting the "Apriori principle," which states that any subset of a frequent itemset must also be frequent. This property allows for efficient pruning of candidate itemsets that cannot be frequent.

Once frequent itemsets are discovered, association rules are derived by evaluating the support and confidence of each rule. The support of a rule is the proportion of transactions that contain both the antecedent and consequent of the rule, while the confidence is the conditional probability of the consequent given the antecedent.

Apriori is a widely used algorithm for mining association rules. However, it can be computationally expensive, especially for datasets with large numbers of items and long itemsets.

5.3.2 FP-growth Algorithm

The FP-growth algorithm (Frequent Pattern growth) is an alternative algorithm for mining frequent itemsets that avoids generating and pruning candidate itemsets like the Apriori algorithm. Instead, FP-growth constructs a compact data structure called an FP-tree to represent the dataset and mines frequent itemsets from this structure.

The steps of the FP-growth algorithm are as follows:

Scan the dataset to build the FP-tree by counting the occurrences of each item and constructing the tree structure.

Identify frequent items by traversing the FP-tree in a bottom-up manner.

For each frequent item, construct conditional pattern bases by following the paths in the FP-tree that contain the item.

Recursively mine frequent itemsets from the conditional pattern bases.

The FP-growth algorithm leverages the compactness of the FP-tree and the concept of conditional pattern bases to efficiently mine frequent itemsets. It has better performance than the Apriori algorithm, especially for datasets with long itemsets and low support thresholds.

5.3.3 Advantages and Considerations

Advantages of association rule learning algorithms include:

Pattern Discovery: Association rule learning allows for the discovery of interesting relationships and patterns in large datasets.

Market Basket Analysis: Association rules are widely used in market basket analysis to identify items that are frequently purchased together, leading to insights for cross-selling and promotional strategies.

Considerations when using association rule learning algorithms:

Memory and Computational Requirements: The Apriori algorithm can have high memory and computational requirements, especially for large datasets and long itemsets. FP-growth is often more efficient in such cases.

Determining Support and Confidence Thresholds: Selecting appropriate support and confidence thresholds is crucial for obtaining meaningful and actionable association rules.

Handling Large Datasets: For very large datasets, efficient implementations and optimizations may be required to handle the scalability of association rule mining.

5.3.4 Applications

Association rule learning algorithms find applications in various domains, including:

Retail and E-commerce: Market basket analysis, recommendation systems, and personalized marketing.

Healthcare: Analysis of medical records, drug interactions, and treatment patterns.

Web Usage Mining: Understanding user behavior, session analysis, and personalized content recommendation.

Customer Relationship Management: Analyzing customer preferences, segmentation, and loyalty programs.

By understanding the principles and characteristics of association rule learning algorithms, you can effectively apply these techniques to discover meaningful associations and patterns in your data.

Chapter 6: Model Evaluation and Validation

In machine learning, model evaluation and validation are essential steps to assess the performance and generalization ability of trained models. In this chapter, we will explore various concepts and techniques related to model evaluation and validation, including performance metrics, cross-validation, and hyperparameter tuning.

6.1 Performance Metrics

Performance metrics provide quantitative measures to evaluate the performance of machine learning models. They help assess how well a model generalizes to unseen data and make comparisons between different models. Some commonly used performance metrics include:

Accuracy: Measures the proportion of correctly classified instances.

Precision: Calculates the proportion of true positive predictions out of the total predicted positive instances, indicating the model's ability to avoid false positives.

Recall: Represents the proportion of true positive predictions out of the total actual positive instances, indicating the model's ability to find all positive instances.

F1 Score: Combines precision and recall into a single metric, providing a balance between the two.

Area Under the Receiver Operating Characteristic Curve (AUC-ROC): Evaluates the model's ability to discriminate between positive and negative instances across different classification thresholds.

The choice of performance metric depends on the specific problem and the desired balance between different evaluation aspects. It is important to consider the context and requirements of the problem at hand.

6.2 Cross-Validation

Cross-validation is a technique used to assess the performance and generalization ability of a machine learning model on unseen data. It helps estimate how well the model will perform on new data by simulating the process of training and testing on multiple subsets of the available data.

Commonly used cross-validation techniques include:

K-Fold Cross-Validation: The data is divided into K equally sized folds. The model is trained on K-1 folds and evaluated on the remaining fold. This process is repeated K times, with each fold serving as the validation set once.

Stratified K-Fold Cross-Validation: Similar to K-fold cross-validation, but it ensures that each fold contains a proportional representation of each class, useful for imbalanced datasets.

Leave-One-Out Cross-Validation (LOOCV): Each data point is treated as a separate validation set, and the model is trained on all other data points. LOOCV is computationally expensive but provides an unbiased estimate of model performance.

Cross-validation helps estimate the performance of a model on unseen data and provides insights into its stability and generalization ability. It can assist in hyperparameter tuning and model selection.

6.3 Hyperparameter Tuning

Hyperparameters are parameters of a machine learning algorithm that are not learned from data but are set prior to training. Examples of hyperparameters include learning rate, regularization strength, and the number of hidden layers in a neural network. Hyperparameter tuning involves selecting the optimal values for these parameters to maximize model performance.

Techniques for hyperparameter tuning include:

Grid Search: Exhaustively searches a predefined hyperparameter grid and evaluates the model's performance for each combination of hyperparameters.

Random Search: Randomly samples hyperparameter combinations from a predefined search space, reducing the computational cost compared to grid search.

Bayesian Optimization: Utilizes a probabilistic model to intelligently search the hyperparameter space, balancing exploration and exploitation.

Hyperparameter tuning aims to find the optimal configuration for a model, enhancing its performance and generalization ability.

6.4 Model Selection and Validation Curves

Model selection involves comparing and choosing the best model from a set of candidate models based on their performance and generalization ability. Validation curves provide a graphical representation of the model's performance as a function of a specific hyperparameter, helping in the selection process.

A validation curve plots a performance metric (such as accuracy or error) against a range of hyperparameter values. It helps identify the optimal value that maximizes the performance metric without overfitting or underfitting the data.

By analyzing validation curves, one can gain insights into the effect of hyperparameters on model performance and make informed decisions during model selection.

6.5 Overfitting and Underfitting

Overfitting occurs when a model performs well on the training data but fails to generalize to unseen data. It is a result of the model capturing noise and irrelevant patterns in the training data, leading to poor performance on new instances.

Underfitting, on the other hand, occurs when a model is too simplistic to capture the underlying patterns in the data. It performs poorly on both the training and test data.

Regularization techniques, such as L1 and L2 regularization, can help prevent overfitting by adding a penalty term to the model's objective function. Other strategies, such as increasing the complexity of the model or collecting more data, can help mitigate underfitting.

6.6 Bias-Variance Trade-off

The bias-variance trade-off is a key concept in machine learning that relates to the model's ability to simultaneously capture the underlying patterns in the data (low bias) and generalize well to new instances (low variance).

A model with high bias may oversimplify the data, leading to underfitting. A model with high variance may overly rely on the training data, capturing noise and resulting in overfitting.

The goal is to strike a balance between bias and variance by selecting an optimal model complexity and applying regularization techniques. Understanding the trade-off helps in making informed decisions during model development.

By understanding the concepts and techniques related to model evaluation and validation, you can effectively assess the performance of machine learning models, select the best model, and optimize its hyperparameters.

6.1 Training and Testing Split

In machine learning, it is crucial to evaluate the performance of a trained model on unseen data to assess its generalization ability. One commonly used technique for this purpose is the training and testing split, where the available data is divided into separate sets for model training and evaluation.

6.1.1 The Training and Testing Split

The training and testing split involves partitioning the available data into two disjoint sets: a training set and a testing set. The training set is used to train the model, while the testing set is used to evaluate its performance.

The general guideline is to allocate the majority of the data to the training set, typically around 70-80% of the total data, and the remaining portion to the testing set. The exact split may depend on factors such as the size of the dataset, the complexity of the model, and the availability of data.

It is important to ensure that the data in the testing set is representative of the real-world data the model will encounter. Therefore, random shuffling of the data is often performed before splitting to avoid any ordering or bias effects.

6.1.2 Benefits of the Training and Testing Split

The training and testing split provides several benefits in model evaluation:

Assessing Generalization: The testing set serves as an unbiased evaluation of the model's performance on unseen data. It helps estimate how well the model will perform when deployed in the real world.

Detecting Overfitting: By evaluating the model on an independent testing set, it is possible to identify whether the model is overfitting the training data. Overfitting occurs when the model learns to fit the training data too closely but fails to generalize to new data.

Hyperparameter Tuning: The testing set can be used to compare the performance of different models or different hyperparameter configurations, aiding in the selection of the best model or hyperparameters.

6.1.3 Limitations and Considerations

While the training and testing split is a commonly used technique, it is important to be aware of its limitations and consider other evaluation techniques when appropriate:

Limited Data: If the available dataset is small, splitting it into separate training and testing sets may result in limited data for either training or evaluation. In such cases, techniques like cross-validation (discussed in Chapter 6.2) can be more effective in utilizing the available data.

Data Distribution: The training and testing sets should have similar data distributions to ensure that the testing set is representative of the real-world data. Random shuffling and stratified sampling techniques can help achieve this balance, especially in cases of imbalanced datasets.

Time-dependent Data: If the data has a temporal nature, such as in time series analysis, a simple random split may not be appropriate. Techniques like forward chaining or sliding window validation can be employed to account for the temporal aspect of the data.

Data Leakage: Care should be taken to ensure that there is no data leakage between the training and testing sets. Data leakage occurs when information from the testing set is inadvertently used during model training, leading to overly optimistic performance estimates. To prevent this, the testing set should remain completely untouched until the final evaluation.

6.1.4 Train-Validation-Test Split

In some cases, a three-way split, known as the train-validation-test split, is used instead of a simple train-test split. The validation set is used during the model development process for hyperparameter tuning and model selection. Once the model has been finalized, it is evaluated on the independent testing set to assess its final performance.

The train-validation-test split is particularly useful when the model has multiple hyperparameters that need tuning or when there is a need to compare multiple models and select the best one.

By employing the training and testing split technique, you can effectively evaluate the performance of machine learning models on unseen data and assess their generalization ability.

6.2 Cross-Validation Techniques

Cross-validation is a technique used in machine learning to assess the performance and generalization ability of a model on unseen data. It involves splitting the available data into multiple subsets, training and testing the model on different combinations of these subsets, and averaging the performance metrics across all evaluations. Cross-validation provides a more robust estimate of model performance compared to a single train-test split. In this chapter, we will explore various cross-validation techniques.

6.2.1 K-Fold Cross-Validation

K-Fold Cross-Validation is one of the most commonly used cross-validation techniques. It involves splitting the data into K equally-sized folds or subsets. The model is trained on K-1 folds and evaluated on the remaining fold. This process is repeated K times, with each fold serving as the validation set once. The performance metrics are averaged across all iterations to obtain an overall estimate of the model's performance.

K-Fold Cross-Validation helps to mitigate the impact of the particular data split on the model's performance. It provides a more reliable estimate of the model's performance by reducing the variance associated with a single train-test split.

6.2.2 Stratified K-Fold Cross-Validation

Stratified K-Fold Cross-Validation is particularly useful for classification tasks, especially when dealing with imbalanced datasets. It ensures that each fold has a proportional representation of each class, maintaining the class distribution of the overall dataset. This helps prevent bias towards the majority class and ensures a fair evaluation across all classes.

Stratified K-Fold Cross-Validation is performed similarly to K-Fold Cross-Validation, but with the additional step of stratifying the data based on the class labels before creating the folds. This ensures that each fold maintains the same class distribution as the original dataset.

6.2.3 Leave-One-Out Cross-Validation (LOOCV)

Leave-One-Out Cross-Validation (LOOCV) is a special case of K-Fold Cross-Validation where K is set to the number of data points in the dataset. Each data point is treated as a separate validation set, and the model is trained on all other data points. LOOCV provides an unbiased estimate of the model's performance but can be computationally expensive, especially for large datasets.

LOOCV is useful when the available data is limited, and every data point contributes valuable information to the model's training.

6.2.4 Repeated Cross-Validation

Repeated Cross-Validation involves repeating the cross-validation process multiple times with different random splits of the data. This technique provides a more robust estimate of model performance by averaging the results across multiple iterations. Repeated Cross-Validation helps account for the variability in model performance that can arise due to different data splits.

The number of repetitions can be specified based on the desired level of confidence in the performance estimate. It is common to perform 5 or 10 repetitions of the cross-validation process.

6.2.5 Nested Cross-Validation

Nested Cross-Validation combines the concept of cross-validation with model selection. It involves an outer loop of K-Fold Cross-Validation for estimating the performance of different models, and an inner loop of K-Fold Cross-Validation for hyperparameter tuning and model selection. This technique helps provide a more unbiased estimate of the model's performance by avoiding data leakage during hyperparameter tuning.

Nested Cross-Validation is particularly useful when there is a need to compare multiple models or when the model has multiple hyperparameters that require tuning.

6.2.6 Benefits and Considerations

Cross-validation techniques offer several benefits:

Robust Performance Estimate: Cross-validation provides a more reliable estimate of a model's performance by reducing the impact of a single train-test split and incorporating the average performance across multiple iterations.

Hyperparameter Tuning: Cross-validation can be used for hyperparameter tuning and model selection, ensuring that the selected model performs well on unseen data.

Better Data Utilization: Cross-validation makes efficient use of available data by maximizing the use of data for both training and evaluation.

Considerations when using cross-validation:

Computational Cost: Cross-validation can be computationally expensive, especially for large datasets or complex models. However, it provides valuable insights into model performance and generalization.

Data Representativeness: It is essential to ensure that the cross-validation splits are representative of the overall dataset to obtain reliable performance estimates. Random shuffling and stratification techniques can be applied to achieve this.

Data Leakage: Care should be taken to prevent any data leakage between the training and validation sets during hyperparameter tuning or model selection.

By employing cross-validation techniques, you can obtain a robust estimate of model performance and make informed decisions regarding model selection, hyperparameter tuning, and generalization.

6.3 Evaluation Metrics (Accuracy, Precision, Recall, F1-score)

Evaluation metrics provide quantitative measures to assess the performance of machine learning models. They help in evaluating the model's ability to make accurate predictions and generalize well to unseen data. In this chapter, we will explore some commonly used evaluation metrics, including accuracy, precision, recall, and F1-score.

6.3.1 Accuracy

Accuracy is a widely used evaluation metric that measures the proportion of correctly classified instances out of the total number of instances. It provides a general measure of overall model performance. The formula for accuracy is:

Accuracy = (Number of Correct Predictions) / (Total Number of Predictions)

Accuracy is suitable for balanced datasets, where the class distribution is roughly equal. However, it can be misleading in the case of imbalanced datasets, where the majority class dominates the accuracy calculation. In such cases, other metrics like precision, recall, and F1-score provide a more comprehensive evaluation.

6.3.2 Precision

Precision is a metric that measures the proportion of true positive predictions out of the total positive predictions made by the model. It focuses on the ability of the model to avoid false positives. Precision is calculated using the formula:

Precision = (True Positives) / (True Positives + False Positives)

Precision is useful in scenarios where false positives are costly or undesirable, such as in medical diagnostics or fraud detection. A higher precision indicates a lower rate of false positives.

6.3.3 Recall

Recall, also known as sensitivity or true positive rate, measures the proportion of true positive predictions out of the total actual positive instances. It quantifies the model's ability to identify all positive instances correctly. Recall is calculated using the formula:

Recall = (True Positives) / (True Positives + False Negatives)

Recall is particularly important when the identification of true positive cases is crucial, such as in disease diagnosis or anomaly detection. A higher recall indicates a lower rate of false negatives.

6.3.4 F1-score

The F1-score is a harmonic mean of precision and recall, providing a balanced evaluation metric that considers both false positives and false negatives. It combines precision and recall into a single score and is calculated using the formula:

F1-score = 2 * ((Precision * Recall) / (Precision + Recall))

The F1-score is useful when there is an imbalance between the classes or when both precision and recall need to be considered simultaneously. It provides a comprehensive evaluation of model performance, considering both false positives and false negatives.

6.3.5 Receiver Operating Characteristic (ROC) Curve and Area Under the Curve (AUC-ROC)

In binary classification tasks, the Receiver Operating Characteristic (ROC) curve is a graphical representation of the trade-off between the true positive rate (recall) and the false positive rate. The ROC curve helps visualize the performance of the model across different classification thresholds.

The Area Under the Curve (AUC-ROC) is a metric that quantifies the overall performance of the model based on the ROC curve. A higher AUC-ROC indicates a better model performance in distinguishing between positive and negative instances.

The ROC curve and AUC-ROC are particularly useful when the classification threshold needs to be adjusted to balance between false positives and false negatives. They provide insights into the model's discrimination ability.

6.3.6 Choosing the Right Evaluation Metric

The choice of evaluation metric depends on the specific problem and the goals of the model. Some considerations include:

Accuracy: Use accuracy when the class distribution is balanced and equal importance is given to all classes.

Precision and Recall: Use precision and recall when the costs of false positives and false negatives are different or when the class distribution is imbalanced.

F1-score: Use the F1-score when both precision and recall need to be considered simultaneously.

ROC-AUC: Use the ROC-AUC when the classification threshold needs to be adjusted to balance between false positives and false negatives.

It is important to select the evaluation metric that aligns with the specific requirements and objectives of the problem at hand.

By utilizing appropriate evaluation metrics, you can assess the performance of machine learning models, understand their strengths and weaknesses, and make informed decisions for model selection and refinement.

6.4 Overfitting and Underfitting

Overfitting and underfitting are common challenges in machine learning that affect the ability of a model to generalize well to unseen data. Understanding these concepts is crucial for developing effective models. In this chapter, we will explore overfitting, underfitting, and techniques to address these issues.

6.4.1 Overfitting

Overfitting occurs when a model performs exceptionally well on the training data but fails to generalize to new, unseen data. The model becomes too complex and starts to capture noise or irrelevant patterns in the training data, rather than learning the underlying patterns that are truly informative.

Signs of overfitting include:

Very high accuracy on the training data but poor performance on the testing data.

Large differences between training and testing performance.

The model is too complex and has many parameters relative to the size of the training data.

Overfitting can occur due to several reasons:

Model Complexity: Complex models, such as those with a large number of parameters or deep neural networks, are more prone to overfitting.

Insufficient Training Data: When the available training data is limited, the model may try to fit noise rather than learning the true underlying patterns.

Incorrect Hyperparameters: Poor choices of hyperparameters, such as high learning rates or low regularization strength, can lead to overfitting.

6.4.2 Underfitting

Underfitting, on the other hand, occurs when a model is too simple to capture the underlying patterns in the data. It fails to learn from the training data and exhibits poor performance both on the training and testing data.

Signs of underfitting include:

Low accuracy on both the training and testing data.

High bias and low variance.

The model fails to capture the important relationships in the data.

Underfitting can occur due to several reasons:

Model Complexity: When the model is too simple or lacks the necessary complexity to represent the underlying patterns in the data, it leads to underfitting.

Insufficient Training or Features: If the training data is limited or lacks important features, the model may struggle to learn the underlying patterns.

Incorrect Hyperparameters: Poor choices of hyperparameters, such as a low number of hidden layers in a neural network or high regularization strength, can lead to underfitting.

6.4.3 Addressing Overfitting and Underfitting

To address overfitting and underfitting, several techniques can be employed:

Regularization: Regularization techniques, such as L1 or L2 regularization, add a penalty term to the model's objective function. This encourages simpler models and helps prevent overfitting.

Cross-Validation: Cross-validation techniques, as discussed in Chapter 6.2, provide a more robust estimate of model performance and help in selecting models that generalize well.

Feature Selection: Removing irrelevant or redundant features can help reduce overfitting and simplify the model.

Early Stopping: Monitoring the model's performance on a validation set during training and stopping the training process when the performance starts to deteriorate can prevent overfitting.

Ensemble Methods: Using ensemble methods, such as random forests or gradient boosting, combines multiple models to reduce overfitting and improve generalization.

Data Augmentation: Increasing the size of the training data through techniques like data augmentation can help the model generalize better.

Hyperparameter Tuning: Choosing appropriate hyperparameters through techniques like grid search or random search can help find the right balance between model complexity and generalization.

By addressing overfitting and underfitting, you can develop models that generalize well and perform effectively on unseen data.

6.5 Hyperparameter Tuning

Hyperparameters are parameters that are not learned by the model during training but are set prior to the training process. They control the behavior and performance of the model. Hyperparameter tuning involves finding the optimal values for these parameters to improve the model's performance and generalization ability. In this chapter, we will explore techniques and strategies for hyperparameter tuning.

6.5.1 Common Hyperparameters

The specific hyperparameters and their ranges depend on the type of model and algorithm being used. Here are some examples of common hyperparameters:

Learning Rate: The step size at each iteration of the optimization algorithm. It determines how quickly the model learns and converges.

Number of Hidden Layers and Units: For neural networks, the number of hidden layers and the number of units in each layer affect the model's capacity to learn complex representations.

Regularization Strength: The parameter that controls the strength of regularization techniques like L1 or L2 regularization. It helps prevent overfitting by adding a penalty term to the loss function.

Dropout Rate: The proportion of units randomly dropped out during training in order to reduce overfitting in neural networks.

Kernel Size: For algorithms like convolutional neural networks (CNNs), the kernel size determines the receptive field and the level of feature extraction.

These are just a few examples, and different models may have different hyperparameters that need to be tuned.

6.5.2 Grid Search

Grid search is a simple but exhaustive technique for hyperparameter tuning. It involves specifying a set of possible values for each hyperparameter and training and evaluating the model for all possible combinations of these values. The performance of the model is then compared across these combinations to find the best hyperparameter values.

While grid search guarantees finding the optimal combination of hyperparameters within the specified range, it can be computationally expensive, especially when dealing with a large number of hyperparameters and a wide range of values.

6.5.3 Random Search

Random search is an alternative technique for hyperparameter tuning that overcomes the computational limitations of grid search. Instead of exhaustively searching over all possible combinations, random search randomly selects combinations of hyperparameters within specified ranges. This random sampling process reduces the computational cost while still exploring a wide range of hyperparameter configurations.

Random search can be more efficient than grid search when the impact of individual hyperparameters on the model's performance is uncertain. It allows for a more comprehensive exploration of the hyperparameter space without evaluating all possible combinations.

6.5.4 Model-based Optimization

Model-based optimization, such as Bayesian optimization, is an advanced technique for hyperparameter tuning. It uses probabilistic models to intelligently search the hyperparameter space based on the performance of previously evaluated hyperparameter configurations. It balances exploration and exploitation, gradually learning from the observed results to identify promising regions of the hyperparameter space.

Model-based optimization is particularly useful when the hyperparameter space is large and complex, and the evaluation of each configuration is expensive or time-consuming. It offers faster convergence and requires fewer evaluations compared to grid search or random search.

6.5.5 Cross-Validation for Hyperparameter Tuning

Cross-validation is often employed during hyperparameter tuning to obtain more reliable performance estimates. Instead of relying on a single train-test split, cross-validation provides a more robust evaluation of the model by averaging the performance across multiple iterations. It helps in assessing the generalization ability of different hyperparameter configurations.

Cross-validation can be combined with grid search, random search, or model-based optimization to identify the best hyperparameter values. The performance metrics obtained from cross-validation can guide the selection of optimal hyperparameters.

6.5.6 Automated Hyperparameter Tuning

Automated hyperparameter tuning tools and libraries, such as scikit-learn's GridSearchCV or Optuna, provide convenient interfaces for hyperparameter tuning. These tools automate the process of hyperparameter search, evaluation, and selection, making it easier to find the best hyperparameter values.

These tools typically support various search strategies, including grid search, random search, and model-based optimization. They also integrate with cross-validation techniques to obtain robust performance estimates.

6.5.7 Considerations and Best Practices

When tuning hyperparameters, consider the following best practices:

Define a reasonable search space for each hyperparameter based on prior knowledge or experimentation.

Use appropriate performance metrics to evaluate the model's performance during hyperparameter tuning. Consider not only accuracy but also other metrics like precision, recall, or F1-score, depending on the problem.

Perform hyperparameter tuning on a separate validation set or using cross-validation to prevent overfitting to the testing set.

Keep track of the performance of different hyperparameter configurations to analyze trends and patterns.

Be mindful of computational resources and time constraints, as exhaustive grid search may not always be feasible.

Hyperparameter tuning should be an iterative process. It may require multiple rounds of experimentation and refinement to find the optimal configuration.

By effectively tuning the hyperparameters, you can enhance the model's performance, improve generalization, and achieve better results.

Chapter 7: Model Deployment

Model deployment is the process of making trained machine learning models available for use in real-world applications. It involves taking the model from the development stage and making it operational to generate predictions or make decisions. In this chapter, we will explore various aspects of model deployment, including considerations, techniques, and best practices.

7.1 Choosing the Deployment Environment

When deploying a machine learning model, it is essential to choose the right environment that suits the requirements of the application. Consider the following options:

7.1.1 On-Premises Deployment

On-premises deployment involves hosting the model on local servers or hardware infrastructure within the organization. This option provides full control over the deployment environment, data security, and integration with existing systems. However, it requires dedicated hardware resources and ongoing maintenance and management.

7.1.2 Cloud Deployment

Cloud deployment involves hosting the model on cloud-based platforms such as Amazon Web Services (AWS), Google Cloud

Platform (GCP), or Microsoft Azure. It offers scalability, flexibility, and the ability to leverage various cloud services and resources. Cloud deployment allows for easy integration with other cloud-based services and facilitates collaboration and accessibility. However, it relies on a stable internet connection and involves ongoing costs based on usage.

7.1.3 Edge Deployment

Edge deployment involves deploying the model directly onto edge devices such as mobile phones, IoT devices, or embedded systems. This enables real-time inference and reduces latency as the predictions are made locally on the device. Edge deployment is useful in scenarios where low latency, offline availability, or privacy concerns are critical. However, it may have resource limitations and requires efficient model architectures and optimization techniques.

7.2 Model Serving

Model serving is the process of exposing the trained model as an API or service to generate predictions or perform inference. There are various techniques for model serving, including:

7.2.1 RESTful APIs

RESTful APIs (Representational State Transfer) provide a standard way to communicate with the model over HTTP protocols. The model is deployed as a web service, and clients can send requests to the API to obtain predictions. This approach allows for flexibility in integrating the model into different applications and frameworks.

7.2.2 Containerization

Containerization technologies such as Docker allow models to be packaged into lightweight, portable containers. Containers encapsulate the model, dependencies, and runtime environment, making it easier to deploy and run consistently across different platforms. Containerization enables seamless deployment and scalability, as well as simplified management and version control of the model.

7.2.3 Serverless Functions

Serverless computing platforms, such as AWS Lambda or Azure Functions, allow models to be deployed as serverless functions. The platform automatically handles the infrastructure provisioning and scaling, and the model is executed in response to specific events or requests. Serverless functions offer cost efficiency, scalability, and automatic resource management, making them suitable for applications with varying workloads.

7.3 Monitoring and Performance Evaluation

Once the model is deployed, it is important to monitor its performance and evaluate its effectiveness in the real-world environment. Some key considerations include:

7.3.1 Logging and Error Handling

Implement logging mechanisms to capture relevant information about the model's performance, usage patterns, and any errors or exceptions encountered during inference. This enables effective debugging, troubleshooting, and continuous improvement of the deployed model.

7.3.2 Performance Metrics

Define and track relevant performance metrics for the deployed model, such as response time, throughput, and prediction accuracy. These metrics provide insights into the model's performance and help identify any performance degradation or anomalies.

7.3.3 Data Drift and Model Drift

Monitor the input data distribution to detect data drift, which occurs when the characteristics of the incoming data change over time. Similarly, monitor the model's performance to detect model drift, which occurs when the model's performance deteriorates due to changes in the underlying data or the model itself. Regularly retraining or updating the model can help address these drift-related challenges.

7.3.4 A/B Testing and Experimentation

Implement A/B testing or experimentation frameworks to compare the performance of different models or variations of the same model. This allows for continuous improvement and optimization by comparing the effectiveness of different approaches in a controlled manner.

7.4 Security and Privacy Considerations

When deploying machine learning models, it is crucial to consider security and privacy aspects:

7.4.1 Model Protection

Take measures to protect the deployed model from unauthorized access, tampering, or theft. Techniques such as model encryption, access control, and secure communication protocols can be employed to enhance model security.

7.4.2 Data Privacy

Ensure that data privacy regulations and requirements are met during model deployment. Anonymization, encryption, and access controls should be implemented to safeguard sensitive data used for model inference.

7.4.3 Ethical Considerations

Consider ethical implications when deploying models, especially those that have a direct impact on individuals or decision-making processes. Evaluate for potential biases, fairness issues, or unintended consequences that may arise from the deployed model's predictions or decisions.

7.5 Continuous Improvement and Iteration

Model deployment is not a one-time activity but an iterative process. It requires continuous monitoring, evaluation, and improvement. Regularly reevaluate the model's performance, collect feedback from users, and incorporate new data or domain knowledge to refine and enhance the deployed model.

By considering the deployment environment, choosing appropriate model serving techniques, monitoring performance, addressing security and privacy concerns, and embracing continuous improvement, you can successfully deploy machine learning models into real-world applications.

7.1 Exporting and Saving Models

Before deploying a machine learning model, it is necessary to export and save the trained model in a format that can be used by the deployment environment. In this chapter, we will explore various techniques for exporting and saving models.

7.1.1 Serialization

Serialization is the process of converting an object into a format that can be stored or transmitted. In the context of machine learning models, serialization involves converting the trained model into a binary representation that can be saved to disk.

Most machine learning libraries provide built-in serialization methods to save and load models. For example, in Python's scikit-learn library, you can use the joblib or pickle module to serialize and deserialize models. In TensorFlow, models can be saved using the tf.saved_model API, while in PyTorch, you can use the torch.save and torch.load functions.

Serialization formats vary depending on the library and framework used. Common formats include binary formats (e.g., .pkl, .joblib) and platform-independent formats (e.g., TensorFlow's SavedModel format, PyTorch's .pt or .pth format).

When serializing models, ensure that you include any necessary metadata, such as preprocessing steps or feature encodings, to ensure the model can be correctly restored during deployment.

7.1.2 Exporting to ONNX

The Open Neural Network Exchange (ONNX) format is an open standard for representing machine learning models. It provides a common format that allows models to be trained in one framework and deployed in another. ONNX supports a wide range of popular frameworks, including PyTorch, TensorFlow, and scikit-learn.

To export a model to the ONNX format, you need to convert it into the ONNX representation using libraries such as onnx, torch.onnx, or tf2onnx. Once exported, the ONNX model can be loaded and used in other frameworks or deployment environments that support the ONNX format.

Exporting models to the ONNX format allows for interoperability and flexibility when deploying models across different platforms and frameworks.

7.1.3 Model Versioning

Model versioning is crucial for maintaining a record of different iterations or versions of the deployed model. Versioning helps in tracking changes, reproducing results, and ensuring reproducibility.

Assigning a version number or label to each model iteration simplifies the process of identifying and managing different versions. This can be done through naming conventions, timestamps, or dedicated version control systems.

When deploying models, it is good practice to store the serialized models along with their associated version information in a versioned repository or storage system. This allows for easy retrieval and management of different model versions.

7.1.4 Packaging Models as Libraries or Containers

In some cases, it may be beneficial to package the model along with any necessary dependencies or preprocessing steps as a library or container. This approach provides a self-contained deployment unit that encapsulates the model and its associated components.

For example, you can create a Python library that includes the model, along with any required preprocessing or post-processing code. This library can then be easily installed and used in other applications or systems.

Alternatively, you can package the model, along with its dependencies and any necessary runtime environment, into a container using technologies like Docker. This containerized approach ensures consistency and portability, as the model and its dependencies are bundled together.

Packaging models as libraries or containers simplifies the deployment process and ensures that all required components are included.

7.1.5 Cloud-Based Model Storage

Cloud platforms like AWS, GCP, and Azure provide storage services that allow you to store and retrieve models efficiently. These services offer scalability, reliability, and easy access to models from different deployment environments.

By uploading serialized models to cloud-based storage services, you can easily manage and distribute models across different deployments. This approach also enables seamless integration with other cloud-based services and allows for versioning and access control.

When using cloud-based model storage, ensure that proper security measures are in place to protect sensitive or proprietary models.

7.1.6 Model Size and Optimization

When exporting and saving models, consider the size of the serialized model file. Large model sizes can impact deployment and inference performance, especially in resource-constrained environments.

You can optimize the model size by applying techniques such as model compression, quantization, or pruning. These techniques reduce the size of the model without significant loss in performance, making the deployment process more efficient.

However, be mindful of the trade-off between model size and performance. Drastic model size reduction may lead to reduced accuracy or increased inference time.

By appropriately exporting and saving models, you can ensure that they are easily deployable and accessible in different environments.

7.2 Building APIs for Model Deployment

When deploying machine learning models, building APIs (Application Programming Interfaces) is a common approach to provide a standardized and flexible way for clients to interact with the model. APIs enable seamless integration of the model into various applications and systems. In this chapter, we will explore techniques and best practices for building APIs for model deployment.

7.2.1 RESTful APIs

RESTful APIs (Representational State Transfer) are a popular choice for building APIs for model deployment. They provide a standard and scalable approach for communication between clients and the deployed model.

A RESTful API typically follows these principles:

Use HTTP methods (GET, POST, PUT, DELETE) to represent different operations on the model.

Use URLs (Uniform Resource Locators) to identify resources and endpoints for different functionalities.

Transfer data using standard data formats such as JSON (JavaScript Object Notation).

To build a RESTful API for model deployment, you can use web frameworks like Flask (Python), Express (Node.js), or Django (Python). These frameworks provide tools and libraries to handle HTTP requests, define routes, and manage responses.

The API endpoints can be designed to handle various functionalities, such as model inference, model training, or data preprocessing. For model inference, the API endpoint receives input data, processes it through the model, and returns the predicted output to the client.

7.2.2 API Documentation

When building APIs, it is crucial to provide clear and comprehensive documentation to facilitate integration and usage. API documentation should include:

Endpoint details: Describe the available endpoints, their functionalities, and the expected input and output formats.

Input validation: Specify the required input data format, data types, and any constraints on the input.

Error handling: Document potential errors or exceptions that can occur during API usage and provide appropriate error codes and error messages.

Examples: Include example requests and responses to demonstrate the API usage.

API documentation can be created using tools like Swagger or OpenAPI Specification (OAS). These tools provide a structured way to describe the API endpoints, data models, and documentation details.

7.2.3 Authentication and Authorization

To ensure secure access to the deployed model API, authentication and authorization mechanisms should be implemented. These mechanisms validate the identity of clients and authorize access based on defined permissions.

Common authentication methods include API keys, JSON Web Tokens (JWT), OAuth, or token-based authentication. These methods require clients to provide valid credentials to access the API.

Authorization mechanisms control the level of access granted to different clients based on their roles or permissions. This ensures that only authorized users or systems can perform specific operations on the model API.

7.2.4 Rate Limiting and Throttling

To manage the usage and prevent abuse of the model API, rate limiting and throttling techniques can be applied. Rate limiting sets limits on the number of requests a client can make within a specified time period. Throttling controls the rate at which requests are processed, preventing excessive load on the API.

Implementing rate limiting and throttling helps maintain API stability, prevent resource exhaustion, and protect against denial-of-service attacks.

7.2.5 Monitoring and Logging

Monitoring and logging are essential for tracking the usage and performance of the deployed model API. Implement mechanisms to capture and analyze relevant metrics, such as response times, error rates, and resource utilization.

Logging should record important events, errors, and exceptions that occur during API usage. This helps in debugging, troubleshooting, and performance optimization.

Integration with monitoring and logging tools or frameworks, such as Prometheus, Grafana, or ELK stack (Elasticsearch, Logstash, Kibana), can facilitate effective monitoring and logging of the API.

7.2.6 Versioning

API versioning is crucial for managing changes and backward compatibility. It allows for the introduction of new features or improvements without breaking existing client integrations.

Versioning can be implemented through URL paths, headers, or query parameters. It ensures that clients can continue using the older version of the API until they are ready to migrate to the newer version.

Properly managing API versions simplifies the deployment of model updates and ensures smooth transitions for clients.

By building APIs for model deployment, you can provide a flexible and standardized interface for clients to interact with the deployed model. APIs enable seamless integration, usage, and scalability of the model in various applications and systems.

7.3 Cloud Deployment (AWS, Azure, Google Cloud)

Cloud deployment offers numerous advantages for deploying machine learning models, including scalability, flexibility, and easy integration with other cloud services. Major cloud providers such as Amazon Web Services (AWS), Microsoft Azure, and Google Cloud Platform (GCP) offer robust infrastructure and services to facilitate model deployment. In this chapter, we will explore cloud deployment options provided by these platforms.

7.3.1 AWS SageMaker

Amazon SageMaker is a fully managed service by AWS that simplifies the process of building, training, and deploying machine learning models. It provides a comprehensive environment for end-to-end machine learning workflows.

With SageMaker, you can:

Use pre-built algorithms and frameworks or bring your own custom code.

Scale your models using auto-scaling capabilities.

Deploy models as real-time endpoints or batch processing jobs.

Monitor and optimize model performance.

Securely manage and version your models.

SageMaker integrates with other AWS services, allowing you to leverage a wide range of capabilities such as data storage, data lakes, and serverless computing.

7.3.2 Azure Machine Learning

Azure Machine Learning is a cloud-based service provided by Microsoft Azure that enables the end-to-end lifecycle management of machine learning models. It offers a rich set of tools and services for building, training, and deploying models.

With Azure Machine Learning, you can:

Develop models using Jupyter notebooks or Azure Machine Learning studio.

Leverage pre-built algorithms and frameworks or bring your own code.

Train models at scale using Azure's infrastructure.

Deploy models as web services or containers.

Monitor and optimize model performance.

Collaborate with team members through version control and deployment pipelines.

Azure Machine Learning integrates seamlessly with other Azure services, enabling easy access to data storage, data processing, and other cloud-based resources.

7.3.3 Google Cloud AI Platform

Google Cloud AI Platform is a managed service by Google Cloud that allows you to build, train, and deploy machine learning models on Google Cloud infrastructure. It provides a suite of tools and services for model development and deployment.

With Google Cloud AI Platform, you can:

Develop models using Jupyter notebooks or the Google Cloud Console.

Utilize pre-built algorithms and frameworks or bring your own code.

Train models at scale using distributed computing.

Deploy models as online prediction services or batch processing jobs.

Monitor and manage model performance.

Collaborate with team members through version control and deployment pipelines.

Google Cloud AI Platform integrates with other Google Cloud services, making it easy to leverage additional cloud-based resources for data storage, processing, and visualization.

7.3.4 Benefits of Cloud Deployment

Cloud deployment offers several benefits for model deployment, including:

Scalability: Cloud platforms provide elastic computing resources, allowing you to easily scale your models based on demand. This ensures high availability and performance even with varying workloads.

Flexibility: Cloud deployment supports a variety of deployment options, including real-time endpoints, batch processing, serverless functions, and containerization. You can choose the most suitable approach based on your application's requirements.

Integration with Cloud Services: Cloud providers offer a wide range of services for data storage, data processing, monitoring, security, and more. These services can be seamlessly integrated with your deployed models, enabling comprehensive solutions.

Managed Services: Cloud platforms provide managed services specifically designed for machine learning, such as AWS

SageMaker, Azure Machine Learning, and Google Cloud AI Platform. These services abstract away the complexities of infrastructure management, allowing you to focus on model development and deployment.

Security and Compliance: Cloud providers offer robust security measures and compliance certifications, ensuring the confidentiality, integrity, and availability of your deployed models and data.

When deploying models on cloud platforms, it is essential to understand the pricing structures, security considerations, and specific features offered by each provider. Careful evaluation and selection of the cloud platform based on your project requirements can optimize the deployment process and enhance the performance and accessibility of your machine learning models.

7.4 Monitoring and Maintenance of Deployed Models

Once a machine learning model is deployed, it is crucial to continuously monitor and maintain its performance to ensure its effectiveness and reliability. In this chapter, we will explore important considerations and strategies for monitoring and maintaining deployed models.

7.4.1 Performance Monitoring

Monitoring the performance of deployed models helps identify potential issues, deviations, or degradation in model performance. Here are some key aspects to monitor:

Prediction Accuracy: Track the accuracy or performance metrics specific to your model's task, such as precision, recall, F1-score, or area under the ROC curve. Deviations from the expected performance levels may indicate model deterioration or changes in the underlying data.

Latency and Throughput: Monitor the time taken for the model to generate predictions (latency) and the number of predictions the model can handle within a given time (throughput). Ensure that the model responds within acceptable time limits and can handle the required workload.

Resource Utilization: Monitor the utilization of computational resources such as CPU, memory, and storage to ensure efficient usage and identify any bottlenecks or resource constraints.

Data Drift: Monitor the incoming data distribution to detect data drift, which occurs when the characteristics of the data change over time. Data drift can impact the model's performance, and detecting it early allows for timely updates or retraining.

Model Drift: Continuously evaluate the model's performance on new data to detect model drift, which occurs when the model's performance deteriorates due to changes in the underlying data or the model itself. Regular model monitoring can help identify when retraining or updates are necessary.

Monitoring can be done using various tools and techniques, including log analysis, performance dashboards, and alerts based on predefined thresholds or anomalies.

7.4.2 Error Analysis and Debugging

When issues or errors arise in the deployed model, it is important to analyze and debug them promptly. Techniques for error analysis and debugging include:

Error Logging: Implement detailed logging mechanisms to capture errors, exceptions, and relevant information during inference. This helps in understanding the context and nature of the errors and facilitates effective debugging.

Error Analysis: Analyze the patterns and characteristics of the errors encountered during model inference. Identify common error types, understand their causes, and explore potential improvements or mitigations.

Feedback Loop: Encourage users or stakeholders to provide feedback on the model's performance or any unexpected behavior. Incorporate user feedback and insights into debugging and improvement processes.

7.4.3 Model Maintenance and Updates

Machine learning models may require periodic maintenance and updates to ensure their continued effectiveness. Consider the following aspects:

Retraining: Regularly assess the model's performance and consider retraining it on updated or additional data. Retraining helps the model adapt to changes in the data distribution and maintain its predictive accuracy.

Model Versioning: Maintain a version control system to manage different versions of the model. This allows you to track changes, compare performance, and roll back to previous versions if necessary.

A/B Testing: When introducing updates or improvements to the model, consider conducting A/B testing. Compare the performance of the updated model against the existing model in a controlled manner, using metrics and user feedback to guide the decision-making process.

Communication and Documentation: Maintain clear documentation on the model's updates, changes, and known limitations. Communicate changes to stakeholders, users, or relevant teams to ensure transparency and facilitate informed decision-making.

7.4.4 Security and Privacy

Continuously assess and reinforce the security and privacy measures implemented for the deployed model. Regularly review access controls, authentication mechanisms, and data handling processes to ensure compliance with security standards and protect sensitive information.

Consider conducting periodic security audits or assessments to identify potential vulnerabilities and implement appropriate mitigation strategies.

7.4.5 Scaling and Resource Management

As the usage of the deployed model grows, it is important to monitor resource utilization and scale the infrastructure accordingly. Monitor computational resources such as CPU, memory, and storage to ensure efficient utilization and plan for scalability as needed.

Implement techniques like load balancing, auto-scaling, or serverless computing to dynamically adjust resource allocation based on demand.

7.4.6 Documentation and Knowledge Sharing

Maintain up-to-date documentation that captures the details of the deployed model, its dependencies, deployment procedures, and troubleshooting guidelines. This documentation serves as a valuable resource for future maintenance, collaboration with team members, and knowledge transfer.

Regularly share knowledge and best practices within the team or organization to ensure consistent understanding and effective collaboration in maintaining the deployed models.

By actively monitoring and maintaining deployed models, you can ensure their ongoing performance, reliability, and effectiveness.

Chapter 8: Handling Large Datasets and Big Data

In machine learning, the size of the dataset plays a crucial role in model performance and generalization. Large datasets, often referred to as big data, pose unique challenges in terms of storage, processing, and analysis. In this chapter, we will explore techniques and strategies for effectively handling large datasets and big data in machine learning workflows.

8.1 Data Storage

Storing and managing large datasets require careful consideration of storage infrastructure and data organization. Here are some techniques to handle data storage for large datasets:

8.1.1 Distributed File Systems

Distributed file systems, such as Hadoop Distributed File System (HDFS) or Apache HBase, are designed to store and manage large volumes of data across a cluster of machines. These file systems provide fault tolerance, scalability, and high throughput for data storage and retrieval.

By distributing the data across multiple machines, distributed file systems allow for parallel processing and efficient data access.

8.1.2 Cloud-Based Storage

Cloud storage services, like Amazon S3, Azure Blob Storage, or Google Cloud Storage, offer scalable and cost-effective solutions for storing large datasets. These services provide high durability, availability, and accessibility of data, making them suitable for handling big data.

Cloud storage services often provide various storage classes or tiers to optimize cost and performance based on data access patterns and retrieval requirements.

8.1.3 Data Compression

Data compression techniques can be applied to reduce the storage footprint of large datasets. Compression algorithms, such as gzip, zlib, or Snappy, can significantly reduce the size of data files without losing critical information.

Compression can be especially useful when dealing with text data, log files, or large numerical datasets. However, it is essential to consider the trade-off between compression ratio and computational overhead during data access and processing.

8.2 Data Processing and Analysis

When working with large datasets, traditional data processing and analysis techniques may not be sufficient. Here are some strategies to handle data processing and analysis for large datasets:

8.2.1 Distributed Computing Frameworks

Distributed computing frameworks, like Apache Hadoop, Apache Spark, or Dask, provide scalable and parallel processing capabilities for large datasets. These frameworks distribute the data across a cluster of machines and execute operations in parallel, allowing for efficient data processing and analysis.

By leveraging distributed computing frameworks, you can perform tasks like data filtering, transformations, aggregations, and complex analytics operations on large datasets.

8.2.2 Sampling and Subset Selection

Instead of processing the entire dataset, sampling techniques can be applied to select representative subsets of the data for analysis. Random sampling or stratified sampling methods allow you to obtain a subset of the data that captures the essential characteristics of the entire dataset.

Sampling reduces computational requirements and speeds up the data analysis process. However, it is important to ensure that the selected samples maintain the statistical properties and representativeness of the original dataset.

8.2.3 Incremental Processing

For streaming or continuously updated datasets, incremental processing techniques can be applied to handle the data as it arrives. Incremental processing allows you to process data in small batches or in a streaming manner, updating the model or performing analysis incrementally.

This approach is useful when dealing with real-time data streams or when the entire dataset cannot fit into memory for processing.

8.2.4 Parallel Algorithms

Designing and implementing parallel algorithms specific to your analysis or machine learning tasks can improve the efficiency of large-scale data processing. Parallel algorithms exploit the parallel nature of operations to distribute the computational workload across multiple cores or machines.

Parallelization techniques, such as map-reduce, divide-and-conquer, or data parallelism, can be applied to speed up computations on large datasets.

8.3 Data Preprocessing and Feature Engineering

Data preprocessing and feature engineering play a vital role in preparing large datasets for machine learning models. Here are some considerations:

8.3.1 Distributed Preprocessing

Distributed preprocessing techniques allow you to perform data transformations and cleaning operations on large datasets efficiently. By leveraging distributed computing frameworks, you can distribute preprocessing tasks across multiple machines, making the process scalable and time-efficient.

8.3.2 Feature Selection

Feature selection techniques help identify the most informative features in large datasets. These techniques can be applied to reduce the dimensionality of the data, eliminate redundant or irrelevant features, and improve model efficiency and performance.

Techniques like correlation analysis, feature importance ranking, or L1 regularization can aid in selecting the most relevant features.

8.3.3 Streaming Data Processing

In scenarios where the data arrives in a streaming fashion, techniques like online feature engineering can be applied. Online feature engineering enables the creation of features in real-time as the data arrives, allowing for immediate analysis or model updates.

Streaming data processing frameworks like Apache Flink or Apache Beam provide capabilities for handling continuous data streams and performing real-time feature engineering.

8.4 Distributed Model Training

Training models on large datasets can be computationally intensive and time-consuming. Here are some techniques for distributed model training:

8.4.1 Distributed Deep Learning

Deep learning frameworks like TensorFlow, PyTorch, or Horovod provide support for distributed model training across multiple GPUs or machines. Distributed training techniques, such as data parallelism or model parallelism, distribute the model and training data to different compute resources, accelerating the training process.

Distributed deep learning allows for scaling model training on large datasets and leveraging the power of parallel computing.

8.4.2 Ensemble Methods

Ensemble methods combine multiple models or model instances to make predictions. These methods, such as bagging or boosting, can be applied to distribute the training process across multiple machines.

Each machine trains a subset of the data or a different model, and the predictions are aggregated to obtain the final result.

Ensemble methods improve model performance and robustness by leveraging the diversity of individual models.

8.5 Data Streaming and Real-Time Analytics

In scenarios where data arrives in real-time or streaming fashion, techniques for handling data streaming and real-time analytics become important. Here are some considerations:

8.5.1 Stream Processing Frameworks

Stream processing frameworks, such as Apache Kafka, Apache Flink, or Apache Spark Streaming, enable real-time processing and analysis of streaming data. These frameworks provide capabilities to handle high-throughput data streams, perform aggregations, windowing operations, and apply machine learning models in real-time.

Stream processing frameworks support real-time analytics, anomaly detection, pattern recognition, and other real-time applications.

8.5.2 Online Learning

Online learning algorithms are specifically designed for streaming or continuously evolving datasets. These algorithms update the model parameters incrementally as new data arrives, allowing the model to adapt to changes in the data distribution.

Online learning is particularly useful when immediate analysis or decision-making is required in dynamic environments.

Handling large datasets and big data in machine learning workflows requires careful consideration of storage, processing, and analysis techniques. By leveraging distributed computing frameworks, data sampling, incremental processing, parallel algorithms, and appropriate preprocessing techniques, you can effectively handle and extract insights from large datasets

8.1 Distributed Computing and Parallel Processing

When dealing with large datasets and big data, traditional sequential processing may not be sufficient. Distributed computing and parallel processing techniques allow for efficient and scalable data processing, analysis, and model training. In this chapter, we will explore the concepts and strategies behind distributed computing and parallel processing in machine learning.

8.1.1 Distributed Computing

Distributed computing involves the use of multiple machines or nodes to work together on a task, allowing for faster and more efficient data processing. This approach breaks down a large problem into smaller subproblems that can be solved concurrently. Here are some key concepts related to distributed computing:

8.1.1.1 Distributed File Systems

Distributed file systems, such as Hadoop Distributed File System (HDFS) or Google File System (GFS), are designed to store and manage large volumes of data across multiple machines. These file systems provide fault tolerance, scalability, and high throughput for distributed data storage and retrieval.

By distributing the data across multiple machines, distributed file systems enable parallel processing and efficient data access.

8.1.1.2 MapReduce

MapReduce is a programming model for distributed computing that allows for parallel processing of large datasets. It consists of two main stages: Map and Reduce.

In the Map stage, the input data is divided into smaller chunks, and each chunk is processed independently by a map function. The map function transforms the input data into key-value pairs.

In the Reduce stage, the intermediate key-value pairs are grouped based on the keys, and a reduce function is applied to each group to generate the final output.

MapReduce is widely used in distributed computing frameworks like Apache Hadoop and Apache Spark for tasks such as data processing, aggregations, and feature extraction.

8.1.2 Parallel Processing

Parallel processing refers to the execution of multiple tasks simultaneously to speed up data processing and analysis. It involves dividing a task into smaller subtasks that can be executed in parallel on multiple cores or machines. Here are some key concepts related to parallel processing:

8.1.2.1 Data Parallelism

Data parallelism involves dividing the data into partitions and processing each partition independently on different processing units, such as CPU cores or GPUs. Each processing unit operates on its assigned data partition, performing the same operations simultaneously.

Data parallelism is commonly used in machine learning for training models on large datasets. Each processing unit updates its own model parameters, and the parameters are then aggregated to obtain the final model.

8.1.2.2 Model Parallelism

Model parallelism involves dividing a deep learning model across multiple processing units, allowing each unit to handle a specific portion of the model. This approach is useful when the model's size exceeds the memory capacity of a single processing unit.

Model parallelism enables the training and inference of large models by distributing the computational load across multiple devices or machines.

8.1.2.3 Task Parallelism

Task parallelism involves dividing a task into smaller independent subtasks that can be executed concurrently. Each subtask can be assigned to a separate processing unit, enabling parallel execution and faster completion of the overall task.

Task parallelism is useful when different parts of a pipeline or workflow can be executed independently and in parallel.

8.1.3 Distributed Computing Frameworks

To implement distributed computing and parallel processing, various frameworks and libraries are available. These frameworks provide the necessary infrastructure and tools for distributed data storage, data processing, and model training. Some popular distributed computing frameworks include:

Apache Hadoop: An open-source framework that supports distributed storage (HDFS) and distributed data processing (MapReduce).

Apache Spark: A fast and general-purpose distributed computing framework that supports distributed data processing, including batch processing, streaming, and machine learning.

TensorFlow: A popular deep learning framework that provides support for distributed training of deep neural networks.

PyTorch: Another popular deep learning framework that offers capabilities for distributed model training and parallel processing.

These frameworks simplify the development and execution of distributed computing and parallel processing tasks, allowing for efficient utilization of computing resources and faster data processing.

By leveraging distributed computing and parallel processing techniques, you can effectively handle large datasets and big data in machine learning workflows. These approaches enable faster data processing, scalable model training, and efficient analysis of big data.

8.2 Apache Hadoop and Spark

Apache Hadoop and Apache Spark are two widely used open-source frameworks for distributed computing and big data processing. These frameworks provide powerful tools and libraries to handle large datasets, perform parallel processing, and enable efficient analysis. In this chapter, we will explore the key features and components of Apache Hadoop and Spark.

8.2.1 Apache Hadoop

Apache Hadoop is an open-source framework that enables distributed storage and processing of large datasets. It consists of the following components:

8.2.1.1 Hadoop Distributed File System (HDFS)

HDFS is a distributed file system designed to store and manage large volumes of data across a cluster of machines. It provides fault tolerance, high availability, and scalability.

HDFS divides data into blocks and distributes them across multiple machines. It replicates data across different nodes to ensure data reliability and availability. HDFS allows for efficient data access and parallel processing by bringing computation closer to the data.

8.2.1.2 MapReduce

MapReduce is a programming model and processing framework in Hadoop for distributed data processing. It enables parallel execution of tasks across a cluster of machines.

In MapReduce, data processing tasks are divided into two stages: Map and Reduce. The Map stage processes the input data in parallel across different machines, generating intermediate key-value pairs. The Reduce stage aggregates and combines the intermediate results to produce the final output.

MapReduce provides fault tolerance, load balancing, and automatic parallelization of tasks. It is suitable for large-scale data processing, such as batch processing, data transformations, and aggregations.

8.2.1.3 YARN (Yet Another Resource Negotiator)

YARN is the resource management framework in Hadoop that allows for efficient allocation and management of computing resources. It manages resources across a cluster of machines, ensuring optimal resource utilization and fair scheduling of tasks.

YARN enables the execution of various data processing frameworks, including MapReduce, Apache Spark, and Apache Flink, on the same Hadoop cluster.

8.2.2 Apache Spark

Apache Spark is an open-source framework for distributed computing and big data processing. It provides an interface for programming and executing data processing tasks in a distributed and parallel manner. Spark offers several key components:

8.2.2.1 Resilient Distributed Datasets (RDDs)

RDDs are the fundamental data structure in Spark. They represent distributed collections of objects that can be processed in parallel across a cluster of machines. RDDs provide fault tolerance, as they can be automatically recovered in case of failure.

RDDs support transformations (e.g., map, filter, reduce) and actions (e.g., count, collect, save) that allow for data processing and analysis.

8.2.2.2 Spark SQL

Spark SQL is a module in Spark that provides a programming interface for working with structured and semi-structured data. It allows for querying and manipulating data using SQL-like queries or DataFrame APIs.

Spark SQL integrates with various data sources, including Hive, HBase, and Parquet, allowing for seamless data integration and analysis.

8.2.2.3 Spark Streaming

Spark Streaming enables real-time processing and analysis of streaming data. It ingests and processes data in mini-batches, allowing for near real-time analytics.

Spark Streaming integrates with various data sources, such as Kafka, Flume, and HDFS, and provides high-level APIs for data transformation and analysis.

8.2.2.4 Machine Learning Library (MLlib)

MLlib is Spark's machine learning library that provides a rich set of algorithms and tools for machine learning tasks. It includes classification, regression, clustering, and recommendation algorithms, among others.

MLlib leverages Spark's distributed computing capabilities, allowing for efficient training and prediction on large datasets.

8.2.2.5 Graph Processing (GraphX)

GraphX is a graph processing library in Spark that allows for efficient analysis and processing of graph-structured data. It provides a set of graph algorithms and high-level APIs for graph computations.

GraphX supports parallel graph processing and enables efficient graph analytics on large-scale datasets.

8.2.3 Benefits of Apache Hadoop and Spark

Apache Hadoop and Spark offer several benefits for handling large datasets and big data:

Scalability: Both frameworks allow for horizontal scalability by distributing data and processing across a cluster of machines.

They can handle massive datasets and scale seamlessly as data volumes increase.

Fault Tolerance: Hadoop and Spark provide fault tolerance mechanisms, ensuring data reliability and availability even in the presence of failures. They can recover and continue processing in case of machine or task failures.

Parallel Processing: Hadoop and Spark enable parallel processing of data, allowing for faster data analysis and model training. They leverage distributed computing capabilities to process tasks concurrently across multiple machines.

Versatility: Hadoop and Spark support various data processing tasks, including batch processing, streaming, machine learning, graph processing, and SQL-based analytics. They provide a unified platform for different types of data processing and analysis.

Ecosystem: Both frameworks have a rich ecosystem of tools, libraries, and integrations. They integrate with various data sources, databases, and analytics platforms, providing flexibility and interoperability with existing systems.

Apache Hadoop and Spark are widely adopted in industry and academia for handling big data and performing large-scale data processing and analysis. They provide powerful capabilities and a robust infrastructure for managing and processing large datasets efficiently.

8.3 Data Streaming and Real-Time Analytics

In many applications, data arrives in a continuous stream, requiring real-time processing and analysis. Data streaming and real-time analytics enable the extraction of insights and decision-making in near real-time. In this chapter, we will explore the concepts and techniques related to data streaming and real-time analytics.

8.3.1 Data Streaming

Data streaming refers to the continuous and real-time ingestion, processing, and analysis of data as it arrives. Streaming data can come from various sources such as sensors, logs, social media feeds, or financial transactions. Here are key concepts related to data streaming:

8.3.1.1 Event-Driven Architecture

Event-driven architecture is a design approach that focuses on the processing and handling of events. An event represents a significant occurrence or change in the system or data, and it triggers specific actions or workflows.

Streaming data processing often follows an event-driven architecture, where events are processed as they occur, enabling real-time responses and insights.

8.3.1.2 Stream Processing

Stream processing involves the continuous and real-time processing of streaming data. It allows for near real-time transformations, aggregations, and analysis of data as it flows through the system.

Stream processing systems, such as Apache Kafka, Apache Flink, or Apache Storm, provide the infrastructure and tools to handle high-throughput data streams and perform real-time analytics.

8.3.1.3 Windowing

Windowing is a technique in stream processing that allows for the grouping and analysis of data over specific time intervals or event counts. Windows provide a way to define boundaries for aggregations, sliding computations, or time-based analytics.

Windowing enables the analysis of data streams in a time-dependent context, allowing for calculations such as rolling averages, sessionization, or anomaly detection.

8.3.1.4 Event Time and Processing Time

In data streaming, there are two key concepts related to time: event time and processing time.

Event time refers to the time at which an event occurred in the real world. It represents the inherent timestamp associated with the data.

Processing time, on the other hand, refers to the time at which the system processes the event or data. It represents the time at which the system observes and processes the event.

Considerations of event time and processing time are crucial for handling out-of-order events, late arrivals, or dealing with time-dependent calculations in stream processing.

8.3.2 Real-Time Analytics

Real-time analytics involves the processing and analysis of streaming data in near real-time, allowing for immediate insights, decision-making, or actions. Here are key concepts related to real-time analytics:

8.3.2.1 Continuous Queries

In real-time analytics, continuous queries are used to specify the desired analysis or computations on streaming data. Continuous queries are executed continuously as data streams in, producing results in real-time.

Continuous queries can involve filtering, aggregating, joining, or transforming streaming data, providing valuable insights and updates as events occur.

8.3.2.2 Complex Event Processing (CEP)

Complex Event Processing is a technique used in real-time analytics to identify patterns, correlations, or complex relationships among events in the streaming data.

CEP allows for the detection of specific event sequences, anomalies, or significant changes in the data stream, triggering actions or generating alerts in real-time.

8.3.2.3 Real-Time Dashboards and Visualization

Real-time analytics often involves the visualization and monitoring of streaming data through real-time dashboards or visualizations. These dashboards provide live updates and visual representations of key metrics, trends, or anomalies in the data stream.

Real-time dashboards enable stakeholders to monitor and respond to changing conditions or events promptly.

8.3.3 Stream Processing Frameworks

To implement data streaming and real-time analytics, various stream processing frameworks are available. These frameworks provide the necessary infrastructure and tools to handle high-throughput data streams and perform real-time analysis. Some popular stream processing frameworks include:

Apache Kafka: A distributed event streaming platform that enables the ingestion and processing of high-throughput data streams.

Apache Flink: A stream processing framework that supports event-driven computations, fault tolerance, and high-performance processing of streaming data.

Apache Storm: A distributed real-time computation system for processing streaming data in a fault-tolerant and scalable manner.

These frameworks provide the necessary abstractions, APIs, and fault-tolerant mechanisms to handle data streaming and perform real-time analytics.

By leveraging data streaming and real-time analytics, organizations can gain immediate insights, make timely decisions, and take proactive actions based on continuously flowing data. These techniques are crucial in various domains, including IoT applications, financial services, social media analytics, and real-time monitoring systems.

8.4 Scalable Machine Learning Techniques

When working with large datasets and big data, it is essential to employ scalable machine learning techniques that can handle the computational and resource challenges that arise. In this chapter, we will explore several strategies and techniques for scaling machine learning algorithms to handle large-scale data effectively.

8.4.1 Mini-Batch and Stochastic Gradient Descent

Mini-batch and stochastic gradient descent (SGD) are popular techniques for training machine learning models on large datasets. Instead of using the entire dataset for each iteration, mini-batch SGD randomly samples a subset of the data (a mini-batch) and performs gradient descent on that mini-batch. This approach significantly reduces the computational burden while still updating the model parameters effectively.

Mini-batch SGD allows for parallelization across multiple processors or machines, as each mini-batch can be processed independently. This technique is particularly useful for training deep learning models on large-scale datasets.

8.4.2 Distributed Machine Learning

Distributed machine learning algorithms aim to parallelize the training process across multiple machines or processors. These algorithms distribute the data and computation, allowing for faster and more efficient training. Some popular distributed machine learning frameworks include TensorFlow, PyTorch, and Apache Spark's MLlib.

Distributed machine learning algorithms can utilize data parallelism or model parallelism. Data parallelism involves dividing the data across multiple machines, with each machine training a subset of the data independently. Model parallelism, on the other hand, involves dividing the model across multiple machines, where each machine handles a portion of the model's parameters.

By distributing the workload, distributed machine learning algorithms can train models faster and handle larger datasets more efficiently.

8.4.3 Online Learning

Online learning techniques are suitable for situations where data arrives in a streaming or incremental manner. Online learning algorithms update the model's parameters iteratively as new data points become available, allowing for continuous model adaptation.

Online learning is particularly useful when working with evolving or dynamic data, as the model can quickly adapt to changes. Additionally, online learning algorithms are memory-efficient, as they update the model in a sequential manner without requiring the entire dataset to be stored in memory.

Online learning can be applied to various machine learning tasks, such as classification, regression, and anomaly detection.

8.4.4 Feature Hashing

Feature hashing, also known as the hashing trick, is a technique used to handle high-dimensional feature spaces efficiently. In feature hashing, the original feature space is mapped to a lower-dimensional space using a hashing function. This technique reduces the memory requirements and computational complexity associated with high-dimensional feature spaces.

Feature hashing is particularly useful when working with text data or data with a large number of categorical features. It allows for efficient storage and computation while still preserving the key characteristics of the original data.

8.4.5 Approximate Algorithms

In situations where exact calculations are computationally expensive or infeasible, approximate algorithms can be used to achieve scalable machine learning. Approximate algorithms provide fast and efficient solutions by sacrificing some level of accuracy.

Examples of approximate algorithms include locality-sensitive hashing (LSH) for nearest neighbor search, random projections for dimensionality reduction, and sampling techniques for data summarization.

Approximate algorithms allow for scalable computations on large datasets while still providing reasonable results for many applications.

8.4.6 Model Compression

Model compression techniques aim to reduce the size of machine learning models without significantly sacrificing performance. These techniques can be beneficial when deploying models to resource-constrained environments or when working with large ensemble models.

Techniques such as pruning, quantization, and knowledge distillation are commonly used for model compression. Pruning involves removing unnecessary or redundant model parameters, while quantization reduces the precision of model weights. Knowledge distillation transfers the knowledge from a large, complex model to a smaller model.

Model compression techniques reduce the memory requirements and improve the inference speed of machine learning models, enabling more efficient deployment on large-scale systems.

By leveraging scalable machine learning techniques, practitioners can effectively handle large-scale data and perform efficient model training and inference. These techniques ensure that machine learning workflows are optimized for scalability, computational efficiency, and resource utilization.

Chapter 9: Reinforcement Learning

Reinforcement Learning (RL) is a branch of machine learning that focuses on training agents to make sequential decisions in an environment to maximize cumulative rewards. RL has gained significant attention due to its ability to tackle complex decision-making problems, such as game playing, robotics control, and autonomous driving. In this chapter, we will explore the fundamental concepts, algorithms, and applications of reinforcement learning.

9.1 Key Concepts in Reinforcement Learning

9.1.1 Agent and Environment

In reinforcement learning, an agent interacts with an environment. The agent takes actions based on its current state, and the environment responds by transitioning to a new state and providing a reward signal. The agent's goal is to learn a policy, a mapping from states to actions, that maximizes the cumulative rewards over time.

9.1.2 Markov Decision Process (MDP)

Reinforcement learning is often formulated as a Markov Decision Process (MDP). An MDP is defined by a set of states, actions, transition probabilities, and rewards. The transition probabilities represent the likelihood of transitioning from one state to another based on the agent's actions, and rewards indicate the immediate feedback received by the agent.

9.1.3 Policy

A policy in reinforcement learning determines the agent's behavior—how it selects actions in response to states. The policy can be deterministic (e.g., always choosing the same action for a given state) or stochastic (e.g., choosing actions based on probabilities). The goal of the agent is to find an optimal policy that maximizes the expected cumulative rewards.

9.1.4 Value Function

The value function estimates the expected cumulative rewards the agent will receive starting from a particular state under a given policy. It quantifies the goodness of states or state-action pairs and is used to guide the agent's decision-making. The two common types of value functions are the state value function (V(s)) and the action value function (Q(s,a)).

9.1.5 Exploration and Exploitation

In reinforcement learning, there is a trade-off between exploration and exploitation. Exploration involves taking actions to gather information about the environment and discover potentially better actions. Exploitation involves choosing actions that the agent believes will maximize immediate rewards based on its current knowledge. Balancing exploration and exploitation is critical to discovering optimal policies.

9.2 Reinforcement Learning Algorithms

9.2.1 Q-Learning

Q-Learning is a popular off-policy reinforcement learning algorithm that learns an optimal action value function (Q-function). It iteratively updates Q-values based on the agent's experience using the Bellman equation. Q-Learning can handle problems with discrete state and action spaces and does not require a model of the environment.

9.2.2 Deep Q-Network (DQN)

Deep Q-Network (DQN) is an extension of Q-Learning that leverages deep neural networks to approximate the Q-function. DQN allows for handling problems with high-dimensional state spaces by using neural networks as function approximators. It utilizes experience replay and target networks to stabilize the learning process.

9.2.3 Policy Gradient Methods

Policy Gradient methods directly learn the policy by optimizing a parameterized policy function through gradient ascent. These methods estimate the policy gradient using techniques such as the REINFORCE algorithm or the Proximal Policy Optimization (PPO) algorithm. Policy Gradient methods are suitable for problems with continuous action spaces and can handle stochastic policies.

9.2.4 Actor-Critic Methods

Actor-Critic methods combine elements of both value-based methods (such as Q-Learning) and policy-based methods (such as Policy Gradient). They maintain an actor network that learns the policy and a critic network that estimates the value function. Actor-Critic methods strike a balance between exploration and exploitation and can handle problems with both discrete and continuous action spaces.

9.3 Applications of Reinforcement Learning

Reinforcement learning has found successful applications in various domains:

9.3.1 Game Playing

Reinforcement learning has achieved remarkable success in game playing, beating human experts in complex games like Chess, Go, and Poker. Deep reinforcement learning algorithms, such as AlphaGo and AlphaZero, have demonstrated the ability to learn high-level strategies and make optimal decisions in game environments.

9.3.2 Robotics Control

Reinforcement learning is used to train robots to perform tasks like object manipulation, locomotion, and grasping. RL enables robots to learn complex control policies from raw sensory inputs and adapt to different environments and tasks.

9.3.3 Autonomous Vehicles

Reinforcement learning plays a crucial role in training autonomous vehicles to navigate complex traffic scenarios, make safe driving decisions, and optimize fuel efficiency. RL algorithms can learn driving policies that adapt to changing road conditions and traffic patterns.

9.3.4 Resource Management

Reinforcement learning is applied to optimize resource allocation and scheduling in various domains, such as energy management, network routing, and supply chain management. RL algorithms learn policies that maximize resource utilization, minimize costs, or optimize other performance metrics.

9.4 Challenges in Reinforcement Learning

Reinforcement learning poses several challenges:

9.4.1 Exploration-Exploitation Trade-off

Finding a balance between exploration and exploitation is critical. Insufficient exploration may lead to suboptimal policies, while excessive exploration can result in slow convergence or inefficient learning.

9.4.2 Credit Assignment

Determining which actions contribute to long-term rewards can be challenging, especially in delayed reward settings. Credit assignment refers to attributing rewards to the actions that led to them, which is crucial for effective learning.

9.4.3 Sample Efficiency

Reinforcement learning often requires significant amounts of data to learn optimal policies, which can be time-consuming and costly. Improving sample efficiency is a key research area to reduce the data requirements for learning.

9.5 Future Directions in Reinforcement Learning

Reinforcement learning is a rapidly evolving field with ongoing research and advancements. Some future directions include:

9.5.1 Deep Reinforcement Learning

Exploring further advancements in deep reinforcement learning, including architectures, algorithms, and training techniques, to improve sample efficiency, stability, and generalization.

9.5.2 Transfer Learning and Multi-Task Learning

Developing methods to transfer learned knowledge from one task to another or to leverage shared information across multiple related tasks, improving learning efficiency and generalization.

9.5.3 Safe Reinforcement Learning

Ensuring the safety and reliability of RL agents, especially in critical domains like healthcare, finance, and autonomous systems. Safe RL involves techniques to handle risk, uncertainty, and ethical considerations in decision-making.

9.5.4 Explainability and Interpretability

Improving the interpretability of RL models and decision-making processes to enhance transparency, trust, and accountability in RL systems.

Reinforcement learning holds great potential for solving complex decision-making problems. As research progresses and new techniques emerge, RL will continue to advance, enabling autonomous agents and systems to make optimal decisions in diverse real-world scenarios.

9.1 Introduction to Reinforcement Learning

Reinforcement Learning (RL) is a subfield of machine learning that focuses on training agents to make sequential decisions in an environment to maximize cumulative rewards. RL differs from other machine learning approaches in that it involves learning through interaction and feedback from the environment rather than relying solely on labeled data. RL is particularly well-suited for problems where the optimal solution is not known in advance and must be discovered through trial and error.

9.1.1 Agent and Environment

In reinforcement learning, an agent interacts with an environment to learn optimal behavior. The agent takes actions based on its current state, and the environment responds by transitioning to a new state and providing feedback in the form of rewards or penalties. The agent's goal is to learn a policy—a mapping from states to actions—that maximizes the expected cumulative rewards over time.

The agent and environment can be represented in the context of a Markov Decision Process (MDP), which is a mathematical framework for modeling sequential decision-making problems. An MDP consists of a set of states, actions, transition probabilities, and rewards. The agent's objective is to find the optimal policy that maximizes the expected cumulative rewards.

9.1.2 Reward Signal

The reward signal is a crucial component of reinforcement learning. It provides immediate feedback to the agent on the quality of its actions in a given state. The agent's objective is to maximize the cumulative rewards it receives over time. The reward signal can be positive (e.g., a high score in a game) or negative (e.g., a penalty for an incorrect move). By receiving rewards, the agent can learn which actions are desirable and which ones should be avoided.

9.1.3 Exploration and Exploitation

Reinforcement learning involves a trade-off between exploration and exploitation. Exploration refers to the agent's desire to try out different actions to discover potentially better strategies and gain more information about the environment. Exploitation, on the other hand, involves using the knowledge the agent has gained so far to choose actions that are likely to yield higher rewards based on its current understanding.

Balancing exploration and exploitation is a fundamental challenge in reinforcement learning. If the agent only explores, it may not take advantage of the knowledge it has acquired. Conversely, if it only exploits, it may miss out on discovering better strategies. Finding the right balance is crucial for effective learning and achieving optimal performance.

9.1.4 Value and Policy

In reinforcement learning, the agent aims to learn a value function and a policy to make informed decisions.

Value Function: The value function estimates the expected cumulative rewards the agent will receive from a particular state or state-action pair. It quantifies the desirability of being in a specific state or taking a specific action. The value function guides the agent's decision-making process by providing a measure of how good each state or action is.

Policy: The policy represents the agent's strategy for selecting actions in different states. It defines the mapping from states to actions, determining how the agent behaves in the environment. The policy can be deterministic (e.g., always selecting the action with the highest value) or stochastic (e.g., selecting actions based on probabilities). The agent's objective is to learn an optimal policy that maximizes the expected cumulative rewards.

9.1.5 Applications of Reinforcement Learning

Reinforcement learning has found successful applications in various domains:

Game Playing: RL algorithms have achieved impressive results in playing complex games, such as Chess, Go, and Atari games, surpassing human performance.

Robotics: RL enables robots to learn control policies to perform tasks such as object manipulation, locomotion, and grasping.

Autonomous Systems: RL is used in autonomous vehicles to learn driving policies, optimize energy consumption, and make real-time decisions in dynamic environments.

Resource Management: RL algorithms are applied to optimize resource allocation, scheduling, and decision-making in domains like energy management, network routing, and supply chain management.

9.1.6 Challenges in Reinforcement Learning

Reinforcement learning presents several challenges:

Exploration vs. Exploitation: Finding the right balance between exploration and exploitation to discover optimal policies without getting stuck in suboptimal solutions.

Credit Assignment: Attributing rewards to the actions that led to them, especially in cases where rewards are delayed or sparse.

Scalability: Dealing with large state and action spaces, long time horizons, and high-dimensional observations.

Safety and Ethics: Ensuring that RL agents operate safely and ethically, taking into account potential risks and unintended consequences.

9.1.7 Future Directions in Reinforcement Learning

Reinforcement learning is an active area of research, and several directions show promise for future advancements:

Deep Reinforcement Learning: Combining reinforcement learning with deep neural networks to handle high-dimensional state and action spaces and learn complex policies.

Transfer Learning: Leveraging knowledge learned from one task to accelerate learning in related tasks, improving sample efficiency and generalization.

Explainability and Interpretability: Developing techniques to make RL models and decision-making processes more transparent and interpretable.

Hierarchical RL: Learning policies at different levels of abstraction to handle problems with long time horizons and complex structures.

Reinforcement learning offers a powerful framework for training agents to make sequential decisions. By understanding the key concepts, algorithms, and challenges in reinforcement learning, practitioners can apply RL techniques to a wide range of problems and contribute to advancements in this exciting field.

9.2 Markov Decision Processes (MDP)

Markov Decision Processes (MDPs) provide a mathematical framework for modeling sequential decision-making problems in reinforcement learning. MDPs capture the essential elements of an agent interacting with an environment, allowing for the formulation and analysis of optimal decision-making policies. In this chapter, we will explore the key concepts and components of MDPs.

9.2.1 Components of an MDP

An MDP is defined by the following components:

9.2.1.1 State Space (S)

The state space represents all possible states that the agent can be in. Each state captures relevant information about the environment at a particular time. The state space can be discrete, where states are explicitly defined, or continuous, where states are represented by a continuous set of values.

9.2.1.2 Action Space (A)

The action space represents all possible actions that the agent can take in each state. Actions are the decisions made by the agent to transition from one state to another. Similar to the state space, the action space can be discrete or continuous.

9.2.1.3 Transition Probabilities (P)

The transition probabilities define the probability of transitioning from one state to another when the agent takes a particular action. For each state-action pair (s, a), P(s'|s, a) represents the probability of transitioning to state s' given that the agent is in state s and takes action a. The transition probabilities capture the dynamics of the environment.

9.2.1.4 Rewards (R)

Rewards provide immediate feedback to the agent based on its actions and the resulting state transitions. In an MDP, a reward function R(s, a, s') assigns a numerical value to the agent for transitioning from state s to state s' after taking action a. The reward can be positive, negative, or zero, depending on the desirability of the state transition.

9.2.1.5 Discount Factor (γ)

The discount factor, denoted as γ (gamma), determines the importance of future rewards compared to immediate rewards. It represents the agent's preference for immediate rewards versus long-term rewards. A discount factor of $\gamma = 0$ means the agent only considers immediate rewards, while $\gamma = 1$ means the agent values future rewards equally to immediate rewards.

9.2.2 Policy and Value Functions

In an MDP, the agent's goal is to find an optimal policy that maximizes the expected cumulative rewards. A policy π is a mapping from states to actions, indicating the action the agent should take in each state. The policy can be deterministic, where it selects a single action, or stochastic, where it chooses actions based on probabilities.

The value functions provide a measure of the expected cumulative rewards under a given policy. There are two types of value functions in an MDP:

9.2.2.1 State Value Function (V(s))

The state value function V(s) represents the expected cumulative rewards the agent will receive starting from state s and following the policy π. It measures the desirability of being in a particular state. The state value function is defined as the expected sum of discounted future rewards:

$$V(s) = E[\Sigma \gamma^t R(s_t, a_t, s_{t+1}) \mid s, \pi]$$

where t represents the time step, γ is the discount factor, and the sum is taken over all future time steps.

9.2.2.2 Action Value Function (Q(s, a))

The action value function Q(s, a) represents the expected cumulative rewards the agent will receive starting from state s, taking action a, and following the policy π thereafter. It measures the desirability of taking a particular action in a specific state. The action value function is defined as the expected sum of discounted future rewards:

$$Q(s, a) = E[\Sigma\gamma^t R(s_t, a_t, s_{t+1}) \mid s, a, \pi]$$

where t represents the time step, γ is the discount factor, and the sum is taken over all future time steps.

9.2.3 Bellman Equations

The value functions in an MDP satisfy the Bellman equations, which define recursive relationships between the values of states and actions. The Bellman equations enable iterative algorithms to compute optimal value functions and policies.

The Bellman equation for the state value function is:

$$V(s) = E[R(s, a, s') + \gamma * V(s') \mid s, a]$$

This equation expresses the value of a state as the sum of the immediate reward R(s, a, s') and the discounted value of the next state V(s').

The Bellman equation for the action value function is:

$$Q(s, a) = E[R(s, a, s') + \gamma * \max_{a'} Q(s', a') \mid s, a]$$

This equation expresses the value of taking an action in a state as the sum of the immediate reward R(s, a, s') and the discounted value of the best action in the next state.

By iteratively solving the Bellman equations, optimal value functions can be obtained, leading to the determination of an optimal policy.

9.2.4 Solving MDPs

There are several algorithms to solve MDPs and find optimal policies:

Value Iteration: Value iteration is an iterative algorithm that repeatedly applies the Bellman equations to update the value functions until convergence. It converges to the optimal value functions and policy.

Policy Iteration: Policy iteration is an iterative algorithm that alternates between policy evaluation and policy improvement steps. It iteratively updates the policy based on the value functions until convergence to the optimal policy.

Q-Learning: Q-Learning is a model-free reinforcement learning algorithm that learns the action value function Q(s, a) directly through exploration and exploitation. It iteratively updates Q-values based on the agent's experience and converges to the optimal Q-function and policy.

9.2.5 Extensions of MDPs

While MDPs provide a solid framework for sequential decision-making, there are extensions that address additional complexities:

Partially Observable MDPs (POMDPs): POMDPs model situations where the agent has limited or noisy observations of the environment, introducing uncertainty and the need for probabilistic reasoning.

Continuous MDPs: Continuous MDPs extend the MDP framework to handle continuous state and action spaces, requiring techniques like function approximation and policy optimization.

MDPs form the foundation for understanding and solving sequential decision-making problems in reinforcement learning. By modeling the environment as an MDP and using appropriate algorithms, agents can learn optimal policies that maximize long-term rewards.

9.3 Q-Learning and Deep Q-Networks (DQN)

Q-Learning is a popular reinforcement learning algorithm that learns the optimal action value function (Q-function) through trial and error. Q-Learning, along with its extension Deep Q-Networks (DQN), has achieved significant success in solving complex reinforcement learning problems, including game playing and robotics control. In this chapter, we will explore the concepts and techniques behind Q-Learning and DQN.

9.3.1 Q-Learning

Q-Learning is a model-free reinforcement learning algorithm that learns the optimal action value function (Q-function) directly from interactions with the environment. The Q-function represents the expected cumulative rewards the agent will receive by taking a particular action in a given state.

The Q-Learning algorithm iteratively updates Q-values based on the agent's experience. The key idea is to estimate the Q-values by bootstrapping from the Q-values of future states, using the Bellman equation:

$$Q(s, a) = Q(s, a) + \alpha * (r + \gamma * \max\_a' \, Q(s', a') - Q(s, a))$$

In the equation, Q(s, a) represents the Q-value of state s and action a, r is the immediate reward obtained by taking action a in state s, s' is the next state after taking action a, a' is the next action in state s', γ is the discount factor, and α is the learning rate.

By iteratively updating the Q-values based on the observed rewards and transitions, Q-Learning converges to the optimal Q-function that maximizes the expected cumulative rewards.

9.3.2 Deep Q-Networks (DQN)

Deep Q-Networks (DQN) is an extension of Q-Learning that leverages deep neural networks to approximate the Q-function. DQN combines reinforcement learning with deep learning, allowing for handling high-dimensional state spaces and learning complex policies.

In DQN, a deep neural network, known as the Q-network, is used to approximate the Q-function. The Q-network takes a state as input and outputs Q-values for all possible actions. The Q-network is trained to minimize the temporal difference error between the predicted Q-values and the target Q-values, defined as:

Loss = (r + γ * max_a' Q_target(s', a') - Q(s, a))^2

In the equation, r is the immediate reward, γ is the discount factor, Q_target(s', a') represents the target Q-value of the next state, and Q(s, a) is the predicted Q-value of the current state.

To stabilize the learning process, DQN employs two techniques: experience replay and target network.

Experience Replay: Experience replay stores the agent's experiences, consisting of state, action, reward, next state, and done flag, in a replay buffer. During training, a random batch of experiences is sampled from the replay buffer to decorrelate the experiences and reduce the impact of temporal correlations.

Target Network: DQN utilizes a target network, a separate copy of the Q-network, to compute the target Q-values. The target network's parameters are updated less frequently, reducing the target value's moving target problem and improving the stability of learning.

By using deep neural networks and the aforementioned techniques, DQN can handle high-dimensional state spaces and learn complex policies effectively.

9.3.3 Extensions and Variants

Several extensions and variants of DQN have been proposed to address specific challenges and improve performance:

Double Q-Learning: Double Q-Learning addresses the issue of overestimation bias in the Q-values by decoupling the action selection and evaluation steps.

Dueling DQN: Dueling DQN separates the Q-function into state-value and advantage components, allowing for better estimation of the value of each state and the importance of different actions.

Rainbow: Rainbow is an integration of several enhancements, including prioritized experience replay, distributional Q-learning, and multi-step returns, to further improve the performance of DQN.

9.3.4 Applications of DQN

DQN and its variants have been successfully applied to various reinforcement learning tasks:

Game Playing: DQN achieved breakthrough results in playing Atari games, surpassing human-level performance in several games.

Robotics Control: DQN has been used to train robots to perform complex manipulation tasks and control systems.

Autonomous Systems: DQN is applied to train agents for autonomous driving, navigation, and decision-making in dynamic environments.

Resource Management: DQN is employed to optimize resource allocation, scheduling, and decision-making in domains such as energy management and network routing.

DQN has demonstrated the ability to learn complex policies and achieve state-of-the-art results in various domains, making it a powerful tool in reinforcement learning.

9.4 Policy Gradient Methods

Policy gradient methods are a class of reinforcement learning algorithms that directly learn policies by optimizing a parameterized policy function through gradient ascent. Unlike value-based methods, which estimate the value functions, policy gradient methods aim to find the optimal policy by iteratively improving the policy parameters. In this chapter, we will explore the concepts and techniques behind policy gradient methods.

9.4.1 Policy Optimization

In reinforcement learning, the policy determines the agent's behavior—how it selects actions in different states. The goal of policy gradient methods is to find the policy parameters that maximize the expected cumulative rewards. The policy is typically represented by a parameterized function, denoted as $\pi(a|s; \theta)$, where θ represents the parameters of the policy.

To optimize the policy, policy gradient methods use gradient ascent to update the policy parameters based on the observed rewards. The policy is updated in the direction that increases the expected cumulative rewards. The update rule for the policy parameters can be expressed as:

$$\theta \leftarrow \theta + \alpha * \nabla_\theta J(\theta)$$

In the equation, α is the learning rate, and $\nabla_\theta J(\theta)$ represents the gradient of the objective function $J(\theta)$ with respect to the policy parameters θ.

9.4.2 Objective Functions

The objective function $J(\theta)$ measures the performance of the policy and determines the direction of the policy update. Commonly used objective functions include:

Average Reward: The objective is to maximize the average reward obtained by following the policy. $J(\theta) = E_{\pi} [R]$, where R represents the cumulative rewards obtained when following the policy π.

Discounted Reward: The objective is to maximize the expected sum of discounted rewards. $J(\theta) = E_{\pi} [\Sigma \gamma^t R_t]$, where γ is the discount factor and R_t represents the reward obtained at time step t.

9.4.3 Policy Gradient Theorem

The policy gradient theorem provides a fundamental result in policy gradient methods. It states that the gradient of the objective function with respect to the policy parameters can be expressed as:

$$\nabla_{\theta} J(\theta) = E_{\pi} [\nabla_{\theta} \log \pi(a|s; \theta) * Q\pi(s, a)]$$

In the equation, $\nabla_{\theta} \log \pi(a|s; \theta)$ represents the gradient of the log-probability of taking action a in state s under the policy π, and $Q\pi(s, a)$ represents the action-value function.

The policy gradient theorem indicates that the gradient of the objective function can be obtained by multiplying the log-probability of actions with the corresponding action-values. This allows for estimating the gradient through sampling and using the observed rewards.

9.4.4 REINFORCE Algorithm

The REINFORCE algorithm is a classic policy gradient method that uses the policy gradient theorem to update the policy parameters. The REINFORCE update rule can be expressed as:

$$\theta \leftarrow \theta + \alpha * \nabla_\theta \log \pi(a|s; \theta) * G$$

In the equation, G represents the return, which is the cumulative rewards obtained after taking action a in state s and following the policy π. The return can be computed as the sum of discounted rewards or the average rewards, depending on the objective function.

The REINFORCE algorithm iteratively samples trajectories by interacting with the environment, computes the returns, and performs gradient ascent updates to improve the policy.

9.4.5 Proximal Policy Optimization (PPO)

Proximal Policy Optimization (PPO) is a state-of-the-art policy gradient method that addresses some limitations of traditional policy gradient algorithms, such as unstable updates and sensitivity to the step size. PPO utilizes a clipped surrogate objective to ensure more stable policy updates.

PPO introduces a surrogate objective function that constrains the policy update to be within a specified range:

$$L(\theta) = E\_min [ratio * A, clip(ratio, 1 - \varepsilon, 1 + \varepsilon) * A]$$

In the equation, ratio represents the ratio of the updated policy probabilities to the old policy probabilities, A represents the advantage function, and ε is a hyperparameter that controls the extent of the policy update.

By constraining the policy update, PPO achieves more reliable and stable improvements in the policy parameters.

9.4.6 Applications of Policy Gradient Methods

Policy gradient methods have been successfully applied to various reinforcement learning tasks:

Continuous Control: Policy gradient methods are well-suited for problems with continuous action spaces, allowing for learning complex policies in robotics control and motor control tasks.

Robotics: Policy gradient methods have been used to train robots to perform dexterous manipulation tasks, locomotion, and other complex control tasks.

Natural Language Processing: Policy gradient methods have been applied to dialogue systems, machine translation, and other language-related tasks.

Game Playing: Policy gradient methods have been used to train agents to play games with complex rules, such as board games and video games.

Policy gradient methods provide a flexible approach to learning policies directly from interactions with the environment. With advancements like PPO, policy gradient methods continue to make significant contributions to reinforcement learning research and applications.

Chapter 10: Natural Language Processing (NLP)

10.1 Introduction to Natural Language Processing

Natural Language Processing (NLP) is a subfield of artificial intelligence and linguistics that focuses on the interaction between computers and human language. NLP encompasses a range of techniques and methodologies to enable computers to understand, analyze, and generate human language in a meaningful way. In this chapter, we will explore the fundamentals of NLP and its applications in various domains.

10.2 Basic Concepts in Natural Language Processing

10.2.1 Tokenization

Tokenization is the process of breaking down a text into individual units called tokens. Tokens can be words, sentences, or even smaller units like characters or subwords. Tokenization serves as a fundamental step in many NLP tasks, as it helps in structuring and organizing the text data for further analysis.

10.2.2 Part-of-Speech Tagging

Part-of-Speech (POS) tagging involves labeling each word in a sentence with its corresponding grammatical category, such as noun, verb, adjective, etc. POS tagging is essential for various NLP tasks, including syntactic analysis, information extraction, and machine translation.

10.2.3 Named Entity Recognition

Named Entity Recognition (NER) aims to identify and classify named entities (such as person names, organizations, locations, etc.) in text. NER plays a crucial role in information extraction, question answering, and text summarization tasks.

10.2.4 Sentiment Analysis

Sentiment analysis, also known as opinion mining, involves determining the sentiment or subjective information expressed in text. It classifies the text into categories like positive, negative, or neutral, enabling the analysis of public opinions, customer feedback, and social media sentiments.

10.2.5 Text Classification

Text classification is the task of assigning predefined categories or labels to text documents. It is used in applications such as spam detection, sentiment analysis, topic categorization, and document classification.

10.2.6 Language Modeling

Language modeling involves predicting the probability distribution of words or characters in a sequence of text. Language models play a crucial role in applications like machine translation, speech recognition, and autocomplete systems.

10.3 Key Techniques in Natural Language Processing

10.3.1 Word Embeddings

Word embeddings are dense vector representations that capture semantic and syntactic relationships between words. Popular word embedding techniques, such as Word2Vec and GloVe, create vector representations by training on large text corpora. Word embeddings enable computers to understand the contextual meaning of words and find semantic similarities.

10.3.2 Neural Machine Translation

Neural Machine Translation (NMT) is an approach to machine translation that utilizes neural networks to translate text from one language to another. NMT models, such as the sequence-to-sequence with attention model, have achieved significant improvements in translation quality compared to traditional statistical machine translation methods.

10.3.3 Named Entity Recognition with Conditional Random Fields

Named Entity Recognition (NER) can be performed using Conditional Random Fields (CRF), a probabilistic graphical model. CRF models take into account the contextual dependencies among words to improve the accuracy of named entity recognition.

10.3.4 Recurrent Neural Networks

Recurrent Neural Networks (RNNs) are neural network architectures designed to process sequential data, such as text. RNNs can capture the dependencies between words in a sentence, making them suitable for tasks like sentiment analysis, machine translation, and text generation.

10.3.5 Transformers

Transformers are a recent advancement in NLP that have achieved state-of-the-art results in various tasks. Transformer models, such as the BERT (Bidirectional Encoder Representations from Transformers) model, use attention mechanisms to capture the contextual relationships between words and enable deeper understanding of the text.

10.4 Applications of Natural Language Processing

10.4.1 Machine Translation

NLP techniques have revolutionized machine translation, enabling accurate and fluent translation between different languages. NMT models have shown significant improvements over traditional statistical machine translation methods, making translation services more accessible and reliable.

10.4.2 Text Generation

NLP techniques like language modeling and recurrent neural networks have been used for text generation tasks, including automatic summarization, chatbots, and dialogue systems. These techniques enable computers to generate human-like text based on learned patterns and structures.

10.4.3 Sentiment Analysis and Opinion Mining

Sentiment analysis techniques are widely used to analyze public opinions, customer feedback, and social media sentiments. Businesses can gain valuable insights into consumer preferences, market trends, and brand reputation by analyzing sentiment in text data.

10.4.4 Question Answering

Question Answering (QA) systems leverage NLP techniques to understand and answer user questions based on available knowledge sources. QA systems have been developed for specific domains like healthcare, customer support, and general knowledge.

10.4.5 Information Extraction

NLP techniques are employed for extracting structured information from unstructured text data. Named Entity Recognition (NER), relationship extraction, and event extraction are some of the techniques used in information extraction tasks.

10.5 Ethical Considerations in Natural Language Processing

As NLP techniques become more advanced and widely used, it is essential to consider ethical considerations and potential biases. Issues such as data privacy, fairness, transparency, and bias in training data should be addressed to ensure responsible and ethical use of NLP technologies.

10.6 Future Directions in Natural Language Processing

Natural Language Processing continues to evolve, driven by advancements in deep learning and large-scale language models. Future directions in NLP include:

Multilingual NLP: Developing techniques that can handle multiple languages and cross-lingual understanding.

Explainable NLP: Enhancing the interpretability of NLP models and providing explanations for their predictions and decisions.

Contextual Understanding: Improving models' ability to understand context and capture complex linguistic phenomena.

Domain-Specific NLP: Tailoring NLP techniques for specific domains, such as healthcare, legal, or scientific texts.

Interactive and Conversational NLP: Advancing dialogue systems and chatbots to have more natural and interactive conversations with users.

Natural Language Processing has immense potential for enabling computers to understand and process human language. As research and development in NLP continue, we can expect further breakthroughs and applications in various domains.

10.1 Text Preprocessing and Tokenization

Text preprocessing is an essential step in natural language processing (NLP) that involves transforming raw text into a format suitable for analysis and modeling. It typically includes tasks such as cleaning the text, removing unnecessary characters, and converting the text into a tokenized representation. Tokenization, specifically, is the process of breaking down text into individual units called tokens, which can be words, sentences, or even smaller units like characters or subwords.

10.1.1 Cleaning the Text

Cleaning the text involves removing any unwanted characters, such as punctuation marks, special symbols, or HTML tags. This step helps in reducing noise and ensuring that the text data is in a standardized format. Common techniques used for text cleaning include:

Removing punctuation marks: Punctuation marks like commas, periods, and question marks are often removed as they do not contribute significantly to the meaning of the text.

Removing special characters: Special characters, such as dollar signs, hashtags, or emoticons, are often removed as they may not add value to the analysis.

Removing HTML tags: If the text contains HTML tags, they are removed to extract the plain text content.

10.1.2 Lowercasing

Lowercasing involves converting all the text to lowercase. This step ensures that the model treats words with the same spelling but different cases (e.g., "apple" and "Apple") as the same word, preventing redundancy and improving generalization.

10.1.3 Stop Word Removal

Stop words are common words like "a," "an," "the," "is," etc., that occur frequently in the language but carry little semantic meaning. In many NLP tasks, removing stop words can help reduce the dimensionality of the data and improve the efficiency of subsequent analysis. Libraries like NLTK (Natural Language

Toolkit) provide pre-defined lists of stop words for different languages.

10.1.4 Tokenization

Tokenization is the process of breaking down text into individual tokens. Tokens can be words, sentences, or even smaller units like characters or subwords, depending on the specific task and requirements. Tokenization helps in structuring the text data for further analysis and modeling.

Word Tokenization: Word tokenization involves splitting the text into individual words. This is a common type of tokenization used in many NLP tasks. For example, the sentence "I love natural language processing" would be tokenized into the following words: ["I", "love", "natural", "language", "processing"].

Sentence Tokenization: Sentence tokenization involves splitting the text into individual sentences. This is useful when analyzing the text at the sentence level. For example, the paragraph "I love NLP. It is fascinating." would be tokenized into the following sentences: ["I love NLP.", "It is fascinating."].

Character Tokenization: Character tokenization involves breaking down the text into individual characters. This level of tokenization is useful when analyzing the text at a character level. For example, the word "hello" would be tokenized into ["h", "e", "l", "l", "o"].

Subword Tokenization: Subword tokenization involves breaking down the text into smaller meaningful units, which are not necessarily full words. This is useful for languages with complex morphology or for handling out-of-vocabulary words. Techniques like Byte Pair Encoding (BPE) and WordPiece are commonly used for subword tokenization.

10.1.5 Lemmatization and Stemming

Lemmatization and stemming are techniques used to reduce words to their base or root form. These techniques help in reducing the dimensionality of the data and treating different forms of a word as the same word.

Lemmatization: Lemmatization involves reducing words to their base form, called the lemma. For example, the word "running" would be lemmatized to "run," and "better" would remain unchanged. Lemmatization considers the context and part of speech of the word.

Stemming: Stemming is a simpler and faster technique that involves removing the suffixes from words to reduce them to their base or root form. For example, the word "running" would be stemmed to "run," and "better" would be reduced to "bett." Stemming does not consider the context or part of speech and may produce less accurate results compared to lemmatization.

10.1.6 Handling Out-of-Vocabulary Words

Out-of-vocabulary (OOV) words are words that are not present in the vocabulary of the model or tokenizer. In NLP tasks, OOV words can pose a challenge, especially when dealing with unfamiliar or domain-specific terms. Techniques such as subword tokenization or using pre-trained word embeddings can help handle OOV words by representing them as subwords or finding similar words in the embedding space.

10.1.7 Regularization and Normalization

Regularization and normalization techniques can be applied to further preprocess the text data. These techniques include:

Removing numeric characters: Numeric characters may not always contribute to the semantic meaning of the text and can be removed to reduce noise.

Removing excessive whitespace: Extra whitespace, tabs, or newlines can be removed or replaced with a single whitespace to ensure consistent spacing between tokens.

Spell checking and correction: Automated spell checking algorithms can be applied to correct common spelling errors in the text.

10.1.8 Handling Imbalanced Data

In some NLP tasks, the data may be imbalanced, meaning that certain classes or labels are overrepresented or underrepresented. Techniques such as oversampling, undersampling, or class weighting can be employed to address the class imbalance issue and ensure fair representation during training and evaluation.

10.1.9 Special Considerations for Multilingual Text

When working with multilingual text, additional considerations arise:

Language identification: It is essential to identify the language of the text before applying language-specific preprocessing techniques.

Transliteration and transliteration normalization: Transliteration involves converting text from one script to another (e.g., from Cyrillic to Latin characters). Transliteration normalization aims to standardize different transliterated forms of the same word.

Handling language-specific characteristics: Different languages may have specific linguistic characteristics, such as word order, morphology, or writing systems, which may require language-specific preprocessing techniques.

Proper text preprocessing and tokenization are crucial for successful NLP tasks. The specific preprocessing steps and techniques may vary depending on the task at hand, the language used, and the characteristics of the text data.

10.2 Word Embeddings (Word2Vec, GloVe)

Word embeddings are vector representations of words in a high-dimensional space, where words with similar meanings or contexts are closer to each other. Word embeddings capture semantic and syntactic relationships between words, enabling NLP models to understand the meaning and context of words in a more effective manner. In this chapter, we will explore two popular word embedding models: Word2Vec and GloVe.

10.2.1 Word2Vec

Word2Vec is a widely used word embedding model that learns continuous vector representations of words from large text corpora. It is based on the idea that words appearing in similar contexts have similar meanings. Word2Vec consists of two main algorithms: Continuous Bag-of-Words (CBOW) and Skip-gram.

Continuous Bag-of-Words (CBOW): CBOW aims to predict a target word based on its context words. It takes a set of context words as input and predicts the target word. CBOW is computationally efficient and works well with frequent words.

Skip-gram: Skip-gram aims to predict the context words given a target word. It takes a target word as input and predicts the context words. Skip-gram is effective for capturing rare words and can handle out-of-vocabulary words better.

Both CBOW and Skip-gram models are trained using a shallow neural network with a single hidden layer. The training process involves adjusting the model's parameters to minimize the prediction error between the predicted and actual target or context words.

10.2.2 GloVe

GloVe (Global Vectors for Word Representation) is another popular word embedding model that leverages global statistics of word co-occurrence to learn word vectors. GloVe aims to capture the relationship between words based on their co-occurrence probabilities in a large corpus.

GloVe constructs a co-occurrence matrix that represents the frequency of word co-occurrences in a corpus. It then factorizes this matrix to obtain word vectors that capture the underlying relationships. The resulting word vectors encode both semantic and syntactic information, making them suitable for various NLP tasks.

GloVe training involves optimizing a weighted least-squares objective function, considering the ratios of co-occurrence probabilities. It achieves a balance between global co-occurrence statistics and local context windows.

10.2.3 Pre-trained Word Embeddings

Both Word2Vec and GloVe can be trained on large corpora, but pre-trained embeddings are also widely available. Pre-trained word embeddings capture general language semantics and can be readily used in various NLP tasks without the need for training from scratch.

Pre-trained word embeddings are often trained on extensive text corpora, such as Wikipedia or news articles. These embeddings capture a wide range of language patterns and can be used as a starting point for NLP models. Popular pre-trained word embeddings include Google's Word2Vec, Stanford's GloVe, and Facebook's FastText.

10.2.4 Applications of Word Embeddings

Word embeddings have various applications in NLP:

Semantic Similarity: Word embeddings enable the measurement of semantic similarity between words. By computing the cosine similarity between word vectors, it is possible to identify words with similar meanings or contexts.

Named Entity Recognition (NER): Word embeddings are useful in NER tasks to capture contextual information and improve entity recognition accuracy.

Sentiment Analysis: Word embeddings help in sentiment analysis tasks by capturing sentiment-related words and their relationships.

Machine Translation: Word embeddings aid in capturing the semantic and syntactic relationships between words, improving translation quality.

Text Classification: Word embeddings are widely used in text classification tasks, enabling models to understand the meaning and context of words in classifying text documents.

10.2.5 Limitations and Considerations

While word embeddings are powerful representations for word semantics, they have certain limitations:

Polysemy: Word embeddings may struggle to capture multiple meanings of polysemous words, as they are represented by a single vector.

Out-of-Vocabulary (OOV) Words: Word embeddings may not have representations for rare or out-of-vocabulary words. Techniques like subword embeddings or handling OOV words separately can help mitigate this issue.

Bias in Word Embeddings: Word embeddings trained on biased data may reflect and amplify biases present in the training corpus. Care should be taken to address bias in word embeddings and ensure fair and unbiased representations.

Contextual Information: Word embeddings are context-independent and do not capture fine-grained contextual information. Contextual word embeddings, such as ELMo and BERT, have been developed to address this limitation.

10.2.6 Training and Integration

To train word embeddings from scratch, a large corpus of text data is required. However, pre-trained word embeddings are readily available and can be integrated into NLP models. Integration involves mapping words from the pre-trained embeddings to the corresponding vectors in the model.

Popular libraries like Gensim and spaCy provide convenient APIs for training and using word embeddings in NLP tasks. These libraries offer pre-trained embeddings and allow for fine-tuning or further training based on specific requirements.

Word embeddings, such as Word2Vec and GloVe, have revolutionized NLP by providing effective representations of word semantics. These embeddings enable models to understand the meaning and context of words, leading to improved performance in various NLP tasks.

10.3 Sentiment Analysis

Sentiment analysis, also known as opinion mining, is a popular natural language processing (NLP) task that involves determining the sentiment or subjective information expressed in text. The goal of sentiment analysis is to classify text into categories such as positive, negative, or neutral based on the sentiment it conveys. Sentiment analysis has a wide range of applications, including social media monitoring, brand reputation management, customer feedback analysis, and market research. In this chapter, we will explore the techniques and methodologies used in sentiment analysis.

10.3.1 Supervised Sentiment Analysis

Supervised sentiment analysis involves training a machine learning model on labeled data, where each text sample is annotated with its corresponding sentiment label. The model learns to recognize patterns in the text and assigns sentiment labels to new, unseen text samples. Common steps in supervised sentiment analysis include:

Data Preparation: Preparing the labeled data by cleaning the text, performing tokenization, and transforming the text into numerical representations (e.g., using bag-of-words or word embeddings).

Feature Extraction: Extracting relevant features from the text data, such as n-grams, word frequencies, or word embeddings, to represent the text samples.

Model Training: Training a machine learning model, such as logistic regression, support vector machines (SVM), or neural networks, on the labeled data. The model learns to classify text samples into sentiment categories based on the extracted features.

Model Evaluation: Evaluating the trained model's performance on a separate test set to assess its accuracy, precision, recall, and

F1-score. Cross-validation techniques can also be employed to estimate the model's generalization performance.

Inference: Using the trained model to classify sentiment in new, unseen text samples. The model assigns sentiment labels, such as positive, negative, or neutral, to the input text based on the learned patterns.

10.3.2 Unsupervised Sentiment Analysis

Unsupervised sentiment analysis aims to determine sentiment in text without relying on labeled data for training. Instead, it leverages techniques such as lexicons, rule-based approaches, or clustering algorithms to infer sentiment from the text. Common approaches in unsupervised sentiment analysis include:

Lexicon-Based Approaches: Lexicons or sentiment dictionaries contain words or phrases annotated with sentiment labels (e.g., positive or negative). Unsupervised sentiment analysis uses these lexicons to assign sentiment scores to words or phrases in the text. Aggregating these scores allows determining the overall sentiment of the text.

Rule-Based Approaches: Rule-based approaches involve defining a set of linguistic rules or patterns that capture sentiment expressions in text. These rules can include syntactic patterns, grammatical structures, or semantic cues associated with positive or negative sentiment. The presence of these patterns determines the sentiment of the text.

Clustering Approaches: Clustering algorithms group similar text samples together based on the similarity of their word usage. Unsupervised sentiment analysis can use clustering techniques to identify clusters of text with similar sentiment expressions. By examining the sentiment expressed in the dominant cluster, the overall sentiment of the text can be inferred.

10.3.3 Deep Learning Approaches

Deep learning approaches have shown promising results in sentiment analysis by leveraging the power of neural networks. These approaches often employ recurrent neural networks (RNNs), convolutional neural networks (CNNs), or transformer models like BERT (Bidirectional Encoder Representations from Transformers) to capture the contextual information in text.

Recurrent Neural Networks (RNNs): RNNs can model the sequential nature of text by processing the words in a sentence one by one. They capture the dependencies between words and can handle variable-length inputs. Long Short-Term Memory (LSTM) and Gated Recurrent Unit (GRU) are popular RNN variants used in sentiment analysis.

Convolutional Neural Networks (CNNs): CNNs excel in capturing local patterns and can be applied to sentiment analysis by treating the text as a one-dimensional sequence. Convolutional filters slide over the text, capturing important features at different levels of abstraction. Pooling operations aggregate the features, and fully connected layers make the final sentiment classification.

Transformer Models: Transformer models, such as BERT, have revolutionized sentiment analysis by capturing contextual information through self-attention mechanisms. These models pre-train on large corpora and can be fine-tuned for specific sentiment analysis tasks, achieving state-of-the-art results.

10.3.4 Aspect-Based Sentiment Analysis

Aspect-Based Sentiment Analysis (ABSA) goes beyond overall sentiment classification and focuses on identifying sentiment towards specific aspects or entities in the text. It involves identifying aspects or targets, extracting sentiment expressions related to those aspects, and determining the sentiment polarity associated with each aspect. ABSA is particularly useful for tasks like product reviews, where sentiment towards different product features or aspects needs to be analyzed.

10.3.5 Challenges and Considerations

Sentiment analysis faces several challenges, including:

Context and Ambiguity: Sentiment can be highly context-dependent, and understanding the nuances of sentiment expressions requires a deep understanding of language and world knowledge. Ambiguities in language, sarcasm, or irony can pose challenges to accurate sentiment analysis.

Domain Adaptation: Sentiment analysis models trained on one domain may not perform well when applied to a different domain.

Domain-specific features and sentiment expressions need to be captured to improve performance in specific contexts.

Data Imbalance: Sentiment analysis datasets often suffer from class imbalance, with a skewed distribution of positive, negative, and neutral samples. Techniques like oversampling, undersampling, or class weighting can be employed to handle imbalanced data.

Multilingual Sentiment Analysis: Analyzing sentiment in languages other than English poses additional challenges due to language-specific characteristics, lack of labeled data, and varying sentiment expressions.

Ethical Considerations: Sentiment analysis should be conducted responsibly, ensuring privacy protection, unbiased analysis, and transparency in handling user-generated content.

10.3.6 Evaluation Metrics

To assess the performance of sentiment analysis models, various evaluation metrics can be employed, including:

Accuracy: Measures the overall accuracy of sentiment predictions.

Precision, Recall, F1-score: Evaluate the precision, recall, and F1-score of each sentiment class (positive, negative, neutral) to measure class-specific performance.

Confusion Matrix: Provides a detailed breakdown of the model's predicted and actual sentiment labels, allowing for a comprehensive analysis of classification errors.

10.3.7 Applications of Sentiment Analysis

Sentiment analysis has numerous applications across different industries:

Social Media Monitoring: Analyzing sentiment in social media posts, tweets, or comments to understand public opinion, brand perception, or customer feedback.

Customer Feedback Analysis: Assessing sentiment in customer reviews, surveys, or support tickets to gain insights into customer satisfaction, product improvement areas, or brand loyalty.

Market Research: Analyzing sentiment in market research data to understand consumer preferences, identify trends, or assess the success of marketing campaigns.

Brand Reputation Management: Monitoring and managing the sentiment surrounding a brand or organization to address potential issues, manage public perception, or enhance customer satisfaction.

Financial Analysis: Analyzing sentiment in financial news, earnings reports, or social media discussions to understand market sentiment, predict stock price movements, or assess investor sentiment.

10.3.8 Limitations and Future Directions

Sentiment analysis still faces certain limitations, such as accurately handling sarcasm, irony, or complex linguistic expressions. Future directions in sentiment analysis research include:

Contextual Sentiment Analysis: Developing models that can capture the contextual information and understand sentiment in a broader context.

Multimodal Sentiment Analysis: Integrating text with other modalities like images, videos, or audio to capture a more comprehensive understanding of sentiment.

Fine-Grained Sentiment Analysis: Moving beyond binary sentiment classification and developing models that can handle fine-grained sentiment analysis, distinguishing between different levels of positivity or negativity.

Cross-Lingual Sentiment Analysis: Extending sentiment analysis techniques to languages other than English and addressing language-specific challenges.

Ethical Considerations: Ensuring ethical practices in sentiment analysis, addressing biases, privacy concerns, and the responsible use of sentiment analysis results.

Sentiment analysis plays a crucial role in understanding public opinion, customer feedback, and market trends. With advances in machine learning and deep learning techniques, sentiment analysis continues to evolve and find applications in various domains.

10.4 Named Entity Recognition

Named Entity Recognition (NER) is a fundamental task in natural language processing (NLP) that involves identifying and classifying named entities in text into predefined categories. Named entities are specific words or phrases that represent entities such as person names, organizations, locations, date and time expressions, monetary values, and more. NER plays a crucial role in various NLP applications, including information extraction, question answering, text summarization, and knowledge graph construction. In this chapter, we will explore the techniques and approaches used in Named Entity Recognition.

10.4.1 Rule-based Approaches

Rule-based approaches in NER involve defining a set of linguistic rules or patterns to identify named entities in text. These rules can be based on syntactic patterns, regular expressions, or gazetteers (lists of entity names). For example, a rule-based approach can define patterns to identify person names based on capitalization and adjacent words like "Mr.," "Mrs.," or "Dr." Rule-based approaches are relatively simple to implement and can be effective for specific domains or entity types. However, they may struggle with complex or ambiguous patterns and require manual effort to define and maintain the rules.

10.4.2 Statistical and Machine Learning Approaches

Statistical and machine learning approaches for NER involve training models on annotated data to learn patterns and make predictions on new, unseen text. These approaches typically involve two main steps: feature extraction and model training.

Feature Extraction: Features are extracted from the text data to represent the input for the NER model. These features can include part-of-speech tags, word embeddings, contextual information, and other linguistic features. The choice of features depends on the specific NER task and the available data.

Model Training: NER models can be trained using various machine learning algorithms, such as conditional random fields (CRF), support vector machines (SVM), or deep learning models like recurrent neural networks (RNNs) or transformers. During training, the model learns to associate words or sequences of words with specific entity labels based on the annotated training data.

10.4.3 Named Entity Recognition with Conditional Random Fields

Conditional Random Fields (CRF) is a popular statistical modeling technique used for sequence labeling tasks like NER. CRF models take into account the dependencies between neighboring words in a sequence and use them to make predictions. CRF models are trained to maximize the likelihood of the correct sequence of entity labels given the input text.

CRF-based NER models typically use a combination of handcrafted features, such as part-of-speech tags, word shapes, and linguistic patterns, along with word embeddings or other contextual representations. These features capture both local and global context information, allowing the model to make informed predictions.

10.4.4 Neural Network Approaches

Neural network approaches have gained popularity in NER due to their ability to capture complex patterns and contextual information in text. These approaches leverage deep learning models such as recurrent neural networks (RNNs), convolutional neural networks (CNNs), or transformer models.

Recurrent Neural Networks (RNNs): RNNs, including variants like Long Short-Term Memory (LSTM) and Gated Recurrent Unit (GRU), can capture sequential dependencies in text. They process the words in a sentence one by one, updating the hidden state at each step and predicting entity labels.

Convolutional Neural Networks (CNNs): CNNs can be applied to NER by treating the text as a one-dimensional sequence. Convolutional filters slide over the text, capturing relevant patterns at different levels of abstraction. Pooling operations aggregate the features, and fully connected layers make the final entity label predictions.

Transformer Models: Transformer models, such as BERT (Bidirectional Encoder Representations from Transformers), have achieved state-of-the-art results in NER. They leverage self-attention mechanisms to capture contextual information and can model bidirectional dependencies in the text. Pre-trained transformer models are fine-tuned on NER data to adapt them to specific entity recognition tasks.

10.4.5 Evaluation Metrics

To evaluate the performance of NER models, several metrics can be used:

Precision: Measures the proportion of correctly predicted named entities out of the total predicted entities.

Recall: Measures the proportion of correctly predicted named entities out of the total true entities in the data.

F1-score: Combines precision and recall into a single metric, providing a balanced measure of the model's performance.

Accuracy: Measures the overall accuracy of the NER model in predicting the entity labels.

10.4.6 Challenges and Considerations

NER faces various challenges and considerations, including:

Ambiguity: Named entities can be ambiguous and can have different interpretations based on the context. Resolving such ambiguities requires a deeper understanding of language and world knowledge.

Out-of-Vocabulary (OOV) Entities: NER models may struggle to recognize entities that are not present in the training data or the predefined entity categories. Handling OOV entities often requires techniques like domain adaptation, transfer learning, or incorporating external knowledge sources.

Multilingual NER: NER in languages other than English poses additional challenges due to language-specific characteristics, lack of labeled data, and variations in named entity types.

Fine-grained Entity Recognition: NER models can be extended to identify more fine-grained entity types, such as specific subcategories or domain-specific entities.

Named Entity Linking: Associating named entities with knowledge bases or resolving entity mentions to unique identifiers (e.g., linking "New York" to the entity "New York City") can enhance NER performance and enable downstream applications like knowledge graph construction.

10.4.7 Applications of Named Entity Recognition

Named Entity Recognition has a wide range of applications:

Information Extraction: NER helps extract structured information from unstructured text by identifying and classifying named entities.

Question Answering: NER is crucial in identifying entities mentioned in questions and finding relevant answers from knowledge sources.

Text Summarization: NER can be used to identify key entities in a text, aiding in the generation of informative and concise summaries.

Machine Translation: NER can improve the accuracy of machine translation systems by properly handling named entities during the translation process.

Text-to-Speech Systems: NER assists in generating natural and context-aware speech synthesis by correctly pronouncing named entities.

10.4.8 Limitations and Future Directions

NER still faces challenges in accurately recognizing named entities in various contexts. Future directions in NER research include:

Developing models that can handle complex linguistic expressions, metaphors, and sarcasm in named entity recognition.

Improving NER performance in low-resource languages by exploring transfer learning techniques or leveraging multilingual models.

Expanding NER to capture more fine-grained entity types and domain-specific entities.

Addressing ethical considerations related to privacy and data protection when handling personally identifiable information in named entity recognition.

Named Entity Recognition is a crucial task in NLP, enabling the extraction of valuable information from unstructured text. By identifying and classifying named entities, NER provides a foundation for various downstream applications and information extraction tasks.

10.5 Language Generation (Chatbots, Machine Translation)

Language generation is a key area of natural language processing (NLP) that involves generating human-like text or speech. It encompasses tasks such as chatbot development, machine translation, text summarization, and dialogue systems. Language generation models aim to produce coherent and contextually appropriate responses, translations, or summaries. In this chapter, we will explore language generation techniques for chatbots and machine translation.

10.5.1 Chatbot Development

Chatbots are computer programs designed to interact with humans through text or speech. They simulate human conversation by understanding user queries and generating appropriate responses. Chatbot development involves two main components: input understanding and response generation.

Input Understanding: Chatbots employ natural language understanding techniques to interpret user inputs. This involves tasks like intent recognition, entity extraction, and sentiment analysis to grasp the user's query and context effectively.

Response Generation: Once the user's query is understood, chatbots generate appropriate responses. Language generation models, such as sequence-to-sequence models, can be employed for response generation. These models learn to map input queries to output responses, capturing the underlying patterns and context of the conversation.

Chatbots can be rule-based, where predefined rules determine the responses, or data-driven, where machine learning models generate responses based on training data. Advanced chatbot systems may incorporate reinforcement learning or transformer-based models to improve response quality and maintain context over longer conversations.

10.5.2 Machine Translation

Machine translation aims to automatically translate text or speech from one language to another. It plays a vital role in breaking language barriers and facilitating cross-lingual communication. Machine translation techniques can be categorized into three main types:

Rule-based Machine Translation: Rule-based systems rely on linguistic rules and dictionaries to translate text. They involve the manual creation of grammar and translation rules, which are applied to input sentences to generate translations. Rule-based approaches are effective for specific language pairs but require significant manual effort and may not handle complex language phenomena well.

Statistical Machine Translation: Statistical machine translation (SMT) models learn translation patterns from parallel corpora, which consist of aligned sentences in the source and target languages. SMT models employ statistical techniques, such as phrase-based models or alignment models, to generate translations based on learned patterns. SMT has been widely used and has achieved good results in many language pairs.

Neural Machine Translation: Neural machine translation (NMT) models have revolutionized machine translation by employing neural networks to learn direct mappings between source and target languages. NMT models, often based on sequence-to-sequence architectures with attention mechanisms, learn to generate translations by capturing complex language dependencies and context. NMT models have shown superior performance compared to traditional SMT approaches.

Advanced NMT models, such as transformer models like BERT or GPT (Generative Pre-trained Transformer), have further improved translation quality. These models are often pre-trained on large-scale multilingual corpora and fine-tuned for specific language pairs or domains.

10.5.3 Evaluation of Language Generation Systems

Evaluating the quality of language generation systems is essential to assess their performance. Evaluation metrics for chatbots and machine translation include:

Perplexity: Measures how well a language model predicts a given sequence of words. Lower perplexity indicates better model performance.

BLEU (Bilingual Evaluation Understudy): A commonly used metric for machine translation that measures the similarity between machine-generated translations and reference translations.

METEOR (Metric for Evaluation of Translation with Explicit ORdering): An evaluation metric that combines precision, recall, and alignment information to measure the quality of machine translations.

Human Evaluation: In addition to automated metrics, human evaluation through crowd-sourced judgments or expert assessment provides valuable insights into the quality, fluency, and relevance of generated text.

10.5.4 Challenges and Considerations

Language generation faces several challenges and considerations, including:

Context and Coherence: Ensuring that generated responses or translations are contextually relevant and coherent with the preceding dialogue or source text.

Handling Ambiguity: Resolving ambiguities in user queries or source sentences to generate accurate and meaningful responses or translations.

Domain Adaptation: Adapting language generation models to specific domains or tasks to improve the quality and relevance of the generated text.

Language Specificity: Handling language-specific challenges, such as idiomatic expressions, cultural references, or language-specific grammatical structures.

Ethical Considerations: Ensuring ethical practices in language generation, addressing issues related to bias, privacy, and the responsible use of generated content.

10.5.5 Future Directions

Language generation continues to evolve, driven by advancements in deep learning and transformer-based models. Future directions in language generation research include:

Contextual and Interactive Models: Developing models that can maintain context and engage in extended interactions, providing coherent and dynamic responses.

Controllable Generation: Enabling users to control specific attributes of the generated text, such as sentiment, style, or formality.

Multimodal Generation: Integrating text with other modalities like images, videos, or audio to generate rich and diverse content.

Explainability and Interpretability: Improving the transparency and interpretability of language generation models, allowing users to understand the reasoning behind generated responses.

Language generation plays a critical role in applications like chatbots, machine translation, and text summarization. By generating human-like text, language generation systems facilitate communication and bridge language gaps.

Chapter 11: Computer Vision

11.1 Introduction to Computer Vision

Computer Vision is a field of study that focuses on enabling computers to understand and interpret visual information from images or videos. It aims to replicate human visual perception and enable machines to analyze, process, and extract meaningful insights from visual data. Computer Vision has a wide range of applications, including object detection, image classification, image segmentation, facial recognition, autonomous vehicles, medical imaging, and more. In this chapter, we will explore the fundamentals of computer vision and its key components.

11.1.1 Image Representation

In computer vision, images are represented as a collection of pixels, each pixel containing information about its color and intensity. Image representation is often based on color spaces, such as RGB (Red, Green, Blue) or grayscale. RGB represents each pixel as a combination of red, green, and blue color channels, while grayscale uses a single channel to represent the intensity of each pixel.

Image representation also includes considerations for image size, aspect ratio, and resolution. Images can be resized, cropped, or transformed to meet specific requirements for processing or analysis.

11.1.2 Image Filtering and Enhancement

Image filtering techniques are used to modify images by applying various operations to enhance their quality or extract specific features. Filtering operations include blurring, sharpening, noise reduction, edge detection, and more. These operations help improve image clarity, remove unwanted noise or artifacts, and enhance important features.

11.1.3 Feature Extraction

Feature extraction is a crucial step in computer vision that involves identifying and extracting meaningful visual patterns or features from images. These features can include edges, corners, textures, color histograms, or higher-level representations like SIFT (Scale-Invariant Feature Transform) or SURF (Speeded-Up Robust Features). Feature extraction methods aim to capture relevant information from images that can be used for further analysis, object recognition, or classification tasks.

11.1.4 Object Detection and Recognition

Object detection involves identifying and localizing specific objects or instances of interest within an image or video. It typically involves algorithms such as Haar cascades, Histogram of Oriented Gradients (HOG), or more advanced deep learning-based approaches like Faster R-CNN or YOLO (You Only Look Once). Object recognition aims to classify the detected objects into predefined categories or labels, such as humans, cars, animals, or specific objects.

11.1.5 Image Classification

Image classification is the task of assigning a label or category to an entire image based on its visual content. It is widely used in applications such as image recognition, medical diagnosis, and autonomous vehicles. Deep learning models, particularly Convolutional Neural Networks (CNNs), have significantly advanced image classification performance, achieving state-of-the-art results on benchmark datasets like ImageNet.

11.1.6 Image Segmentation

Image segmentation involves dividing an image into multiple regions or segments based on similarities in color, texture, or other visual attributes. It allows for fine-grained analysis of specific objects or regions within an image. Segmentation methods include region-based algorithms, such as GrabCut or watershed, as well as deep learning-based approaches like Fully Convolutional Networks (FCNs) or U-Net.

11.1.7 Facial Recognition

Facial recognition is a specialized area of computer vision that focuses on identifying and verifying individuals based on their facial features. It involves tasks like face detection, facial feature extraction, and face recognition. Facial recognition systems utilize techniques like Viola-Jones algorithm, eigenfaces, or deep learning-based models like FaceNet or VGGFace for accurate and reliable identification.

11.1.8 Optical Character Recognition (OCR)

Optical Character Recognition (OCR) is the process of extracting text from images or documents and converting it into machine-readable text. OCR enables the automated analysis and extraction of textual information from sources like scanned documents, license plates, or handwritten text. OCR techniques involve image preprocessing, text detection, character segmentation, and character recognition using algorithms like Tesseract or deep learning-based models.

11.2 Computer Vision Techniques

11.2.1 Traditional Computer Vision Techniques

Traditional computer vision techniques encompass a range of algorithms and methods developed before the advent of deep learning. These techniques include edge detection, corner detection, scale-space representation, image registration, motion estimation, and more. These algorithms often rely on handcrafted features and mathematical operations to extract relevant information from images.

11.2.2 Deep Learning in Computer Vision

Deep learning has revolutionized computer vision by leveraging deep neural networks to automatically learn features directly from raw image data. Convolutional Neural Networks (CNNs) have emerged as a dominant architecture for computer vision tasks, achieving exceptional performance in areas like image classification, object detection, and segmentation. Pretrained CNN models like AlexNet, VGGNet, ResNet, and EfficientNet are commonly used as a starting point for various computer vision tasks.

11.2.3 Transfer Learning and Fine-tuning

Transfer learning is a technique that allows leveraging pre-trained models on large-scale datasets and adapting them to specific computer vision tasks with limited labeled data. By reusing the learned features from pre-trained models, transfer learning enables faster convergence, improved performance, and reduced data requirements. Fine-tuning involves updating a pre-trained model on task-specific data to further enhance its performance on the target task.

11.2.4 Data Augmentation

Data augmentation is a technique used to increase the diversity and size of training datasets by applying various transformations to the existing images. Common augmentations include rotations, translations, flips, scaling, cropping, and adding noise. Data augmentation helps prevent overfitting, improves model generalization, and enhances the robustness of computer vision models.

11.3 Applications of Computer Vision

Computer vision has numerous applications across various domains:

Autonomous Vehicles: Computer vision enables object detection, lane detection, traffic sign recognition, and pedestrian detection, contributing to autonomous driving and advanced driver assistance systems.

Medical Imaging: Computer vision techniques aid in medical image analysis, assisting with diagnosis, tumor detection, segmentation, and disease classification.

Surveillance and Security: Computer vision-based surveillance systems enable video analysis, object tracking, and activity recognition for enhanced security and monitoring.

Robotics: Computer vision plays a critical role in robot perception, object manipulation, navigation, and human-robot interaction.

Augmented Reality (AR) and Virtual Reality (VR): Computer vision technologies support the alignment of virtual objects with the real world, enabling immersive AR and VR experiences.

Retail and E-commerce: Computer vision enables product recognition, visual search, virtual try-on, and personalized shopping experiences.

Quality Control and Inspection: Computer vision systems assist in quality control and inspection tasks by detecting defects, identifying anomalies, and ensuring manufacturing accuracy.

11.4 Challenges and Future Directions

Computer vision still faces various challenges, including:

Limited Labeled Data: Annotated datasets for specific computer vision tasks can be limited, requiring the development of techniques for effective learning with small amounts of labeled data.

Robustness to Variations: Computer vision models should be robust to variations in lighting conditions, viewpoint changes, occlusions, and image quality to ensure reliable performance in real-world scenarios.

Explainability and Interpretability: Deep learning models in computer vision often lack interpretability, making it challenging to understand the reasoning behind their predictions. Developing explainable models is crucial, especially in safety-critical applications.

Ethical Considerations: Computer vision systems should address ethical concerns related to privacy, bias, fairness, and the responsible use of visual data.

Future directions in computer vision research include:

Continual Learning: Developing models that can learn and adapt incrementally over time, allowing for lifelong learning and handling dynamic environments.

Multi-modal Learning: Integrating computer vision with other modalities like text, audio, or sensor data to enable more comprehensive and multimodal understanding of the environment.

Weakly Supervised and Self-Supervised Learning: Exploring learning paradigms that require less annotation effort, such as leveraging weak supervision or unsupervised learning techniques.

Attention Mechanisms: Developing attention mechanisms that focus on important regions or features in an image to improve efficiency and performance.

Human-Centric Vision: Advancing computer vision technologies that can understand human actions, intentions, and emotions for improved human-computer interaction and assistive applications.

Computer vision has made significant progress in recent years, driven by deep learning and advancements in hardware capabilities. With ongoing research and development, computer vision will continue to play a critical role in various industries, transforming the way we perceive and interact with visual information.

11.1 Image Preprocessing and Augmentation

Image preprocessing and augmentation are essential steps in computer vision workflows. Preprocessing involves preparing images before feeding them into a computer vision model, while augmentation involves creating new variations of existing images to expand the training dataset. In this chapter, we will explore image preprocessing and augmentation techniques commonly used in computer vision tasks.

11.1.1 Image Preprocessing Techniques

Image preprocessing techniques aim to improve the quality, enhance relevant features, and standardize images before analysis or model training. Some commonly used image preprocessing techniques include:

Resizing: Images are resized to a fixed dimension to ensure consistency and compatibility across the dataset or model requirements.

Normalization: Normalizing the pixel values of images helps bring them within a standardized range, such as [0, 1] or [-1, 1]. Common normalization techniques include min-max scaling or z-score normalization.

Grayscale Conversion: Converting color images to grayscale reduces the dimensionality of the data and simplifies processing, especially for tasks where color information is not crucial.

Cropping and Padding: Cropping removes unwanted parts of an image, focusing on the region of interest. Padding adds extra pixels to the image to ensure a consistent size or maintain aspect ratio.

Noise Reduction: Applying filters, such as Gaussian blur or median blur, helps reduce noise or smooth out image details that are not essential for analysis.

Contrast Enhancement: Techniques like histogram equalization or adaptive histogram equalization can enhance image contrast and improve visibility of important features.

Edge Detection: Edge detection algorithms, such as the Canny edge detector, identify the boundaries and edges within an image, which can be useful for subsequent analysis or feature extraction.

Rotation and Flipping: Rotating or flipping images can help increase the diversity of the dataset or correct orientation issues.

11.1.2 Image Augmentation Techniques

Image augmentation is a technique used to create variations of existing images by applying transformations that preserve the underlying semantic information. Augmentation expands the training dataset, reduces overfitting, and improves the generalization ability of computer vision models. Some commonly used image augmentation techniques include:

Horizontal and Vertical Flipping: Flipping images horizontally or vertically creates new samples with mirror-reversed versions, increasing the dataset size and allowing the model to learn invariant features.

Random Rotation: Applying random rotations to images introduces variations in object orientations and reduces sensitivity to rotation during training.

Zooming and Scaling: Randomly zooming or scaling images creates variations in object sizes, simulating different distances or perspectives.

Translation: Randomly shifting the image horizontally or vertically can simulate changes in object position or perspective.

Brightness and Contrast Variation: Adjusting the brightness or contrast of images introduces variations in lighting conditions and helps the model generalize better.

Noise Injection: Adding random noise to images can help the model become more robust to noisy or imperfect data.

Elastic Deformation: Applying elastic transformations to images deforms them locally, simulating natural distortions and introducing robustness to local variations.

Occlusion: Introducing occlusions or overlays on images can help models learn to handle occluded objects or partial information.

It's important to apply image augmentation techniques judiciously, considering the specific task requirements and potential domain-specific constraints. Care should be taken to ensure that the augmented images remain semantically meaningful and preserve their underlying properties.

11.1.3 Data Augmentation Libraries

Several popular libraries offer convenient implementations of image preprocessing and augmentation techniques, including:

OpenCV: An open-source computer vision library that provides a wide range of image processing and augmentation functions.

TensorFlow Image Preprocessing: Part of the TensorFlow ecosystem, this library offers various image preprocessing functions and utilities.

Keras Image Preprocessing: The Keras library provides a comprehensive set of tools for image preprocessing and augmentation, including data generators and transformations.

Albumentations: A powerful library for image augmentation, Albumentations supports a diverse range of augmentation techniques with efficient implementations.

imgaug: Another popular library for image augmentation, imgaug offers a wide range of augmentation methods and supports complex augmentation pipelines.

These libraries provide flexible and efficient solutions for image preprocessing and augmentation, simplifying the implementation and integration of these techniques into computer vision pipelines.

11.1.4 Considerations and Best Practices

When applying image preprocessing and augmentation techniques, consider the following best practices:

Preserve Semantic Information: Ensure that the preprocessing and augmentation operations do not distort or remove crucial information relevant to the task. The modified images should remain semantically meaningful.

Consistent Application: Apply the same preprocessing and augmentation operations consistently across the dataset to maintain data integrity and ensure fairness in model training.

Validate Augmentation Effects: Inspect augmented images to ensure that the transformations effectively capture the desired variations and align with the task requirements.

Domain-Specific Considerations: Consider domain-specific factors when applying preprocessing and augmentation techniques. For example, medical imaging may require specialized preprocessing techniques to handle specific imaging modalities or artifacts.

Balance Augmentation Intensity: Adjust the intensity or probability of augmentation operations based on the dataset size, model complexity, and task requirements. Over-augmentation can introduce synthetic noise and adversely affect model performance.

Evaluate the Impact: Assess the impact of preprocessing and augmentation techniques on model performance through rigorous evaluation and validation experiments.

Image preprocessing and augmentation play a crucial role in preparing and expanding the dataset for computer vision tasks. These techniques enable models to learn from a diverse range of data variations and improve their robustness and generalization abilities.

11.2 Object Detection and Tracking

Object detection and tracking are fundamental tasks in computer vision that involve identifying and locating objects of interest in images or videos. These tasks have numerous applications, including surveillance, autonomous driving, augmented reality, and robotics. In this chapter, we will delve into object detection and tracking techniques commonly used in computer vision.

11.2.1 Object Detection

Object detection aims to identify and locate objects within an image or video. It involves two primary components: object localization and object classification.

Object Localization: Object localization determines the precise location of objects by drawing bounding boxes around them. This provides spatial information about the objects' positions in the image.

Object Classification: Object classification involves assigning a label or category to each detected object, such as person, car, or dog. It determines the semantic meaning of the objects.

11.2.1.1 Traditional Object Detection Techniques

Traditional object detection techniques often relied on handcrafted features and machine learning algorithms. Some popular approaches include:

Sliding Window: The sliding window technique involves scanning different regions of an image with fixed-size windows and applying a classifier to each window. It requires defining multiple window sizes and positions and evaluating the classifier's output to identify objects.

Haar Cascades: Haar cascades utilize Haar-like features and a cascade classifier to detect objects. These features are rectangular areas with specific intensity patterns, and the cascade classifier combines them to differentiate between objects and non-objects.

Histogram of Oriented Gradients (HOG): HOG extracts local gradients of an image and represents them as histograms of gradient orientations. These histograms capture shape and edge information, which can be used for object detection.

11.2.1.2 Deep Learning-Based Object Detection

Deep learning-based approaches have revolutionized object detection, achieving remarkable performance. Some notable methods include:

Region-Based Convolutional Neural Networks (R-CNN): R-CNN and its variants, such as Fast R-CNN and Faster R-CNN, use region proposal methods to generate potential object regions. These regions are then fed into a CNN for feature extraction and object classification.

Single Shot MultiBox Detector (SSD): SSD is a single-stage object detection model that directly predicts object bounding boxes and class probabilities at multiple scales within a single network architecture.

You Only Look Once (YOLO): YOLO is another single-stage object detection model that simultaneously predicts object bounding boxes and class probabilities in one pass through the network. YOLO models are known for their real-time performance.

EfficientDet: EfficientDet is a recent family of object detection models that achieve high accuracy with fewer parameters, making them computationally efficient. They are based on the

EfficientNet architecture and incorporate compound scaling techniques.

11.2.2 Object Tracking

Object tracking involves following a specific object across consecutive frames in a video sequence. It enables the estimation of an object's position and movement over time. Object tracking techniques can be categorized into two main types:

Model-based Tracking: Model-based tracking utilizes a predefined model of the target object to track it over time. This can involve modeling the object's appearance, motion, or both. Techniques such as Kalman filters, particle filters, and correlation filters are commonly used in model-based tracking.

Feature-based Tracking: Feature-based tracking relies on tracking distinct features or keypoints on the object. These features can include corners, edges, or texture descriptors. Techniques like the Kanade-Lucas-Tomasi (KLT) algorithm, Scale-Invariant Feature Transform (SIFT), or Speeded-Up Robust Features (SURF) are commonly used for feature-based tracking.

11.2.3 Object Detection and Tracking Applications

Object detection and tracking find applications in various domains:

Surveillance and Security: Object detection and tracking systems are crucial for monitoring activities, identifying suspicious objects or individuals, and enhancing security measures.

Autonomous Vehicles: Object detection and tracking play a vital role in autonomous driving systems, enabling the detection of vehicles, pedestrians, traffic signs, and other objects for navigation and collision avoidance.

Augmented Reality (AR): Object detection and tracking are essential for placing virtual objects accurately in the real world, aligning them with the detected objects.

Robotics: Object detection and tracking enable robots to interact with and manipulate objects in their environment, facilitating tasks like pick-and-place, navigation, and human-robot interaction.

Sports Analysis: Object tracking can be used to analyze player movements, ball trajectories, and team formations in sports events, providing valuable insights for coaching and analysis.

11.2.4 Challenges and Future Directions

Object detection and tracking still face challenges and ongoing research efforts:

Occlusion: Handling object occlusion, where objects are partially or completely hidden, remains a challenge. Developing robust algorithms that can handle occlusion is crucial for accurate object detection and tracking.

Real-time Performance: Real-time object detection and tracking are essential for applications like autonomous vehicles or robotics. Optimizing algorithms and models for efficient inference on resource-constrained devices is an area of active research.

Scalability: Scaling object detection and tracking algorithms to handle large-scale scenes or complex environments remains a challenge. Efficient algorithms that can handle high-resolution images or videos are needed.

Multi-Object Tracking: Tracking multiple objects simultaneously in crowded scenes with occlusions is a complex task. Advancements in multi-object tracking techniques are necessary for robust and accurate tracking.

Few-Shot or Zero-Shot Learning: Enabling object detection and tracking in scenarios with limited labeled data or unseen object classes is an ongoing research area. Techniques that leverage few-shot or zero-shot learning are being explored.

Object detection and tracking techniques continue to advance, driven by deep learning and advancements in hardware capabilities. Further research and development in these areas will continue to improve their accuracy, efficiency, and applicability in various computer vision domains.

11.3 Image Segmentation

Image segmentation is a critical task in computer vision that involves dividing an image into meaningful and coherent regions or segments. Unlike object detection, which focuses on identifying specific objects within an image, image segmentation provides a more detailed and pixel-level understanding of the image. It plays a crucial role in various applications, including medical imaging, autonomous driving, object recognition, and scene understanding. In this chapter, we will explore image segmentation techniques commonly used in computer vision.

11.3.1 Types of Image Segmentation

Image segmentation techniques can be categorized into several types based on their underlying principles and methodologies:

Thresholding: Thresholding-based segmentation involves setting a threshold value to separate image regions based on pixel intensity or color. It is a simple and fast technique but may not be effective in handling complex images with varying lighting conditions or intricate textures.

Edge-based Segmentation: Edge-based segmentation detects edges in the image by identifying significant changes in pixel intensity or color gradients. Techniques like the Canny edge detector or the Sobel operator can be used to extract edge information.

Region-based Segmentation: Region-based segmentation treats similar pixels or regions as belonging to the same object or region. Common algorithms for region-based segmentation include the Watershed algorithm, Mean-Shift clustering, and Graph-Cut-based methods.

Contour-based Segmentation: Contour-based segmentation aims to detect and extract the boundaries of objects within an image. Techniques like the Active Contour Model (Snakes) or the Chan-Vese model can be used to identify object contours.

Semantic Segmentation: Semantic segmentation assigns a semantic label to each pixel in the image, classifying them into predefined categories or object classes. Deep learning-based approaches, particularly convolutional neural networks (CNNs), have achieved state-of-the-art results in semantic segmentation tasks.

Instance Segmentation: Instance segmentation goes a step further by not only segmenting objects but also distinguishing individual instances of each object class. It provides pixel-level masks for each object instance within the image. Methods like Mask R-CNN combine object detection and semantic segmentation to achieve instance segmentation.

11.3.2 Deep Learning-Based Image Segmentation

Deep learning techniques, particularly convolutional neural networks (CNNs), have significantly advanced the field of image segmentation. Fully Convolutional Networks (FCNs) are a popular class of CNNs specifically designed for pixel-wise prediction and image segmentation tasks. FCNs leverage the power of deep learning and capture both local and global context information to produce accurate segmentation maps.

Other deep learning architectures used for image segmentation include U-Net, SegNet, DeepLab, and PSPNet. These models often employ encoder-decoder architectures with skip connections, allowing the fusion of low-level and high-level features for improved segmentation performance.

11.3.3 Evaluation Metrics for Image Segmentation

To evaluate the quality and accuracy of image segmentation algorithms, various evaluation metrics can be used:

Intersection over Union (IoU) or Jaccard Index: IoU measures the overlap between the predicted segmentation mask and the ground truth mask. It computes the ratio of the intersection to the union of the two masks.

Dice Coefficient: The Dice coefficient is another metric commonly used for evaluating segmentation results. It measures the similarity between the predicted mask and the ground truth mask.

Pixel Accuracy: Pixel accuracy measures the percentage of correctly classified pixels in the segmentation mask.

Mean Average Precision (mAP): mAP is commonly used for evaluating instance segmentation models. It combines precision and recall across different object classes and varying levels of overlap.

11.3.4 Applications of Image Segmentation

Image segmentation has numerous applications in computer vision:

Medical Imaging: Image segmentation plays a crucial role in medical image analysis, aiding in tasks such as tumor detection, organ segmentation, and disease diagnosis.

Autonomous Driving: Image segmentation is vital for understanding the road scene in autonomous driving systems. It helps detect and segment different objects, such as cars, pedestrians, traffic signs, and lanes.

Object Recognition and Tracking: Image segmentation assists in isolating and identifying objects of interest within an image, enabling subsequent recognition and tracking tasks.

Image Editing and Augmentation: Image segmentation allows for precise editing and manipulation of specific regions or objects within an image. It facilitates tasks like background removal, object replacement, or image synthesis.

Scene Understanding: Image segmentation provides a detailed understanding of the scene by segmenting objects and regions, allowing for higher-level analysis and understanding of visual content.

11.3.5 Challenges and Future Directions

Image segmentation still faces several challenges and ongoing research efforts:

Handling Complex Scenes: Segmenting objects in complex scenes with occlusions, clutter, or intricate object boundaries remains challenging. Developing robust algorithms that can handle these scenarios is an active area of research.

Efficient Inference: Deep learning-based segmentation models can be computationally expensive, limiting their real-time applications. Optimizing the models and developing efficient inference strategies are important research directions.

Small Object Segmentation: Accurately segmenting small objects or objects with fine details poses a challenge, particularly when dealing with limited resolution or noise.

Weakly Supervised and Unsupervised Segmentation: Developing techniques that require less manual annotation effort, such as weakly supervised or unsupervised segmentation, is an active research area. These approaches aim to leverage limited or unlabeled data for training segmentation models.

3D Image Segmentation: Extending segmentation techniques to handle three-dimensional (3D) volumetric data, such as medical scans or point cloud data, is an important research direction.

Image segmentation continues to evolve, driven by deep learning advancements, larger datasets, and computational capabilities. Future directions in research include developing more accurate and efficient segmentation models, addressing domain-specific challenges, and exploring novel techniques for weakly supervised and unsupervised segmentation.

11.4 Facial Recognition

Facial recognition is a computer vision technique that involves identifying and verifying individuals based on their facial features. It has gained significant attention and adoption due to its wide range of applications, including security systems, access control, surveillance, biometric authentication, and personalized experiences. In this chapter, we will explore the fundamentals of facial recognition and its underlying techniques.

11.4.1 Facial Feature Extraction

Facial recognition begins with the extraction of key facial features from an input image. Some common facial features used for recognition include:

Facial Landmarks: Facial landmarks are specific points on the face, such as the corners of the eyes, the tip of the nose, or the edges of the mouth. These landmarks provide geometric information about the face and help align and normalize facial images.

Eigenfaces: Eigenfaces represent the principal components of facial variation in a dataset. They are obtained through techniques like Principal Component Analysis (PCA) applied to a set of face images. Eigenfaces capture the main facial characteristics and can be used to measure similarity between faces.

Local Binary Patterns (LBP): LBP is a texture descriptor that captures patterns in facial regions. It encodes the relationship between a pixel and its neighbors, producing a binary pattern that describes the texture properties of a face.

Deep Learning Features: Deep learning models, such as Convolutional Neural Networks (CNNs), can extract high-level facial features directly from raw images. Pretrained CNN models, like VGGFace, FaceNet, or OpenFace, have achieved remarkable performance in facial recognition tasks.

11.4.2 Face Detection

Before facial recognition can be applied, the first step is to detect and locate faces within an image or video frame. Face detection algorithms identify regions in the image that are likely to contain faces. Common face detection techniques include:

Haar Cascades: Haar cascades utilize a cascade classifier to detect faces based on Haar-like features. These features capture local image patterns that are characteristic of faces.

Viola-Jones Algorithm: The Viola-Jones algorithm combines Haar-like features with the AdaBoost algorithm to achieve efficient face detection. It scans the image with a sliding window and applies a strong classifier to detect faces.

Deep Learning-Based Face Detectors: Deep learning models, such as Single Shot MultiBox Detector (SSD) or You Only Look Once (YOLO), can be used for face detection. These models can detect faces in real-time with high accuracy.

11.4.3 Face Recognition

Once faces are detected and facial features are extracted, face recognition algorithms compare these features to a database of known faces to identify or verify individuals. Common face recognition techniques include:

Euclidean Distance: The Euclidean distance is a simple metric used to measure the similarity between two sets of facial features. It calculates the geometric distance between feature vectors and determines similarity based on the distance threshold.

Cosine Similarity: Cosine similarity measures the cosine of the angle between two feature vectors. It is commonly used to compare the similarity of deep learning-based facial features.

One-Shot Learning: One-shot learning techniques aim to recognize individuals with very limited or single training examples. These methods leverage similarity measures or metric learning approaches to generalize from a small set of known faces.

Siamese Networks: Siamese networks are neural network architectures designed for comparing and matching pairs of inputs. They are often used for face recognition tasks, where two images are compared to determine if they belong to the same person.

11.4.4 Challenges and Considerations

Facial recognition still faces challenges and considerations:

Variations in Pose, Lighting, and Expression: Facial recognition performance can be affected by variations in pose (viewpoint), lighting conditions, and facial expressions. Robust algorithms and preprocessing techniques are required to handle these variations.

Privacy and Ethical Concerns: Facial recognition raises concerns related to privacy, surveillance, and potential misuse of biometric data. It is crucial to adhere to privacy regulations and ensure transparent and responsible use of facial recognition technologies.

Demographic Bias: Facial recognition algorithms can exhibit bias and lower accuracy rates on certain demographic groups, particularly women and people of color. Ensuring fairness and addressing bias in algorithm design and training data is an ongoing challenge.

Dataset Size and Diversity: Facial recognition models benefit from large, diverse datasets that include individuals from different demographics, ages, and ethnicities. Collecting and curating representative datasets is important for improving accuracy and fairness.

11.4.5 Applications of Facial Recognition

Facial recognition finds applications in various domains:

Security and Access Control: Facial recognition is used for access control systems, surveillance, and identifying individuals for security purposes.

Biometric Authentication: Facial recognition provides a convenient and secure method for biometric authentication, replacing traditional passwords or PINs.

Personalized Experiences: Facial recognition can personalize experiences by recognizing individuals in smart devices, smart homes, or personalized marketing.

Law Enforcement and Forensics: Facial recognition assists law enforcement agencies in identifying suspects or missing persons.

It aids in forensic investigations by matching faces to existing databases.

Attendance Management: Facial recognition systems can automate attendance management in educational institutions or workplaces, reducing administrative efforts.

11.4.6 Future Directions

Future research and development in facial recognition aim to address existing challenges and improve its capabilities:

Robustness to Variations: Advancements are needed to improve the robustness of facial recognition algorithms to variations in pose, lighting, expression, and occlusion.

Bias Mitigation: Research focuses on addressing bias in facial recognition algorithms to ensure fairness and accuracy across different demographic groups.

Privacy and Ethical Considerations: Continued efforts are required to address privacy concerns, adhere to regulations, and ensure responsible use of facial recognition technologies.

Real-Time Performance: Optimizing algorithms for real-time processing is crucial for applications like surveillance, access control, or mobile devices.

Multimodal Recognition: Exploring multimodal approaches that combine facial recognition with other biometric modalities, such as voice or iris recognition, can improve accuracy and reliability.

Facial recognition technology continues to evolve, driven by advancements in deep learning, hardware capabilities, and ethical considerations. With ongoing research and development, facial recognition holds promise for various applications while emphasizing the need for responsible and ethical deployment.

11.5 Convolutional Neural Networks (CNN)

Convolutional Neural Networks (CNNs) have revolutionized the field of computer vision and are widely used for a variety of image-related tasks, including image classification, object detection, image segmentation, and more. In this chapter, we will explore the fundamentals of CNNs, their architecture, and their applications in computer vision.

11.5.1 Understanding CNN Architecture

CNNs are designed to process data with a grid-like structure, such as images. They consist of multiple layers, each serving a specific purpose in the overall network architecture. The key components of a CNN include:

Convolutional Layers: Convolutional layers are the core building blocks of CNNs. They apply convolution operations to input images using learnable filters or kernels. Convolutional layers capture local patterns and features, extracting increasingly complex representations as the network deepens.

Pooling Layers: Pooling layers reduce the spatial dimensions of feature maps, helping to achieve translation invariance and spatial hierarchy. Max pooling and average pooling are common pooling operations used in CNNs.

Activation Functions: Activation functions introduce non-linearity into the network, enabling the modeling of complex relationships. Rectified Linear Units (ReLU) activation is widely used due to its simplicity and effectiveness.

Fully Connected Layers: Fully connected layers connect every neuron in one layer to every neuron in the next layer. They aggregate high-level features extracted by convolutional layers and map them to specific output classes or labels.

Dropout: Dropout is a regularization technique commonly used in CNNs. It randomly sets a fraction of the neurons to zero during training, preventing overfitting and improving generalization.

11.5.2 CNN Training and Optimization

Training a CNN involves the following steps:

Data Preparation: Preparing the dataset involves splitting it into training, validation, and testing sets. It may also involve data augmentation techniques to increase the diversity and robustness of the training data.

Forward Propagation: During forward propagation, input data passes through the network layer by layer, applying convolution, pooling, activation functions, and fully connected layers to generate predictions.

Loss Function: The loss function quantifies the difference between predicted and actual labels. Common loss functions for classification tasks include categorical cross-entropy and softmax loss.

Backpropagation: Backpropagation calculates the gradients of the network parameters with respect to the loss. The gradients are then used to update the network weights and biases using optimization algorithms like Stochastic Gradient Descent (SGD), Adam, or RMSprop.

Iterative Training: Training the CNN involves iteratively repeating the forward and backward propagation steps using mini-batches of data until convergence or a predefined number of epochs.

11.5.3 Transfer Learning with CNNs

Transfer learning is a technique that leverages pre-trained CNN models on large-scale datasets and adapts them to new tasks with limited labeled data. It involves using the learned features from the pre-trained model as a starting point and fine-tuning the network on the target task-specific data. Transfer learning enables faster convergence, improved performance, and reduced data requirements, especially in scenarios with limited training data.

11.5.4 Applications of CNNs

CNNs have found extensive applications in computer vision tasks:

Image Classification: CNNs excel at image classification tasks, accurately assigning labels to images from predefined classes. Notable CNN architectures for image classification include AlexNet, VGGNet, ResNet, and InceptionNet.

Object Detection: CNN-based object detection models like Faster R-CNN, SSD, and YOLO enable accurate localization and recognition of objects within images.

Image Segmentation: CNNs, particularly fully convolutional networks (FCNs), are widely used for pixel-level image segmentation, providing detailed semantic understanding of images.

Facial Recognition: CNNs have greatly advanced facial recognition, allowing for accurate identification and verification of individuals based on facial features.

Autonomous Driving: CNNs play a crucial role in autonomous driving systems, enabling object detection, lane detection, and scene understanding for safe navigation.

11.5.5 Future Directions

The field of CNNs continues to evolve with ongoing research and development. Future directions include:

Model Efficiency: Developing more efficient CNN models that achieve high accuracy with fewer parameters and computational resources.

Explainability and Interpretability: Enhancing the interpretability of CNN models to understand their decision-making processes and provide explanations for their predictions.

Handling Limited Data and Few-Shot Learning: Exploring techniques to train CNNs with limited labeled data or adapt them to new classes with few examples.

Self-Supervised and Unsupervised Learning: Advancing self-supervised and unsupervised learning techniques to train CNNs without relying on manual annotation.

Multimodal Learning: Investigating approaches that integrate visual information from CNNs with other modalities, such as text or audio, to enable multimodal understanding.

CNNs have made significant strides in advancing the field of computer vision. Their ability to learn hierarchical representations from visual data has transformed the way we solve complex image-related tasks. With ongoing research, CNNs will continue to evolve, enabling more sophisticated and accurate computer vision systems.

Chapter 12: Time Series Analysis

12.1 Introduction to Time Series Analysis

Time series analysis is a statistical technique that focuses on analyzing and modeling data points collected over time. Time series data can be found in various domains, including finance, economics, weather forecasting, stock market analysis, and many others. In this chapter, we will explore the basics of time series analysis, its applications, and the key concepts involved.

12.1.1 What is a Time Series?

A time series is a sequence of data points collected at successive time intervals. It represents the evolution of a variable or phenomenon over time. The data points are typically recorded at regular intervals, such as daily, monthly, or yearly. Examples of time series data include stock prices, temperature readings, sales data, and energy consumption records.

12.1.2 Key Characteristics of Time Series Data

Time series data has several key characteristics:

Trend: The long-term movement or pattern in the data, which may be increasing, decreasing, or stationary.

Seasonality: Repeating patterns or fluctuations that occur at fixed intervals, such as daily, weekly, or yearly. Seasonality can be observed in various domains, such as retail sales during holidays or temperature variations across seasons.

Cyclicity: Patterns that occur over longer periods, often exceeding a year. Cyclical patterns are different from seasonality as they don't have fixed intervals.

Irregularity or Noise: Random fluctuations or irregularities in the data that cannot be explained by the trend, seasonality, or cyclical patterns. Noise represents unpredictable variations or measurement errors.

Autocorrelation: The correlation between observations at different time points within the same series. Autocorrelation captures dependencies and patterns within the data.

12.2 Time Series Analysis Techniques

Time series analysis involves various techniques to understand, model, and forecast the data. Some commonly used techniques include:

12.2.1 Data Visualization

Data visualization techniques, such as line plots, scatter plots, and histograms, are used to gain insights into the underlying patterns, trends, and seasonalities within the time series data.

Visualization helps in identifying outliers, understanding data distributions, and making initial assessments about the presence of trends and seasonality.

12.2.2 Time Series Decomposition

Time series decomposition aims to separate the different components of a time series, including trend, seasonality, cyclicity, and noise. Decomposition techniques, such as additive and multiplicative decomposition, help in understanding the individual contributions of each component and facilitate further analysis.

12.2.3 Stationarity Analysis

Stationarity is an important assumption in many time series models. A stationary time series has a constant mean, variance, and autocorrelation structure over time. Stationarity analysis involves checking for stationarity using statistical tests like the Augmented Dickey-Fuller (ADF) test or analyzing the autocorrelation function (ACF) and partial autocorrelation function (PACF) plots.

12.2.4 Smoothing Techniques

Smoothing techniques, such as moving averages and exponential smoothing, are used to remove noise and short-term fluctuations from the time series. Moving averages calculate the average of a subset of consecutive data points, while exponential smoothing assigns weights to the data points based on their recency.

12.2.5 Time Series Forecasting

Time series forecasting aims to predict future values based on historical data patterns. Various methods can be employed for forecasting, including autoregressive integrated moving average (ARIMA) models, exponential smoothing methods, and more advanced techniques like seasonal ARIMA (SARIMA) or Prophet.

12.3 Time Series Modeling and Advanced Techniques

12.3.1 Autoregressive Integrated Moving Average (ARIMA)

ARIMA models are widely used for time series analysis and forecasting. ARIMA combines autoregressive (AR), differencing (I), and moving average (MA) components to model the dependencies and fluctuations in the data. The model requires tuning of parameters like the order of autoregressive, differencing, and moving average components.

12.3.2 Seasonal ARIMA (SARIMA)

SARIMA extends the ARIMA model to account for seasonality in the data. It incorporates additional seasonal components to capture the seasonal patterns and variations.

12.3.3 Vector Autoregression (VAR)

VAR models are used to analyze and forecast multiple time series variables simultaneously. VAR models capture the dependencies and interactions among multiple time series variables.

12.3.4 State Space Models

State space models represent time series data as a combination of hidden states and observed states. Kalman filters and particle filters are commonly used to estimate the hidden states and perform forecasting.

12.3.5 Neural Network Models

Neural network models, such as recurrent neural networks (RNNs) and Long Short-Term Memory (LSTM) networks, have shown promise in time series analysis. These models can capture complex temporal dependencies and are particularly useful for sequential data.

12.4 Applications of Time Series Analysis

Time series analysis has various applications, including:

Financial Forecasting: Time series analysis is used for predicting stock prices, currency exchange rates, and financial market trends.

Demand Forecasting: Time series analysis helps in predicting demand for products and services, enabling efficient inventory management and supply chain optimization.

Sales and Revenue Analysis: Time series analysis aids in understanding sales patterns, identifying seasonality, and forecasting future revenues.

Weather Forecasting: Time series models are employed for weather prediction, enabling meteorologists to forecast temperature, precipitation, and other meteorological variables.

Energy Consumption Analysis: Time series analysis assists in understanding energy consumption patterns, optimizing energy usage, and forecasting future energy demands.

12.5 Conclusion

Time series analysis is a valuable tool for understanding, modeling, and forecasting data collected over time. By considering the underlying patterns, trends, and seasonality in the data, time series analysis provides insights that can be leveraged for decision-making and prediction tasks. With a wide range of techniques and models available, time series analysis is a powerful tool for extracting valuable information from time-dependent data.

12.1 Handling Time Series Data

Time series data presents unique challenges compared to other types of data due to its temporal nature. In this section, we will explore key considerations and techniques for handling time series data effectively.

12.1.1 Data Collection and Sampling

When collecting time series data, it is crucial to ensure that the data points are recorded at regular intervals. Irregularly sampled data can introduce challenges in analysis and modeling. If the data is not collected at regular intervals, interpolation techniques can be applied to fill in missing values or resampling techniques can be used to convert the data into a regular time series.

12.1.2 Time Series Visualization

Visualizing time series data is essential for gaining insights and understanding the underlying patterns. Line plots, scatter plots, and area plots can be used to visualize the temporal evolution of the data. Time series plots can reveal trends, seasonality, outliers, and other important characteristics of the data.

12.1.3 Time Series Decomposition

Time series decomposition helps in understanding the different components present in the data, such as trend, seasonality, and residual (error) components. Decomposition techniques like additive or multiplicative decomposition can be applied to separate these components and analyze them individually. This decomposition aids in modeling and forecasting the time series accurately.

12.1.4 Handling Missing Values

Time series data often contains missing values, which can arise due to various reasons such as sensor failures, data corruption, or incomplete data collection. Handling missing values requires careful consideration. Techniques like forward filling, backward filling, or interpolation can be used to fill in missing values based on neighboring data points. However, the choice of technique should be made cautiously to avoid introducing biases into the analysis.

12.1.5 Handling Outliers

Outliers are data points that significantly deviate from the normal pattern in the time series. Outliers can arise due to measurement errors or exceptional events. Handling outliers depends on the specific context and goal of the analysis. Outliers can be removed, transformed, or treated separately based on their impact on the analysis and the underlying reasons for their occurrence.

12.1.6 Stationarity and Transformation

Stationarity is a desirable property in time series analysis. A stationary time series exhibits constant mean, variance, and autocorrelation structure over time. Many time series models, such as ARIMA, require stationarity for accurate modeling and forecasting. If a time series is non-stationary, techniques like differencing, logarithmic transformation, or seasonal adjustment can be applied to achieve stationarity.

12.1.7 Feature Engineering

Feature engineering plays a crucial role in time series analysis. Transforming the raw time series into meaningful features can enhance the performance of models. Feature engineering techniques for time series data include lagged variables, moving averages, exponential smoothing, Fourier transformations, and wavelet transformations. These techniques extract relevant information from the time series to capture patterns and relationships.

12.1.8 Time Series Forecasting

Time series forecasting involves predicting future values based on historical patterns. Numerous techniques, such as ARIMA, exponential smoothing, and machine learning algorithms, can be applied for forecasting. It is important to evaluate the performance of different models using appropriate metrics and validation techniques, such as train-test splits or cross-validation, to select the best forecasting approach for the specific time series.

12.1.9 Handling Multiple Time Series

In some cases, multiple related time series need to be analyzed together. This can include multivariate time series analysis, where multiple variables are observed over time, or panel data analysis, where multiple time series are observed across different entities. Techniques like vector autoregression (VAR), structural time series models, or machine learning approaches can be used to analyze and model multiple time series simultaneously.

12.1.10 Seasonality and Periodicity

Seasonality refers to patterns that repeat at fixed intervals, such as daily, weekly, or yearly. Identifying and accounting for seasonality is crucial in time series analysis. Seasonal decomposition, seasonal adjustment, or using seasonal models like SARIMA can help capture and model the seasonal patterns in the data.

12.1.11 Long-Term Dependencies and Memory

Some time series exhibit long-term dependencies, where past values have a significant influence on future values. Models like recurrent neural networks (RNNs), including Long Short-Term Memory (LSTM) networks, are designed to capture long-term dependencies and memory in time series data. These models are effective for sequence prediction and forecasting tasks.

12.1.12 Advanced Time Series Techniques

Time series analysis also includes advanced techniques such as state space models, Gaussian processes, spectral analysis, and wavelet analysis. These techniques are used for specific scenarios where more sophisticated modeling and analysis are required.

Handling time series data requires careful consideration of its unique characteristics and challenges. Understanding the patterns, trends, and dependencies within the data is crucial for accurate modeling, forecasting, and decision-making. By applying appropriate techniques, preprocessing steps, and modeling approaches, valuable insights can be derived from time series data.

12.2 Time Series Forecasting (ARIMA, SARIMA, LSTM)

Time series forecasting is a critical task in analyzing and predicting future values in a time-dependent sequence of data points. Several models and techniques have been developed for time series forecasting, including ARIMA, SARIMA, and LSTM. In this section, we will explore these popular methods and their applications in time series forecasting.

12.2.1 Autoregressive Integrated Moving Average (ARIMA)

Autoregressive Integrated Moving Average (ARIMA) is a widely used model for time series forecasting. It combines three components: autoregression (AR), differencing (I), and moving average (MA). The AR component captures the relationship between an observation and a lagged value, the MA component models the dependency between an observation and the residual errors, and the differencing component handles non-stationarity in the data.

The ARIMA model is defined by three parameters: p, d, and q. The parameter p represents the order of the autoregressive component, d represents the order of differencing, and q represents the order of the moving average component. By fitting an ARIMA model to historical data, future values can be forecasted based on the estimated parameters.

12.2.2 Seasonal ARIMA (SARIMA)

Seasonal ARIMA (SARIMA) extends the ARIMA model to handle time series data with seasonal patterns. In addition to the p, d, and q parameters, SARIMA incorporates seasonal components denoted by P, D, and Q. The parameters P, D, and Q represent the seasonal autoregressive, seasonal differencing, and seasonal moving average orders, respectively.

SARIMA models are effective for forecasting time series data that exhibit both non-seasonal and seasonal patterns. By accounting for seasonal variations, SARIMA can provide accurate predictions for seasonal data, such as monthly sales data or quarterly financial indicators.

12.2.3 Long Short-Term Memory (LSTM)

Long Short-Term Memory (LSTM) is a type of recurrent neural network (RNN) that has proven to be highly effective in modeling and forecasting time series data. LSTMs are particularly well-suited for capturing long-term dependencies and patterns in sequential data.

Unlike traditional statistical models, LSTM models learn from both past and present observations to make predictions. LSTMs employ a memory cell, which allows them to selectively remember or forget information based on the relevance and importance of past observations. This ability to capture and retain long-term dependencies makes LSTMs powerful tools for time series forecasting.

LSTM models require careful design and configuration of network architecture, including the number of layers, number of neurons, and the activation functions. Additionally, LSTMs can be enhanced by incorporating techniques such as dropout regularization and bidirectional processing.

12.2.4 Choosing the Right Model

The choice of the forecasting model depends on several factors, including the characteristics of the time series data, the presence of seasonality, the amount of available data, and the forecasting horizon. ARIMA and SARIMA models are suitable for data without strong temporal dependencies, while LSTM models are more appropriate when capturing long-term dependencies and complex patterns is crucial.

It is important to evaluate the performance of different models using appropriate metrics such as mean squared error (MSE), root mean squared error (RMSE), or mean absolute error (MAE). Additionally, validation techniques like train-test splits or cross-validation can provide insights into the model's generalization ability and forecast accuracy.

12.2.5 Advanced Techniques and Considerations

Time series forecasting is an active area of research, and numerous advanced techniques and models have been developed. These include ensemble methods, such as combining multiple models for improved accuracy, and hybrid models that integrate statistical models with machine learning algorithms.

When applying time series forecasting techniques, it is essential to consider potential challenges, such as handling missing values, outliers, and non-stationarity. Preprocessing steps like data imputation, outlier detection, and differencing can help address these challenges and improve forecast accuracy.

Furthermore, it is crucial to monitor and evaluate the forecast performance regularly. As new data becomes available, the forecast models should be updated and refined to ensure accurate predictions.

12.2.6 Applications of Time Series Forecasting

Time series forecasting has a wide range of applications, including:

Sales and Demand Forecasting: Accurate demand forecasting enables optimized inventory management and production planning.

Financial Forecasting: Forecasting stock prices, exchange rates, and financial indicators aids in investment decision-making.

Energy Load Forecasting: Predicting energy demand helps utilities optimize resource allocation and ensure efficient energy distribution.

Weather Forecasting: Forecasting weather patterns and conditions is crucial for agriculture, transportation, and disaster preparedness.

Supply Chain Optimization: Forecasting demand and lead times enables efficient supply chain management, reducing costs and improving customer satisfaction.

12.2.7 Conclusion

Time series forecasting plays a vital role in understanding and predicting future values in time-dependent data. ARIMA, SARIMA, and LSTM are widely used models for time series forecasting, each with its own strengths and suitability for different scenarios. By selecting the appropriate model and applying suitable preprocessing techniques, accurate and reliable forecasts can be obtained.

12.3 Seasonality and Trend Analysis

Seasonality and trend analysis are essential components of time series analysis that help in understanding and modeling the underlying patterns in data. In this section, we will explore the concepts of seasonality and trend, along with techniques for analyzing and incorporating them into time series analysis.

12.3.1 Seasonality

Seasonality refers to recurring patterns or fluctuations that occur at regular intervals within a time series. These patterns can be daily, weekly, monthly, or yearly, depending on the time scale of the data. Seasonality is often observed in data related to sales, demand, weather, or other cyclic phenomena.

To analyze seasonality, techniques such as seasonal decomposition of time series (e.g., additive or multiplicative decomposition) can be used. These techniques separate the time series into its seasonal, trend, and residual components, allowing for a clear understanding of the seasonality pattern.

Once the seasonality pattern is identified, it can be incorporated into forecasting models such as SARIMA or seasonal Holt-Winters. These models explicitly account for the seasonal component and help in producing more accurate forecasts by considering the cyclical nature of the data.

12.3.2 Trend Analysis

Trend analysis focuses on identifying the long-term direction or movement in a time series. Trends can be upward (increasing), downward (decreasing), or stationary (no significant change).

Analyzing trends helps in understanding the underlying growth or decline patterns in the data.

Several techniques can be used for trend analysis, including:

Moving Averages: Moving averages smooth out short-term fluctuations and highlight the long-term trend. Simple moving averages (SMA) or weighted moving averages (WMA) can be used to calculate the average over a specific window size.

Regression Analysis: Regression models can be applied to capture the linear or nonlinear trend in the data. Linear regression, polynomial regression, or exponential regression are commonly used approaches.

Exponential Smoothing: Exponential smoothing methods, such as single, double, or triple exponential smoothing, provide a flexible framework for trend estimation and forecasting.

Seasonal-Trend Decomposition: Seasonal-trend decomposition using LOESS (STL) is a robust method that decomposes a time series into its trend, seasonal, and remainder components. It is particularly effective in handling time series with complex trends and seasonality.

Once the trend is identified, it can be used to make informed decisions, assess long-term growth or decline, and identify potential turning points or anomalies in the data.

12.3.3 Seasonal and Trend Interactions

In many cases, seasonality and trend interact in a time series. For example, there may be a seasonal component superimposed on an increasing trend. Understanding these interactions is important for accurate modeling and forecasting.

One approach to capturing the interactions between seasonality and trend is to employ models like seasonal exponential smoothing or seasonal ARIMA (SARIMA). These models incorporate both the seasonal and trend components into the forecasting process, enabling more accurate predictions.

Another approach is to deseasonalize the data by removing the seasonal component and then modeling the detrended series. Deseasonalization techniques like the ratio-to-moving-average method or seasonal adjustment through regression can be used to extract the trend component from the original time series.

12.3.4 Forecasting with Seasonality and Trend

In time series forecasting, incorporating seasonality and trend is crucial for accurate predictions. Models like SARIMA or Holt-Winters can handle the interaction between seasonality and trend and provide forecasts that capture both components.

Alternatively, exponential smoothing methods, such as Holt's linear exponential smoothing or Holt-Winters' additive or multiplicative method, can be employed to explicitly account for trend and seasonality.

Machine learning techniques like LSTM neural networks can also capture both long-term dependencies (trend) and seasonal patterns in the data. LSTM models excel in capturing complex interactions and nonlinear relationships, making them effective for forecasting time series data with seasonality and trend.

12.3.5 Conclusion

Seasonality and trend analysis are essential components of time series analysis. Identifying and incorporating seasonality and trend patterns into forecasting models can greatly improve the accuracy of predictions and aid in decision-making. By employing appropriate decomposition techniques, trend analysis methods, and forecasting models, valuable insights can be derived from time series data.

12.4 Anomaly Detection in Time Series Data

Anomaly detection is a critical task in time series analysis that involves identifying data points or patterns that deviate significantly from the expected behavior. Anomalies, also known as outliers or aberrations, can provide valuable insights into unusual events, errors, or potential problems within a system. In this section, we will explore techniques for detecting anomalies in time series data.

12.4.1 Types of Anomalies

Anomalies in time series data can take different forms:

Point Anomalies: These anomalies refer to individual data points that deviate significantly from the normal behavior of the time series.

Collective Anomalies: Collective anomalies occur when a group or subset of data points collectively exhibit abnormal behavior, even if individual points may not be anomalous.

Contextual Anomalies: Contextual anomalies are data points that are considered anomalous in a specific context or condition but may be normal in another context.

12.4.2 Statistical Techniques

Statistical techniques form the basis for many anomaly detection methods. Common statistical approaches include:

Z-Score: The z-score measures how many standard deviations a data point deviates from the mean. Points with a z-score above a certain threshold are considered anomalies.

Percentile: Percentile-based approaches identify anomalies based on the rank of a data point within the distribution. Points falling above or below a certain percentile threshold are considered anomalous.

Median Absolute Deviation (MAD): MAD measures the median deviation of each data point from the median of the time series. Points with a deviation above a certain threshold are flagged as anomalies.

12.4.3 Machine Learning Approaches

Machine learning techniques can be applied to detect anomalies in time series data. Some popular approaches include:

Supervised Learning: Anomaly detection can be treated as a supervised learning problem by training a model on labeled data, where anomalies are labeled as such. Classification algorithms like Support Vector Machines (SVM), Random Forests, or Neural Networks can be used for anomaly detection.

Unsupervised Learning: Unsupervised learning methods are commonly employed for anomaly detection when labeled data is scarce or unavailable. Techniques like clustering (e.g., k-means), density estimation (e.g., Gaussian Mixture Models), or autoencoders can be used to identify data points that deviate from the norm.

Time Series Decomposition: Anomalies can be detected by analyzing the residual component obtained from decomposing the time series into its trend, seasonality, and noise. Unusual patterns in the residuals indicate the presence of anomalies.

12.4.4 Time Series Modeling and Forecasting

Anomaly detection can also be achieved through time series modeling and forecasting techniques. By comparing the observed data with the predicted values from a forecasting model (such as ARIMA, SARIMA, or LSTM), significant differences can indicate the presence of anomalies. Additionally, models that explicitly incorporate anomalies in the form of level shifts or change points (e.g., Change Point Detection) can be used for anomaly detection.

12.4.5 Domain-Specific Approaches

In some cases, domain-specific knowledge and techniques can be employed for anomaly detection. These approaches leverage specific characteristics and domain expertise to identify abnormal patterns or events. For example, in manufacturing, sensor data analysis and control charts can be used to detect anomalies in production processes.

12.4.6 Evaluation and Validation

Evaluating the performance of an anomaly detection system is crucial. Metrics such as precision, recall, F1-score, or Area Under the Receiver Operating Characteristic Curve (AUROC) can be used to assess the effectiveness of the detection methods. Validation techniques like cross-validation or holdout testing can provide insights into the system's performance on unseen data.

12.4.7 Conclusion

Anomaly detection in time series data is a challenging task, but it is essential for identifying unusual patterns or events. By applying statistical techniques, machine learning approaches, time series modeling, or domain-specific knowledge, anomalies can be effectively detected. Choosing the appropriate method depends on the characteristics of the data, available resources, and the specific requirements of the application.

Chapter 13: Feature Importance and Interpretability

13.1 Introduction

In machine learning, understanding the importance of features and interpreting the model's decisions are crucial for gaining insights, building trust, and making informed decisions. In this chapter, we will explore techniques and methods for assessing feature importance and enhancing model interpretability.

13.2 Feature Importance

Feature importance refers to the quantification of the impact or relevance of input features on the model's predictions. Understanding feature importance helps in identifying the most influential factors and gaining insights into the underlying relationships in the data. Here are some commonly used techniques for assessing feature importance:

13.2.1 Statistical Measures

Statistical measures, such as correlation coefficients, p-values, or information gain, can provide insights into the relevance of features. For example, correlation coefficients measure the linear relationship between features and the target variable. Features with higher correlation coefficients are considered more important.

13.2.2 Univariate Feature Selection

Univariate feature selection methods evaluate each feature individually based on statistical tests or scoring functions. Common techniques include chi-squared test, ANOVA F-test, or mutual information. Features with higher scores or lower p-values are deemed more important.

13.2.3 Model-Based Feature Importance

Model-based feature importance techniques assess the contribution of features by examining the impact on the model's performance. Methods like permutation feature importance, feature importance based on decision trees (e.g., Gini importance), or coefficients in linear models can provide insights into feature relevance.

13.2.4 Ensemble Feature Importance

Ensemble models, such as random forests or gradient boosting, can estimate feature importance by aggregating the importance scores across multiple models or trees. These methods consider the collective wisdom of multiple models to determine feature importance.

13.3 Model Interpretability

Model interpretability refers to the ability to understand and explain how a model arrives at its predictions. Interpretability is particularly important in sensitive domains, such as healthcare or finance, where decisions impact human lives or have legal implications. Here are some techniques for enhancing model interpretability:

13.3.1 Linear Models

Linear models, such as linear regression or logistic regression, offer inherent interpretability as the coefficients indicate the influence of features on the predictions. Positive coefficients indicate a positive relationship, while negative coefficients suggest a negative relationship.

13.3.2 Decision Trees and Rule-Based Models

Decision trees and rule-based models are inherently interpretable. The hierarchical structure of decision trees allows for easy interpretation of the decision-making process. Rules, such as if-then statements, can be extracted from decision trees to provide understandable explanations.

13.3.3 Partial Dependence Plots

Partial dependence plots show how the predictions change as a single feature varies while keeping other features fixed. These plots provide insights into the relationship between a feature and the model's predictions, allowing for interpretability.

13.3.4 Local Interpretable Model-Agnostic Explanations (LIME)

LIME is a technique that provides explanations for individual predictions of complex models. It approximates the model's decision locally around a specific instance by training an interpretable model on locally perturbed samples.

13.3.5 SHAP Values

SHAP (Shapley) values provide a unified framework for feature attribution in machine learning models. They assign each feature a value indicating its contribution to the prediction for a specific instance. SHAP values offer a comprehensive understanding of feature importance and can be visualized in various ways.

13.4 Balancing Complexity and Interpretability

While complex models like neural networks or ensemble models often achieve high predictive performance, they are typically less interpretable. Balancing complexity and interpretability depends on the specific use case and requirements. It may involve using simpler models, incorporating model-agnostic interpretability techniques, or seeking a trade-off between performance and interpretability.

13.5 Conclusion

Assessing feature importance and enhancing model interpretability are essential for understanding the underlying relationships in data and gaining insights into the decision-making process of machine learning models. By employing techniques such as statistical measures, model-based feature importance, or interpretable models, we can extract valuable insights and build trust in machine learning systems.

13.1 Understanding Feature Importance Methods

Feature importance methods provide insights into the relevance and impact of input features on the model's predictions. Understanding feature importance is crucial for feature selection, model optimization, and gaining insights into the underlying relationships in the data. In this section, we will explore common feature importance methods and their interpretations.

13.1.1 Statistical Measures

Statistical measures assess the relationship between features and the target variable to determine their importance. Some commonly used statistical measures include:

Correlation Coefficients: Correlation coefficients, such as Pearson's correlation coefficient, quantify the linear relationship between two variables. Features with higher correlation coefficients (positive or negative) with the target variable are considered more important.

p-values: In statistical hypothesis testing, p-values indicate the significance of the relationship between a feature and the target variable. Lower p-values suggest a stronger association and higher feature importance.

Information Gain: Information gain measures the reduction in uncertainty about the target variable when splitting data based on a particular feature. Features with higher information gain are considered more important in decision tree-based models.

13.1.2 Univariate Feature Selection

Univariate feature selection methods evaluate each feature individually based on statistical tests or scoring functions. These methods rank features based on their individual relevance to the target variable. Some common techniques include:

Chi-squared Test: The chi-squared test measures the dependence between categorical features and a categorical target variable. Features with higher chi-squared values are considered more important.

ANOVA F-test: The ANOVA F-test assesses the difference in means among groups defined by a categorical feature. Features with higher F-statistics and lower p-values are deemed more important.

Mutual Information: Mutual information quantifies the amount of information shared between a feature and the target variable. Higher mutual information values indicate higher feature importance.

13.1.3 Model-Based Feature Importance

Model-based feature importance methods assess the contribution of features by examining their impact on the model's performance. These methods are often model-specific and can provide insights into the relevance of features within a particular model. Some common model-based feature importance techniques include:

Permutation Feature Importance: Permutation feature importance measures the decrease in model performance when permuting the values of a feature. Features that cause a significant drop in performance when permuted are considered more important.

Gini Importance: Gini importance is a measure used in decision tree-based models, such as random forests. It calculates the total reduction in impurity (Gini index) achieved by a feature across all decision trees in the ensemble.

Coefficients in Linear Models: Linear models, such as linear regression or logistic regression, provide coefficients that indicate the magnitude and direction of the feature's influence on the target variable. Features with larger absolute coefficients are considered more important.

13.1.4 Ensemble Feature Importance

Ensemble models, such as random forests or gradient boosting, can estimate feature importance by aggregating the importance scores across multiple models or trees. Ensemble feature importance methods consider the collective wisdom of multiple models to determine the overall importance of features.

It's important to note that feature importance methods provide relative importance rankings rather than absolute measures. The interpretation of feature importance may vary depending on the specific context and the model being used. Additionally, feature importance is not always indicative of causality but rather highlights the predictive power of the feature within the given model.

13.1.5 Conclusion

Understanding feature importance is vital for extracting valuable insights from machine learning models and making informed decisions. By employing statistical measures, univariate feature selection, model-based feature importance, or ensemble feature importance techniques, we can identify the most relevant features in the data. However, it's essential to consider the limitations of each method and select the most appropriate technique based on the specific problem and model at hand.

13.2 Explainable AI Techniques

Explainable AI (XAI) techniques aim to enhance the interpretability and transparency of machine learning models, allowing humans to understand how the models arrive at their decisions. Interpretable models build trust, facilitate debugging, and enable compliance with legal and ethical requirements. In this section, we will explore some common techniques for achieving explainability in AI.

13.2.1 Linear Models

Linear models, such as linear regression or logistic regression, are inherently interpretable. The coefficients assigned to each feature provide insights into their influence on the model's predictions. Positive coefficients indicate a positive relationship with the target variable, while negative coefficients suggest a negative relationship. The magnitude of the coefficients reflects the strength of the influence.

13.2.2 Decision Trees and Rule-Based Models

Decision trees and rule-based models offer interpretability due to their hierarchical structure and explicit if-then rules. Decision trees partition the feature space based on certain thresholds and make predictions based on the majority class within each partition. The decision paths in a tree can be easily interpreted, enabling an understanding of the decision-making process.

Rule-based models, such as association rule learning or rule-based classifiers, use if-then rules to make predictions. These rules are typically in a human-readable format, allowing for easy interpretation and understanding of the decision logic.

13.2.3 Partial Dependence Plots

Partial dependence plots provide insights into the relationship between a feature and the model's predictions while keeping other features fixed. These plots illustrate how the model's predictions change as the value of a specific feature varies. By examining the shape and direction of the curve, we can understand the impact of a feature on the model's output.

13.2.4 Local Interpretable Model-Agnostic Explanations (LIME)

Local Interpretable Model-Agnostic Explanations (LIME) is a technique for explaining individual predictions of black-box models. LIME approximates the model's decision-making process locally by training an interpretable model (e.g., linear regression) on locally perturbed samples around the instance of interest. The interpretable model provides explanations specific to the instance, offering insights into how the black-box model arrived at its prediction.

13.2.5 SHAP Values

SHAP (Shapley) values provide a unified framework for feature attribution and explanation in machine learning models. SHAP values assign each feature a value indicating its contribution to the prediction for a specific instance. They offer a comprehensive understanding of feature importance and can be visualized in various ways, such as summary plots or individual contribution plots.

13.2.6 Model Distillation

Model distillation involves training a simpler, more interpretable model to mimic the behavior of a complex model. The complex model serves as a teacher, providing the target outputs for the training data, while the interpretable model, such as a linear model or decision tree, learns to approximate the complex model's predictions. The distilled model is easier to interpret while maintaining a similar level of performance.

13.2.7 Domain-Specific Techniques

In some domains, specific techniques can enhance interpretability. For example:

Feature Importance in Image Processing: Techniques such as saliency maps or Grad-CAM (Gradient-weighted Class Activation Mapping) can highlight important regions in an image that contribute to the model's decision.

Natural Language Processing: Attention mechanisms in neural networks can be visualized to understand which parts of the input text are most important for predictions.

13.2.8 Human-AI Collaboration and Explanations

In addition to technical techniques, human-AI collaboration plays a crucial role in achieving explainability. Explanation interfaces, interactive visualizations, or conversational AI systems can facilitate a dialogue between humans and AI systems, allowing users to ask questions and receive interpretable explanations about the model's decisions.

13.2.9 Conclusion

Explainable AI techniques enable humans to understand and trust machine learning models. By utilizing interpretable models, generating partial dependence plots, employing LIME or SHAP values, applying model distillation, or leveraging domain-specific techniques, we can enhance the interpretability and transparency of AI systems.

13.3 LIME (Local Interpretable Model-Agnostic Explanations)

LIME (Local Interpretable Model-Agnostic Explanations) is a technique for explaining individual predictions of black-box machine learning models. It provides local, interpretable explanations by approximating the decision-making process of the black-box model using a simpler, interpretable model. LIME helps us understand why a specific prediction was made by highlighting the important features and their contributions.

13.3.1 How LIME Works

The main idea behind LIME is to generate local explanations for individual predictions. Here are the steps involved in LIME:

Select Instance of Interest: Choose the instance for which you want an explanation.

Perturb the Instance: Create perturbed samples by randomly perturbing the values of the features around the instance of interest. These perturbed samples are generated by adding random noise or making small modifications to the feature values.

Obtain Model's Predictions: Feed the perturbed samples into the black-box model and obtain its predictions for these perturbed instances.

Build Local Surrogate Model: Train an interpretable model, such as linear regression or decision tree, on the perturbed samples and their corresponding predictions. This surrogate model approximates the black-box model's behavior locally.

Weigh Perturbed Samples: Assign weights to the perturbed samples based on their similarity to the instance of interest. Closer samples or those that share similar feature values with the instance of interest will receive higher weights.

Explain the Prediction: Use the local surrogate model to explain the prediction made by the black-box model for the instance of interest. The interpretable model's coefficients or feature importance values provide insights into the relative importance of the features and their contributions to the prediction.

13.3.2 Benefits of LIME

LIME offers several benefits for model interpretability:

Model-Agnostic: LIME is not restricted to a specific type of model. It can be applied to any black-box model, including complex models like neural networks or ensemble models.

Local Explanations: LIME provides explanations specific to individual predictions, offering insights into why a particular instance was classified in a certain way.

Interpretable Models: By training interpretable models as local surrogates, LIME generates explanations that can be easily understood and interpreted by humans.

Feature Importance: LIME highlights the important features that influenced the model's prediction for a specific instance. This information helps in understanding the decision-making process.

Trust and Transparency: LIME enhances trust and transparency by providing explanations for black-box models, which are often considered less interpretable.

13.3.3 Limitations of LIME

While LIME is a powerful technique for local interpretability, it has some limitations:

Local Scope: LIME provides explanations for individual predictions but does not offer a global view of the model's behavior or feature importance across the entire dataset.

Surrogate Model Approximation: The surrogate model used in LIME approximates the behavior of the black-box model in the local region. The accuracy of the approximation depends on the quality and representativeness of the perturbed samples.

Perturbation Sensitivity: LIME's explanations can be sensitive to the choice of perturbation method and the magnitude of perturbations applied to the features. Different perturbation strategies can yield different explanations.

Simplified Model Representation: Interpretable models used as surrogate models in LIME provide simplified representations of the black-box model's decision boundary, potentially overlooking complex interactions between features.

13.3.4 Applications of LIME

LIME finds applications in various domains, including:

Healthcare: LIME can help in explaining medical predictions, such as disease diagnosis or treatment recommendations, providing transparency to healthcare professionals and patients.

Finance: LIME can be used to explain credit risk assessments, fraud detection, or investment decisions, enabling stakeholders to understand the factors influencing the outcomes.

Image and Text Classification: LIME can highlight the important regions or words in an image or text that contribute to the model's prediction, aiding in understanding the model's decision process.

13.3.5 Conclusion

LIME is a powerful technique for generating local, interpretable explanations for individual predictions of black-box machine learning models. By approximating the model's behavior locally using interpretable surrogate models, LIME helps us understand the important features and their contributions to the predictions. LIME enhances the interpretability and transparency of black-box models, facilitating trust and informed decision-making.

13.4 SHAP (SHapley Additive exPlanations)

SHAP (SHapley Additive exPlanations) is a unified framework for feature attribution and explanation in machine learning models. It provides a comprehensive and consistent way to measure the importance of features and understand their contributions to individual predictions. SHAP values offer a flexible and interpretable approach to feature importance analysis.

13.4.1 How SHAP Works

SHAP builds upon cooperative game theory concepts and uses the Shapley value, a concept from cooperative game theory, to allocate contributions to each feature. Here's an overview of how SHAP works:

Define a Reference: Choose a reference point that represents a baseline or neutral prediction. It could be the average prediction of the model or a specific reference instance.

Create Coalitions: Form coalitions by selecting subsets of features along with the reference point. Each coalition represents a different combination of features.

Calculate Contributions: Determine the contribution of each feature to the prediction by comparing the predictions made with and without the feature in the coalition. The contribution is calculated based on the difference in predictions and the Shapley value formula.

Calculate Shapley Values: Apply the Shapley value formula to allocate the contributions fairly among the features. The Shapley value considers all possible coalitions and the marginal contributions of each feature within those coalitions.

Interpret Feature Importance: Interpret the Shapley values as measures of feature importance. Higher absolute Shapley values indicate greater importance, and positive/negative signs indicate positive/negative impacts on the prediction.

13.4.2 Benefits of SHAP

SHAP offers several benefits for feature importance analysis and model interpretability:

Model-Agnostic: SHAP is model-agnostic, meaning it can be applied to any machine learning model, including complex models like neural networks, support vector machines, or ensemble models.

Consistency and Fairness: SHAP adheres to axiomatic properties of feature importance, ensuring consistency, and fairness in the attribution of contributions.

Global and Local Explanations: SHAP provides both global and local explanations. Global SHAP values offer an overall view of feature importance across the entire dataset, while local SHAP values explain the contributions of features to individual predictions.

Interaction Effects: SHAP values can capture interaction effects between features, allowing for a more nuanced understanding of how different features interact to influence predictions.

Interpretability: SHAP values provide interpretable feature importance measures that can be easily understood and communicated to stakeholders.

13.4.3 Limitations of SHAP

While SHAP is a powerful technique for feature importance analysis, it has some limitations:

Computational Complexity: Calculating SHAP values can be computationally expensive, especially for large datasets or complex models with a high-dimensional feature space. Approximation techniques may be used to alleviate computational burden.

Interpretability of Complex Models: Although SHAP provides feature-level insights, interpreting complex models with a large number of features and intricate interactions can still be challenging.

Reference Point Selection: The choice of the reference point can impact the interpretation of SHAP values. Different reference points can yield different feature importance rankings.

High-Dimensional Data: In high-dimensional feature spaces, the number of possible coalitions grows exponentially, making the calculation of SHAP values more challenging.

13.4.4 Applications of SHAP

SHAP has a wide range of applications in various domains, including:

Healthcare: SHAP can help interpret predictions in medical diagnosis, treatment planning, or personalized medicine, enabling doctors and patients to understand the reasons behind the model's recommendations.

Finance: SHAP can provide insights into credit risk assessment, fraud detection, or investment decision-making, assisting financial institutions in understanding the factors driving the model's predictions.

Natural Language Processing: SHAP can explain predictions in text classification, sentiment analysis, or machine translation, shedding light on the important words or phrases influencing the model's decisions.

13.4.5 Conclusion

SHAP (SHapley Additive exPlanations) offers a unified and flexible framework for feature attribution and explanation in machine learning models. By leveraging cooperative game theory concepts and the Shapley value, SHAP provides interpretable and consistent measures of feature importance. SHAP values enable us to understand the contributions of features to individual predictions, enhancing model interpretability and transparency.

Chapter 14: Handling Bias and Fairness in Machine Learning

14.1 Introduction

As machine learning algorithms increasingly play a significant role in decision-making processes, it becomes crucial to address potential biases and ensure fairness in their outcomes. Biases can arise from historical data, biased labeling, or algorithmic design, leading to unfair and discriminatory outcomes. In this chapter, we will explore techniques for identifying, mitigating, and handling bias and promoting fairness in machine learning models.

14.2 Understanding Bias in Machine Learning

Bias in machine learning refers to the systematic and unfair favoritism or discrimination towards certain groups or individuals in the data or model predictions. It can occur due to various factors:

Data Bias: Biases present in the training data, such as underrepresentation or overrepresentation of certain groups, can lead to biased model predictions.

Label Bias: Biased or inaccurate labels assigned to the training data can perpetuate and amplify existing biases.

Algorithmic Bias: Biases can be introduced during the algorithm design or implementation, leading to discriminatory outcomes.

14.3 Measuring Bias and Fairness

To address bias and fairness issues, it is essential to measure and quantify them. Several metrics and approaches can help in assessing bias and fairness:

Disparate Impact: Disparate impact measures the difference in the outcomes between different groups. It compares the proportion of positive outcomes for different groups and identifies disparities.

Statistical Parity: Statistical parity examines whether different groups receive similar proportions of positive outcomes, regardless of the protected attributes (e.g., race or gender).

Equalized Odds: Equalized odds ensures that the true positive rates and false positive rates are similar across different groups, guaranteeing fairness in both predictions of positive and negative outcomes.

Conditional Independence: Conditional independence assesses whether the prediction remains independent of the protected attribute when conditioned on the outcome.

Individual Fairness: Individual fairness focuses on treating similar individuals or cases similarly, regardless of the protected attributes.

14.4 Mitigating Bias and Promoting Fairness

To address bias and promote fairness in machine learning models, various techniques can be employed:

Data Collection and Preprocessing: Ensure diverse and representative training data that includes different groups and avoids underrepresentation or overrepresentation.

Bias-Aware Preprocessing: Apply preprocessing techniques, such as reweighting or resampling, to mitigate biases in the training data.

Fairness Constraints: Integrate fairness constraints into the model training process to explicitly optimize for fairness and prevent biased outcomes.

Bias Mitigation Algorithms: Employ bias mitigation algorithms that aim to reduce the influence of protected attributes on the model's predictions.

Model Evaluation and Testing: Regularly evaluate models for bias and fairness using appropriate metrics and conduct rigorous testing to identify and rectify any disparities.

Human-in-the-Loop Approaches: Involve human domain experts and stakeholders to provide insights, validate fairness, and ensure ethical considerations are upheld.

14.5 Ethical Considerations and Trade-Offs

Addressing bias and promoting fairness in machine learning models involves ethical considerations and trade-offs. It is crucial to strike a balance between fairness, accuracy, and other performance metrics:

Trade-offs between Fairness and Accuracy: Fairness measures can sometimes conflict with accuracy, and achieving perfect fairness may lead to a degradation in overall predictive performance. Consider the appropriate trade-offs based on the specific application and domain.

Transparency and Explainability: Ensure transparency and explainability in the decision-making process to build trust and allow stakeholders to understand how biases are being addressed.

Continuous Monitoring and Evaluation: Regularly monitor and evaluate models for bias and fairness, as biases can emerge or evolve over time. Address biases as part of a continuous improvement process.

User Feedback and Redress: Establish mechanisms to gather user feedback, address concerns, and provide avenues for redress in case of unfair treatment.

14.6 Conclusion

Addressing bias and promoting fairness in machine learning models is crucial to ensure ethical, transparent, and equitable outcomes. By understanding the sources of bias, measuring fairness, employing mitigation techniques, and considering ethical trade-offs, we can develop models that align with societal values and promote equal treatment. Handling bias and promoting fairness is an ongoing process that requires continuous monitoring, evaluation, and stakeholder involvement.

14.1 Recognizing Bias in Data and Models

Bias can manifest in both the data used for training machine learning models and the models themselves. Recognizing and understanding bias is a crucial step in addressing fairness issues. In this section, we will explore methods for recognizing bias in data and models.

14.1.1 Data Bias

Data bias refers to systematic inaccuracies or imbalances in the training data that can lead to biased model predictions. It can arise from various sources, including societal biases, data collection processes, or biased labeling. Here are some methods for recognizing data bias:

Exploratory Data Analysis (EDA): Conducting EDA helps identify potential bias in the data. Look for disparities in the distribution of features or target variables across different groups of interest, such as gender, race, or age.

Data Visualization: Visualizing the data can reveal imbalances or disparities. Plotting histograms, bar charts, or heatmaps can highlight unequal representation or skewed distributions.

Bias Detection Tools: Utilize bias detection tools that leverage statistical techniques or machine learning algorithms to detect potential biases in the data. These tools can identify disparities in the distribution of data or the representation of different groups.

Proxy Variables: Be cautious of using proxy variables that may indirectly capture sensitive attributes and introduce bias. Proxy variables can lead to discriminatory outcomes if they correlate strongly with protected attributes.

Bias in Labels: Examine potential biases in the labeling process. Biased or subjective labeling can perpetuate and amplify biases in the data. Manual review and quality assurance processes can help identify and address label bias.

14.1.2 Model Bias

Model bias refers to biases that arise from the algorithms or model design choices. Even if the training data is unbiased, the model itself can still learn and perpetuate biases. Recognizing model bias is essential for ensuring fairness in predictions. Here are some methods for recognizing model bias:

Performance Disparities: Evaluate model performance across different groups and protected attributes. Assess whether the model exhibits significant disparities in prediction accuracy or error rates for different groups.

Confusion Matrices: Examine confusion matrices for different groups to identify discrepancies in true positive, true negative, false positive, and false negative rates. Significant differences may indicate bias.

Fairness Metrics: Utilize fairness metrics to quantify disparities and measure fairness. Metrics such as disparate impact, statistical parity, equalized odds, or conditional independence can help assess fairness in predictions.

Group-Based Analysis: Conduct group-based analysis to compare model predictions and performance for different groups. This analysis can reveal potential biases in favor of or against specific groups.

Error Analysis: Perform an error analysis to identify whether the model is making consistent errors or biases in certain types of predictions. Analyzing false positive or false negative cases can provide insights into potential biases.

Model Interpretability: Utilize interpretable models or techniques such as LIME or SHAP values to understand the factors driving model predictions. Interpretable models can provide insights into how the model uses different features and whether biases are present.

14.1.3 Human Review and Evaluation

In addition to automated techniques, involving human reviewers and evaluators is crucial for recognizing bias. Human reviewers can provide domain expertise, identify contextual biases, and evaluate the fairness and ethical considerations of the models. They can review model outputs, analyze potential biases, and ensure alignment with societal values.

14.1.4 Limitations and Challenges

Recognizing bias in data and models is a complex task, and there are challenges and limitations to be aware of:

Contextual Understanding: Recognizing bias often requires understanding the social and cultural context in which the data is collected and the models are used. Some biases may be subtle and require domain expertise for identification.

Data Availability: Recognizing bias may be challenging when data is limited or lacks representation from diverse groups. In such cases, careful consideration should be given to potential biases and their impact on model predictions.

Evolving Biases: Biases can evolve over time, and models trained on historical data may perpetuate outdated biases. Regular monitoring and updates are necessary to address evolving biases.

14.1.5 Conclusion

Recognizing bias in data and models is a crucial step in addressing fairness issues in machine learning. By employing exploratory data analysis, data visualization, bias detection tools, evaluating model performance and fairness metrics, and involving human reviewers, we can gain insights into the biases present in the data and models. Understanding bias is the first step towards developing strategies to mitigate bias and promote fairness in machine learning systems.

14.2 Mitigating Bias in Preprocessing and Training

To address bias and promote fairness in machine learning models, it is crucial to incorporate mitigation techniques during the preprocessing and training stages. By mitigating bias early in the pipeline, we can reduce the potential for biased model predictions. In this section, we will explore techniques for mitigating bias in preprocessing and training.

14.2.1 Data Preprocessing Techniques

Data preprocessing plays a critical role in addressing bias in the training data. Here are some techniques that can be employed:

Data Collection and Sampling: Ensure diverse and representative data collection to avoid underrepresentation or overrepresentation of certain groups. Use appropriate sampling techniques to ensure balanced representation.

Oversampling and Undersampling: Apply oversampling techniques, such as SMOTE (Synthetic Minority Over-sampling Technique), to increase the representation of underrepresented groups. Similarly, undersampling techniques can be used to reduce the dominance of overrepresented groups.

Reweighting: Assign weights to training instances to rectify imbalances. Assign higher weights to underrepresented instances and lower weights to overrepresented instances.

Fairness-Aware Data Augmentation: Augment the data with techniques that explicitly address fairness concerns. For example, generate augmented data for underrepresented groups or create synthetic data that promotes equal representation.

Subgroup Analysis: Conduct subgroup analysis to identify and address biases within specific subgroups. Analyze the performance of the model across different demographic or protected attribute subgroups and apply preprocessing techniques accordingly.

14.2.2 Algorithmic Techniques

In addition to preprocessing techniques, algorithmic techniques can be employed during model training to mitigate bias and promote fairness. Here are some approaches:

Fairness Constraints: Introduce fairness constraints during the model training process to explicitly optimize for fairness. Constraints can be applied to minimize disparate impact, equalize odds, or ensure conditional independence.

Regularization and Penalization: Incorporate regularization or penalization terms that discourage biased predictions or mitigate the influence of protected attributes. For example, use regularization terms that penalize models for relying heavily on sensitive attributes.

Predefined Fairness Metrics: Define fairness metrics as part of the training objective to ensure that fairness is explicitly optimized. These metrics can be customized based on the specific fairness concerns of the problem domain.

Adversarial Training: Utilize adversarial training approaches where the model is simultaneously trained to predict the target variable accurately while being resistant to predicting sensitive attributes. Adversarial training aims to remove the correlation between predictions and protected attributes.

Model Selection and Evaluation: Consider fairness metrics as part of the model selection process. Evaluate and compare models based on their performance and fairness across different demographic or protected attribute subgroups.

14.2.3 Model Regularization and Auditing

Regularly audit models for bias and fairness to ensure ongoing mitigation efforts. Here are some strategies:

Bias Testing: Conduct statistical tests or evaluation methods to identify potential biases in the model's predictions. Assess whether the model exhibits disparities in performance or fairness across different groups.

External Validation: Validate model predictions against external, unbiased sources of information or domain experts to ensure fairness and mitigate potential biases.

Continuous Monitoring: Implement monitoring systems to track the performance and fairness of deployed models in real-time. Monitor for shifts in biases over time and trigger corrective actions when necessary.

Model Explainability and Interpretability: Utilize techniques such as LIME (Local Interpretable Model-Agnostic Explanations) or SHAP (SHapley Additive exPlanations) to understand how the model's decisions are influenced by different features and protected attributes.

14.2.4 Limitations and Considerations

While mitigating bias in preprocessing and training is crucial, it's important to consider the limitations and potential challenges:

Trade-offs: Addressing bias and promoting fairness may involve trade-offs with other performance metrics, such as accuracy or precision. Consider the trade-offs and choose the appropriate balance based on the specific application and domain.

Contextual Understanding: Mitigating bias requires a contextual understanding of the problem domain, the potential sources of bias, and the implications of different fairness measures. Involve domain experts and stakeholders to ensure a comprehensive approach.

Ethical Considerations: Consider the ethical implications of addressing bias, including potential unintended consequences. Strive for fairness while being mindful of the broader societal impacts.

14.2.5 Conclusion

Mitigating bias in preprocessing and training stages is a critical step towards promoting fairness in machine learning models. By employing techniques such as data sampling, reweighting, fairness-aware data augmentation, fairness constraints, and model regularization, we can reduce bias and ensure equitable model predictions. Ongoing model auditing and monitoring are essential to ensure continued fairness and mitigate biases that may arise over time.

14.3 Fairness Metrics and Evaluation

Ensuring fairness in machine learning models requires the use of appropriate fairness metrics and evaluation techniques. Fairness metrics provide quantitative measures to assess the degree of bias and fairness in model predictions. Evaluation allows us to identify and address any disparities or discriminatory outcomes. In this section, we will explore fairness metrics and evaluation techniques for promoting fairness in machine learning.

14.3.1 Types of Fairness Metrics

Fairness metrics measure disparities in model predictions across different groups or protected attributes. Here are some commonly used fairness metrics:

Disparate Impact: Disparate impact, also known as the impact ratio or between-group fairness, measures the difference in the outcomes between different groups. It compares the proportion of positive outcomes for different groups and identifies disparities.

Statistical Parity: Statistical parity, or demographic parity, ensures that different groups receive similar proportions of positive outcomes, regardless of their protected attributes. It focuses on equalizing the overall representation of positive outcomes.

Equalized Odds: Equalized odds, or equal opportunity, aims to ensure that the true positive rates and false positive rates are similar across different groups. It guarantees fairness in both the prediction of positive outcomes and the avoidance of false positives.

Conditional Independence: Conditional independence examines whether the prediction remains independent of the protected attribute when conditioned on the outcome. It assesses whether the model's predictions are fair and unbiased, irrespective of the protected attribute.

Treatment Equality: Treatment equality, or treatment parity, compares the treatment received by different groups. It ensures that groups with similar characteristics receive similar levels of treatment, avoiding discrepancies based on protected attributes.

Calibration: Calibration measures the agreement between predicted probabilities and observed frequencies. It ensures that the model's predicted probabilities are well-calibrated across different groups, irrespective of the protected attributes.

Overall Accuracy vs. Group Accuracy: Comparing overall accuracy with group-specific accuracies can reveal disparities in prediction performance across different groups. Significant differences may indicate biased outcomes.

14.3.2 Evaluation Techniques

Evaluating fairness involves assessing model performance and fairness across different demographic or protected attribute subgroups. Here are some techniques for evaluating fairness:

Group-Based Analysis: Evaluate the model's performance and fairness metrics for different subgroups defined by protected attributes, such as gender, race, or age. Compare metrics such as accuracy, false positive rate, or disparate impact across groups to identify disparities.

Intersectional Analysis: Conduct intersectional analysis by considering multiple protected attributes simultaneously. This allows for a more comprehensive understanding of fairness concerns among different intersectional groups.

Fairness Dashboards: Create fairness dashboards or visualizations that provide an intuitive overview of model fairness across different groups. These dashboards can aid in identifying disparities and tracking changes over time.

Model Bias Testing: Perform statistical tests or bias evaluation techniques to identify potential biases in the model's predictions. Compare model outputs with unbiased reference datasets or ground truth labels to identify disparities.

Human Review and Evaluation: Involve human reviewers or domain experts to evaluate model outputs and assess fairness. Human judgment and domain expertise can provide valuable insights into fairness considerations.

14.3.3 Limitations and Considerations

Fairness metrics and evaluation techniques have certain limitations and considerations:

Contextual Understanding: Fairness metrics should be applied in the appropriate context, considering the specific domain and societal norms. Some fairness metrics may be more relevant in certain contexts than others.

Trade-offs: Fairness considerations often involve trade-offs with other performance metrics, such as accuracy or precision. Striking the right balance between fairness and other metrics is essential.

Subgroup Size and Representation: Adequate representation of different groups is important for reliable fairness evaluation. Ensure that subgroup sizes are sufficient to draw meaningful conclusions and avoid biased assessments based on small sample sizes.

Intersectionality: Consider the intersectionality of protected attributes when evaluating fairness. Intersectional analysis provides a more nuanced understanding of how multiple attributes may interact and impact fairness.

14.3.4 Conclusion

Fairness metrics and evaluation techniques are vital for assessing and promoting fairness in machine learning models. By utilizing appropriate fairness metrics, conducting group-based and intersectional analyses, and involving human evaluation, we can identify disparities and mitigate biases. Evaluating fairness allows us to ensure equitable outcomes and address any discriminatory or biased predictions.

14.4 Ethical Considerations in Machine Learning

Ethical considerations are of paramount importance when developing and deploying machine learning models. Machine learning algorithms have the potential to influence and impact individuals, society, and decision-making processes. It is crucial to address ethical concerns to ensure fairness, transparency, and accountability in the development and use of machine learning systems. In this section, we will explore some key ethical considerations in machine learning.

14.4.1 Transparency and Explainability

Transparency and explainability are fundamental ethical considerations in machine learning. It is important to understand how machine learning models make decisions and the factors that influence those decisions. Explainable AI techniques, such as LIME (Local Interpretable Model-Agnostic Explanations) or SHAP (SHapley Additive exPlanations), help in interpreting and providing explanations for model predictions. Transparent and interpretable models instill trust, allow for better scrutiny, and facilitate understanding of potential biases or unfairness.

14.4.2 Bias and Fairness

Addressing bias and promoting fairness are ethical imperatives in machine learning. Bias in data or models can lead to discriminatory outcomes, reinforce inequalities, or perpetuate historical biases. It is essential to recognize, mitigate, and monitor biases throughout the machine learning pipeline. Fairness metrics, algorithmic techniques, and continuous evaluation help in identifying and rectifying biases, ensuring equitable treatment and decision-making.

14.4.3 Data Privacy and Security

Respecting data privacy and ensuring data security are critical ethical considerations. Machine learning models often rely on large amounts of data, including personal and sensitive information. Protecting individuals' privacy and ensuring the security of data against unauthorized access or misuse is essential. Adhering to data protection regulations, implementing secure data storage and transmission practices, and obtaining informed consent when handling personal data are crucial steps in ethical machine learning.

14.4.4 Accountability and Responsibility

Accountability and responsibility are important ethical principles in machine learning. Developers, organizations, and stakeholders should be accountable for the impact of their machine learning models. It is essential to consider the potential consequences of model predictions on individuals or communities. Establishing mechanisms for redress, providing explanations for decisions, and ensuring the ability to rectify errors or biases are key elements of ethical responsibility.

14.4.5 Algorithmic Transparency and Governance

Algorithmic transparency and governance refer to the need for oversight, regulation, and accountability in the development and use of machine learning models. As machine learning algorithms increasingly make decisions with significant impacts, there is a need for ethical guidelines, regulations, and standards. Transparency in model development processes, auditability, and external review mechanisms contribute to responsible and ethical deployment of machine learning systems.

14.4.6 Human-Centered Design and Human-in-the-Loop

Human-centered design and involving humans in the decision-making loop are crucial ethical considerations. Machine learning should augment human capabilities and decision-making rather than replace or undermine them. Engaging domain experts, incorporating diverse perspectives, and considering the societal and ethical implications of machine learning applications are important steps in ensuring responsible and ethical deployment.

14.4.7 Socioeconomic Impact and Bias Mitigation

Machine learning models can have socioeconomic impacts, and it is important to consider potential biases and mitigate their effects. Models should be designed and deployed in a manner that minimizes harm, reduces inequalities, and avoids exacerbating existing social biases. Proactive measures, such as evaluating the impact on different demographic groups, monitoring for disparate outcomes, and incorporating feedback mechanisms, contribute to ethical machine learning.

14.4.8 Continuous Monitoring and Improvement

Ethical considerations in machine learning are not one-time tasks but require ongoing monitoring and improvement. As societal norms evolve, biases change, and new ethical challenges emerge, it is crucial to continuously evaluate models, retrain them with updated data, and adapt to changing ethical standards. Ethical responsibility requires a commitment to continuous improvement and vigilance.

14.4.9 Conclusion

Ethical considerations are integral to responsible and meaningful deployment of machine learning models. Transparency, fairness, privacy, accountability, and human-centered design are crucial pillars of ethical machine learning. By addressing ethical concerns throughout the machine learning pipeline and actively engaging in ongoing evaluation and improvement, we can ensure that machine learning benefits society while upholding ethical principles.

Chapter 15: Transfer Learning and Model Adaptation

15.1 Introduction to Transfer Learning

Transfer learning is a machine learning technique that allows models to leverage knowledge learned from one task or domain to improve performance on a different but related task or domain. Instead of starting the learning process from scratch, transfer learning enables models to transfer knowledge and representations learned from previous tasks, leading to faster convergence and better generalization. In this chapter, we will explore transfer learning and model adaptation techniques.

15.2 Benefits of Transfer Learning

Transfer learning offers several benefits in machine learning:

Improved Performance: By leveraging pre-trained models or learned representations, transfer learning can enhance model performance on new tasks, especially when training data is limited.

Faster Training: Transfer learning reduces the need for extensive training on new tasks by initializing models with pre-trained weights. This saves time and computational resources.

Generalization: Transfer learning helps models generalize well to new and unseen data by capturing meaningful and transferable patterns from previous tasks or domains.

Data Efficiency: When labeled data is scarce or costly to obtain, transfer learning enables models to leverage large amounts of labeled data from a related task or domain, boosting performance.

Adaptability: Transfer learning allows models to adapt and specialize in different target tasks or domains by fine-tuning or modifying pre-trained models.

15.3 Transfer Learning Approaches

There are different approaches to transfer learning, depending on the availability of labeled data and the similarity between the source and target tasks or domains:

Pre-trained Models: Pre-trained models, such as convolutional neural networks (CNNs) pre-trained on ImageNet, are widely used in computer vision. These models learn generic features from large-scale datasets and can be fine-tuned or used as feature extractors for specific tasks.

Feature Extraction: In feature extraction, the pre-trained model's early layers are frozen, and the later layers are replaced or augmented with task-specific layers. The frozen layers act as feature extractors, capturing meaningful representations for the new task.

Fine-tuning: Fine-tuning involves training the entire pre-trained model on the new task with a smaller learning rate. By updating the pre-trained weights while preserving learned representations, fine-tuning adapts the model to the new task.

Domain Adaptation: Domain adaptation focuses on transferring knowledge from a source domain to a target domain when the distributions of the data differ. Techniques like domain adaptation aim to reduce domain shift and align the feature distributions across domains.

Multi-task Learning: Multi-task learning trains a model to perform multiple tasks simultaneously, leveraging shared representations and exploiting relationships between tasks to improve performance on individual tasks.

15.4 Guidelines for Transfer Learning

When applying transfer learning, consider the following guidelines:

Task Similarity: Choose a source task or domain that is similar to the target task or domain. The more similarities in the data distribution and task objectives, the more effective transfer learning is likely to be.

Model Selection: Select a pre-trained model that is suitable for the target task. Different pre-trained models excel in different domains, so choose one that captures relevant features for the new task.

Data Availability: Assess the availability of labeled data for the target task. If labeled data is limited, transfer learning with pre-trained models becomes especially beneficial.

Fine-tuning Strategies: Decide whether to freeze certain layers or fine-tune the entire model. This choice depends on the similarity between the source and target tasks, the amount of available labeled data, and the risk of overfitting.

Regularization: Regularize the model during transfer learning to prevent overfitting. Techniques such as dropout, weight decay, or early stopping can be applied to avoid excessive reliance on the source task.

15.5 Model Adaptation Techniques

Model adaptation involves modifying or updating existing models to address changes in the task, data distribution, or system requirements. Here are some techniques for model adaptation:

Incremental Learning: Incremental learning enables models to learn from new data while retaining knowledge from previous tasks. It facilitates lifelong learning and adaptation to evolving environments.

Online Learning: Online learning allows models to continuously adapt and update their parameters as new data arrives in a streaming fashion. Online learning is particularly useful when data distribution or concept drift occurs over time.

Active Learning: Active learning involves iteratively selecting informative samples for labeling, reducing the need for extensive labeled data. Models actively query the user or domain expert to label instances that are most valuable for improving performance.

Meta-Learning: Meta-learning, or learning to learn, focuses on training models that can quickly adapt to new tasks or domains. Meta-learning algorithms learn from multiple tasks and generalize across them, enabling rapid adaptation to new situations.

15.6 Challenges and Considerations

When applying transfer learning and model adaptation techniques, be mindful of the following challenges and considerations:

Bias Transfer: Transfer learning can inadvertently transfer biases from the source task or domain to the target task or domain. Careful examination and mitigation of biases are necessary to ensure fair and unbiased predictions.

Overfitting: Transfer learning runs the risk of overfitting, especially when fine-tuning models with limited labeled data. Regularization techniques and careful selection of training strategies help mitigate this risk.

Task Dependency: The success of transfer learning depends on the similarity between the source and target tasks. Dissimilar tasks may require more extensive modifications or domain adaptation techniques.

Generalization Limitations: Transfer learning does not guarantee improved performance on all tasks. The effectiveness of transfer learning depends on the quality of the source data, the availability of labeled data for the target task, and the complexity of the target task.

15.7 Conclusion

Transfer learning and model adaptation techniques provide powerful tools to leverage existing knowledge and improve model performance on new tasks or domains. By transferring learned representations, fine-tuning models, or adapting to new environments, machine learning models can adapt, generalize, and perform effectively with limited data. Understanding the principles, guidelines, and challenges of transfer learning and model adaptation enables practitioners to harness the full potential of existing models and drive advancements in various domains.

15.1 Leveraging Pretrained Models

Pretrained models are pre-trained on large-scale datasets and capture valuable knowledge and representations from the training data. Leveraging pretrained models is a popular approach in transfer learning and model adaptation, as it allows models to benefit from the learned features and parameters. In this section, we will explore how to leverage pretrained models effectively.

15.1.1 Understanding Pretrained Models

Pretrained models are typically trained on large, publicly available datasets such as ImageNet for computer vision tasks or large text corpora for natural language processing tasks. These models have learned generic features that can be valuable for a wide range of related tasks. By utilizing pretrained models, you can save time and computational resources compared to training models from scratch.

15.1.2 Benefits of Pretrained Models

Leveraging pretrained models offers several benefits:

Feature Extraction: Pretrained models can be used as feature extractors, where the early layers of the model are used to extract meaningful representations from the input data. These extracted features can then be fed into a new model or classifier for the target task.

Transferable Representations: Pretrained models capture transferable representations that generalize well across different tasks and domains. The models have learned to recognize common patterns and features, which can be beneficial for related tasks.

Faster Convergence: By starting with pretrained weights, models can converge faster on the target task, especially when the target task has limited labeled data. The pretrained weights provide a good initialization point for the model.

Improved Generalization: Pretrained models, being trained on large and diverse datasets, have learned to generalize well to different inputs. By leveraging their representations, models can benefit from this improved generalization ability.

Domain-Specific Adaptation: Pretrained models can be fine-tuned or adapted to the target task by updating their weights with task-specific data. This process allows the model to adapt to the nuances and specificities of the target task.

15.1.3 Techniques for Leveraging Pretrained Models

To effectively leverage pretrained models, consider the following techniques:

Feature Extraction: Use the pretrained model as a feature extractor by freezing its early layers and using the activations from these layers as input features for a new classifier. This technique works well when the dataset for the target task is small or when the low-level features captured by the pretrained model are relevant to the target task.

Fine-Tuning: Fine-tuning involves training the pretrained model on the target task while updating its weights. This technique is useful when the target task has sufficient labeled data and the pretrained model's representations need to be adapted to the specific characteristics of the target task.

Architectural Modifications: Modify the architecture of the pretrained model to suit the requirements of the target task. This can involve adding or removing layers, changing the number of neurons, or adjusting the model's structure to better fit the target task.

Ensemble Methods: Combine multiple pretrained models or variants of the same pretrained model to create an ensemble. Each model in the ensemble contributes its learned representations and predictions, leading to improved performance and robustness.

Knowledge Distillation: Use a pretrained model as a teacher model to transfer its knowledge to a smaller student model. This technique is beneficial when deploying models with limited computational resources while still benefiting from the knowledge of the pretrained model.

15.1.4 Choosing the Right Pretrained Model

Choosing the right pretrained model depends on the nature of the target task and the availability of pretrained models in the relevant domain. Consider the following factors:

Task Similarity: Select a pretrained model that was trained on a task similar to the target task. For example, for computer vision tasks, pretrained models trained on ImageNet or COCO datasets are commonly used.

Dataset Size: If the target task has a small dataset, choose a pretrained model that has been trained on a large and diverse dataset. The representations learned by the pretrained model can generalize better to the target task.

Domain Expertise: Consider pretrained models that have been specifically trained or fine-tuned for the target domain, as they may capture domain-specific features and nuances more effectively.

Computational Resources: Take into account the computational resources available for training and inference. Some pretrained models may be more resource-intensive than others, so choose models that align with your resource constraints.

15.1.5 Evaluation and Fine-Tuning

After leveraging a pretrained model, it is important to evaluate its performance on the target task and fine-tune it if necessary. Evaluate the model's performance metrics and assess whether it is meeting the desired objectives. If required, fine-tune the model by updating its weights using the labeled data specific to the target task. Fine-tuning allows the model to adapt to the nuances and specific requirements of the target task, further improving its performance.

15.1.6 Ethical Considerations

When leveraging pretrained models, ethical considerations should be taken into account. Pretrained models may inadvertently capture biases present in the training data, which can lead to biased predictions on the target task. It is essential to evaluate the pretrained model for potential biases and mitigate them through appropriate preprocessing, data augmentation, or algorithmic techniques. Regular monitoring and audits should be conducted to ensure fair and unbiased outcomes.

15.1.7 Conclusion

Leveraging pretrained models is a powerful technique in transfer learning and model adaptation. By utilizing the knowledge and representations captured by pretrained models, you can improve model performance, save time and resources, and benefit from their generalization capabilities. Careful selection of pretrained models, evaluation of their suitability, and fine-tuning when necessary contribute to successfully leveraging pretrained models for the target task.

15.2 Fine-Tuning and Feature Extraction

Fine-tuning and feature extraction are two common techniques for leveraging pretrained models in transfer learning and model adaptation. These techniques allow models to benefit from the knowledge captured by pretrained models and adapt them to the specific requirements of the target task. In this section, we will delve into fine-tuning and feature extraction techniques.

15.2.1 Fine-Tuning

Fine-tuning involves updating the weights of a pretrained model using task-specific data. By fine-tuning a pretrained model, you enable it to learn task-specific patterns and improve its performance on the target task. The steps involved in fine-tuning are as follows:

Pretrained Model Initialization: Start with a pretrained model that has been trained on a large and relevant dataset, such as ImageNet for computer vision tasks or a language model for natural language processing tasks.

Task-Specific Architecture Modification: Modify the architecture of the pretrained model, if necessary, to suit the requirements of the target task. This may involve adding or removing layers, adjusting the number of neurons, or incorporating task-specific components.

Freeze Pretrained Layers: Freeze the initial layers of the pretrained model, especially the early layers that capture low-level features. By freezing these layers, you preserve the generic representations learned by the pretrained model, preventing them from being modified during training.

Initialize Optimizer: Set up an optimizer, such as stochastic gradient descent (SGD) or Adam, to update the weights of the trainable layers in the model during fine-tuning.

Training on Task-Specific Data: Train the modified model using task-specific labeled data. This involves feeding the data through the model, calculating the loss between the model's predictions and the ground truth labels, and backpropagating the gradients to update the trainable weights.

Gradual Unfreezing: After an initial period of training with frozen layers, gradually unfreeze more layers of the pretrained model. This allows the model to learn more task-specific representations while retaining the useful features learned from the pretrained model.

Fine-Tuning Parameters: Adjust the learning rate and other hyperparameters during fine-tuning. A lower learning rate is typically used during fine-tuning to ensure that the pretrained weights are updated more gradually, avoiding catastrophic forgetting of the pretrained knowledge.

Fine-tuning enables models to adapt to the specific characteristics of the target task while still benefiting from the initial knowledge captured by the pretrained model. It is particularly effective when the target task has limited labeled data or when the pretrained model's representations are relevant to the target task.

15.2.2 Feature Extraction

Feature extraction involves using the pretrained model as a feature extractor, where the early layers of the model are used to extract meaningful representations from the input data. These representations, also known as feature vectors, can then be used as input features for a new classifier or a downstream model specific to the target task. The steps involved in feature extraction are as follows:

Pretrained Model Initialization: Start with a pretrained model, similar to the one used in fine-tuning.

Freeze Pretrained Layers: Freeze the initial layers of the pretrained model, preserving the learned representations and preventing them from being modified during training.

Remove or Replace Classification Layers: Remove or replace the classification layers of the pretrained model, as they are task-specific and not relevant to the target task.

Feature Extraction: Pass the input data through the pretrained model and extract the activations from the chosen layers. These activations serve as the feature vectors that capture the meaningful representations of the input data.

Train a New Classifier: Use the extracted feature vectors as input features to train a new classifier specific to the target task. This classifier can be a simple linear classifier or a more complex model depending on the task requirements.

Feature extraction is useful when the target task has limited labeled data or when the low-level features captured by the pretrained model are relevant to the target task. By leveraging the learned representations from the pretrained model, feature extraction enables the model to benefit from the knowledge captured in a different domain or task.

15.2.3 Choosing Fine-Tuning or Feature Extraction

The choice between fine-tuning and feature extraction depends on several factors:

Available Labeled Data: If the target task has limited labeled data, fine-tuning with the task-specific data is beneficial as it allows the model to learn task-specific patterns. Feature extraction is also effective in this scenario, as it leverages the pretrained model's representations without requiring extensive labeled data.

Task Similarity: Fine-tuning is more suitable when the source and target tasks are closely related, and the pretrained model's representations are directly applicable to the target task. Feature extraction is effective when the low-level features captured by the pretrained model are relevant to the target task, regardless of the overall task similarity.

Model Complexity: Fine-tuning allows for more flexibility in adapting the pretrained model's architecture to the target task. If the target task requires significant architectural modifications or if you need to incorporate task-specific components, fine-tuning provides more flexibility. Feature extraction, on the other hand, is simpler and may be more suitable when architectural modifications are not required.

Resource Constraints: Fine-tuning can be more computationally expensive than feature extraction, as it involves training the entire model on the target task. If computational resources are limited, feature extraction provides a more efficient approach by using the pretrained model as a fixed feature extractor.

15.2.4 Conclusion

Fine-tuning and feature extraction are valuable techniques for leveraging pretrained models in transfer learning and model adaptation. Fine-tuning allows models to adapt to the specific characteristics of the target task while still benefiting from the knowledge captured by the pretrained model. Feature extraction, on the other hand, enables the use of pretrained model's representations as input features for downstream tasks. Understanding when to use fine-tuning or feature extraction based on available data, task similarity, model complexity, and resource constraints allows for effective utilization of pretrained models in various domains.

15.3 Domain Adaptation Techniques

Domain adaptation is a transfer learning technique that aims to address the distribution mismatch between the source domain (where the model is pretrained) and the target domain (where the model will be applied). In many real-world scenarios, models trained on one domain may not generalize well to another domain due to differences in data distributions. Domain adaptation techniques help mitigate this issue by aligning the feature distributions or adapting the model to the target domain. In this section, we will explore some commonly used domain adaptation techniques.

15.3.1 Domain Discrepancy

Domain discrepancy refers to the differences in data distributions between the source and target domains. It can manifest in variations in visual appearance, data statistics, or domain-specific characteristics. To perform effective domain adaptation, it is crucial to understand and measure the domain discrepancy. Various metrics and techniques can be used to quantify the dissimilarity between domains, such as Maximum Mean Discrepancy (MMD), Kullback-Leibler (KL) divergence, or Wasserstein distance.

15.3.2 Unsupervised Domain Adaptation

Unsupervised domain adaptation techniques aim to align the feature distributions of the source and target domains without using target domain labels. These techniques leverage only the source domain labeled data and the unlabeled target domain data. Here are some common methods used in unsupervised domain adaptation:

Domain Adversarial Neural Networks (DANN): DANN introduces a domain discriminator that encourages the model to learn domain-invariant features. The model is trained to confuse the domain discriminator while performing well on the source domain task. This adversarial training helps align the feature distributions across domains.

Self-Ensembling: Self-ensembling methods leverage consistency regularization to align the predictions of a model on different perturbations of the unlabeled target domain data. By enforcing consistency, the model learns to produce consistent predictions across different transformations, encouraging domain-invariant representations.

Domain-Confusion Learning: Domain-confusion learning minimizes the difference between the predictions of the model on the source and target domains, forcing the model to learn domain-invariant features. This technique can be combined with traditional supervised learning objectives to align the feature representations.

15.3.3 Supervised Domain Adaptation

Supervised domain adaptation techniques utilize both the source domain labeled data and a limited amount of labeled data from the target domain. These techniques aim to align the feature distributions and adapt the model to the target domain while leveraging the target domain labels. Some commonly used methods in supervised domain adaptation include:

Adversarial Discriminative Domain Adaptation (ADDA): ADDA introduces a domain adversarial network that encourages the model to learn domain-invariant features, similar to DANN. However, ADDA also incorporates a task-specific network to ensure good performance on the target domain task.

Joint Distribution Adaptation (JDA): JDA learns a joint feature representation that captures both the discriminative information for the source domain task and the domain-invariant information across domains. It optimizes a joint distribution alignment criterion to align the feature distributions.

Target Category Confusion (TCC): TCC leverages labeled target domain data to adapt the model by introducing target category confusion. The model is trained to confuse its predictions between source and target categories while preserving accurate predictions for the source domain categories.

15.3.4 Transfer Learning with Auxiliary Tasks

Another approach to domain adaptation is to introduce auxiliary tasks that are related to the target domain. By jointly training the model on both the main task and auxiliary tasks, the model can leverage the shared representations across tasks to adapt to the target domain. Auxiliary tasks can include tasks such as domain classification, style recognition, or attribute prediction.

15.3.5 Multi-Source Domain Adaptation

In scenarios where multiple source domains are available, multi-source domain adaptation techniques aim to leverage information from all source domains to improve adaptation to the target domain. These techniques explore methods such as domain selection, domain weighting, or domain combination to effectively utilize information from multiple sources.

15.3.6 Conclusion

Domain adaptation techniques play a vital role in transferring knowledge from the source domain to the target domain, mitigating the distribution mismatch between them. By aligning feature distributions or adapting models to the target domain, these techniques enable models to generalize better and perform well on the target task. Understanding the domain discrepancy, choosing appropriate unsupervised or supervised domain adaptation methods, and leveraging auxiliary tasks or multiple sources contribute to successful domain adaptation.

15.4 Multi-Task Learning

Multi-task learning is a transfer learning technique that involves training a model to perform multiple tasks simultaneously. By jointly learning from multiple related tasks, the model can leverage shared knowledge and improve its performance on each individual task. In this section, we will explore the concept of multi-task learning and its benefits.

15.4.1 Understanding Multi-Task Learning

In traditional machine learning, models are typically trained to perform a single task by optimizing a specific objective function. However, in many real-world scenarios, related tasks often share underlying patterns or dependencies. Multi-task learning aims to exploit these shared patterns by jointly training a model on multiple tasks.

In multi-task learning, a single model is designed to predict multiple outputs, each corresponding to a specific task. The model is trained on a combined dataset that includes labeled examples for all tasks. By optimizing a joint objective function that considers all tasks simultaneously, the model can learn to extract shared features and improve performance on each individual task.

15.4.2 Benefits of Multi-Task Learning

Multi-task learning offers several benefits:

Improved Generalization: By leveraging shared patterns across tasks, multi-task learning allows models to generalize better. The model learns to extract relevant features that are beneficial for multiple tasks, leading to improved performance and robustness.

Data Efficiency: Multi-task learning can enhance performance even when the individual tasks have limited labeled data. The shared representations learned from the combined dataset can compensate for the lack of data in specific tasks, reducing the need for large task-specific datasets.

Transfer of Knowledge: Multi-task learning facilitates the transfer of knowledge between related tasks. By jointly learning multiple tasks, the model can transfer knowledge learned from one task to improve performance on others. This is particularly useful when there is a scarcity of labeled data for some tasks.

Regularization and Reduced Overfitting: Training a model on multiple tasks introduces regularization effects. The model is encouraged to learn shared features, reducing the risk of overfitting and improving generalization performance.

Implicit Feature Selection: In multi-task learning, the model learns to identify the most relevant features for each task. This implicit feature selection mechanism can help identify important features and discard noisy or irrelevant ones.

15.4.3 Training Strategies in Multi-Task Learning

There are different strategies to train models in multi-task learning:

Hard Parameter Sharing: In this approach, the model shares the lower layers (representational layers) across all tasks, while each task has its own separate task-specific layers. The shared layers capture common features, while the task-specific layers allow task-specific learning.

Soft Parameter Sharing: Soft parameter sharing allows more flexibility by allowing task-specific layers to share some parameters. Each task has its own set of parameters, but they are encouraged to be similar across tasks by applying regularization techniques such as weight sharing or parameter tying.

Architecture Selection: Different tasks may require different model architectures or network topologies. In this approach, each task can have its own distinct architecture tailored to its specific requirements. The overall model may consist of task-specific subnetworks connected in parallel or hierarchical structures.

Learning to Learn: Learning to learn, or meta-learning, is another approach where the model learns how to quickly adapt to new tasks by training on a distribution of tasks. The model learns to extract and generalize task-specific knowledge, enabling it to adapt rapidly to new tasks.

15.4.4 Task Relationship and Task Design

The success of multi-task learning relies on the relationships and design of the tasks involved. The tasks should be related and share common underlying patterns or dependencies. Task selection and task design should consider factors such as task similarity, task complexity, and the availability of labeled data for each task.

15.4.5 Conclusion

Multi-task learning is a powerful transfer learning technique that allows models to learn from multiple related tasks simultaneously. By leveraging shared knowledge, multi-task learning improves generalization, data efficiency, and knowledge transfer among tasks. Careful task selection, training strategy design, and understanding the relationships between tasks contribute to the success of multi-task learning.

Chapter 16: Ensembling and Model Stacking

16.1 Introduction to Ensembling

Ensembling is a powerful technique in machine learning that combines the predictions of multiple models to make more accurate and robust predictions. By leveraging the diversity and complementary strengths of individual models, ensembling can significantly improve overall performance. In this chapter, we will explore different ensembling methods, including model averaging, voting, and stacking.

16.2 Model Averaging

Model averaging is a simple ensembling technique that involves aggregating the predictions of multiple models. Each model is trained independently, and their predictions are combined by taking the average or weighted average. This technique is effective when the individual models have diverse strengths and capture different aspects of the data. Model averaging helps reduce the impact of outliers or individual model biases, leading to more reliable predictions.

16.3 Voting

Voting is another popular ensembling technique that combines the predictions of multiple models through a voting scheme. There are three common types of voting:

Majority Voting: In majority voting, each model in the ensemble predicts the class label, and the class that receives the majority of votes is selected as the final prediction. This technique is commonly used for classification tasks.

Weighted Voting: Weighted voting assigns different weights to each model's prediction based on its performance or confidence level. The weighted predictions are combined, and the class with the highest weighted sum is chosen as the final prediction.

Soft Voting: Soft voting is applicable to models that provide probability estimates for each class. Each model's probability predictions are averaged, and the class with the highest average probability is selected as the final prediction. Soft voting can provide more nuanced and accurate predictions compared to majority voting.

Voting can be used for both classification and regression tasks and is especially effective when the individual models have different strengths or use different algorithms.

16.4 Model Stacking

Model stacking, also known as meta-learning, is an advanced ensembling technique that involves training a meta-model to make predictions based on the outputs of multiple base models. The process consists of the following steps:

Base Model Training: Train multiple diverse base models on the training data. These models can use different algorithms, architectures, or hyperparameters.

Base Model Predictions: Generate predictions on the validation data using the trained base models.

Meta-Model Training: Use the base model predictions as input features and the ground truth labels as target variables to train a meta-model. The meta-model learns to combine the base model predictions and make a final prediction.

Meta-Model Prediction: Apply the trained meta-model to the test data. The base models generate predictions on the test data, which are then used as input to the meta-model to obtain the final prediction.

Model stacking allows the meta-model to learn the optimal way of combining the predictions from the base models, considering their individual strengths and weaknesses. It can lead to improved performance compared to using individual models or simple ensembling techniques.

16.5 Selecting Ensemble Members

When creating an ensemble, it is essential to consider the diversity and quality of the individual models. Here are some factors to consider when selecting ensemble members:

Diversity: Ensure that the individual models in the ensemble are diverse. They should capture different aspects of the data or use different algorithms/techniques. Diversity helps reduce the risk of overfitting and improves the ensemble's generalization capability.

Performance: Evaluate the performance of each individual model on validation data or through cross-validation. Select models that perform well individually, as they are likely to contribute more to the ensemble's overall performance.

Independence: Choose models that are as independent as possible. Models that rely on similar features or suffer from the same biases are likely to provide similar predictions, limiting the ensemble's effectiveness. Ensuring independence helps capture a broader range of insights and perspectives.

Complexity: Consider the complexity of the models in the ensemble. Combining models of varying complexities can provide a good balance between accuracy and computational efficiency.

16.6 Combining Ensembling with Other Techniques

Ensembling can be combined with other techniques to further improve model performance. Here are a few examples:

Feature Engineering: Ensembling can be combined with feature engineering techniques to create more informative input features for the models. The ensemble can then learn from these enhanced features and make more accurate predictions.

Hyperparameter Optimization: Optimize the hyperparameters of individual models before creating the ensemble. Grid search, random search, or Bayesian optimization can be used to find the optimal hyperparameters for each model.

Bagging: Bagging, short for bootstrap aggregating, is a technique where multiple models are trained on different bootstrap samples of the training data. The models' predictions are then combined using model averaging or voting. Bagging can improve robustness and reduce variance.

16.7 Conclusion

Ensembling techniques, such as model averaging, voting, and model stacking, can significantly enhance model performance and robustness. By leveraging the diversity and strengths of multiple models, ensembling provides more accurate predictions and reduces the risk of overfitting. When combined with other techniques like feature engineering or hyperparameter optimization, ensembling can further boost model performance and generalization capabilities.

16.1 Bagging and Random Forest Ensembles

In addition to model averaging, voting, and model stacking, bagging and random forest ensembles are popular ensembling techniques that can improve model performance and robustness. These techniques leverage the power of combining multiple models through bootstrap aggregation and decision tree ensembles. In this chapter, we will explore bagging and random forest ensembles in detail.

16.1.1 Bagging

Bagging, short for bootstrap aggregating, is an ensembling technique that involves training multiple models on different bootstrap samples of the training data. Each model in the ensemble is trained independently on its own subset of the data. The key steps in bagging are as follows:

Data Sampling: Generate multiple bootstrap samples by randomly selecting data points with replacement from the original training data. Each bootstrap sample has the same size as the original dataset, but some data points may be duplicated, while others may be left out.

Model Training: Train a separate model on each bootstrap sample using the same learning algorithm. Each model is trained independently without any knowledge of the other models.

Model Aggregation: Combine the predictions of all models in the ensemble by averaging (for regression tasks) or voting (for classification tasks) to obtain the final prediction. This aggregation helps reduce the variance and improve the overall prediction accuracy.

Bagging is particularly effective when the underlying base models are high-variance models, such as decision trees. By training multiple models on different subsets of the data, bagging reduces overfitting and produces a more robust ensemble model.

16.1.2 Random Forest Ensembles

Random forest is an extension of bagging that further improves the performance of decision tree ensembles. In addition to training multiple models on different bootstrap samples, random forest introduces two key techniques:

Feature Randomness: At each split in the decision tree, a random subset of features is considered for splitting. This randomness ensures that each tree in the ensemble focuses on different features, leading to more diverse and accurate predictions.

Voting or Averaging: In classification tasks, random forest ensembles use majority voting to determine the final prediction. In regression tasks, the ensemble predictions are averaged to obtain the final prediction.

Random forests are powerful ensembles that are robust to noisy data, handle high-dimensional feature spaces well, and provide estimates of feature importance. They are widely used for a variety of machine learning tasks, including classification and regression.

16.1.3 Benefits of Bagging and Random Forest Ensembles

Bagging and random forest ensembles offer several benefits:

Reduced Variance: By training models on different bootstrap samples or incorporating feature randomness, these ensembles reduce the variance and overfitting compared to individual models.

Improved Accuracy: The aggregation of multiple models leads to more accurate predictions by leveraging the collective knowledge and diversity of the ensemble.

Robustness: Ensembles are robust to noisy data and outliers, as the models' predictions are combined, reducing the impact of individual errors.

Feature Importance: Random forest ensembles provide estimates of feature importance, allowing for better understanding of the underlying data and insights into the importance of different features.

Scalability: Bagging and random forest ensembles can be parallelized, making them scalable and suitable for large datasets and distributed computing environments.

16.1.4 Considerations for Bagging and Random Forest Ensembles

When using bagging and random forest ensembles, consider the following:

Model Diversity: Ensure that the individual models in the ensemble are diverse. Diversity helps capture different aspects of the data and leads to more accurate ensemble predictions.

Hyperparameter Tuning: Tune the hyperparameters of individual models, such as the maximum depth of decision trees, the number of trees in the ensemble, or the number of features considered at each split. Hyperparameter tuning can further improve ensemble performance.

Computational Resources: Bagging and random forest ensembles can be computationally intensive, especially for large datasets and complex models. Consider the available computational resources and scalability requirements when using these ensembling techniques.

16.1.5 Conclusion

Bagging and random forest ensembles are powerful ensembling techniques that combine multiple models to improve prediction accuracy and robustness. By training models on different subsets of the data or incorporating feature randomness, these ensembles reduce overfitting, handle noise, and provide estimates of feature importance. Understanding the principles, benefits, and considerations of bagging and random forest ensembles allows for effective utilization of these techniques in machine learning tasks.

16.2 Boosting Algorithms (AdaBoost, Gradient Boosting)

In addition to bagging and random forest ensembles, boosting algorithms are powerful ensembling techniques that combine multiple weak learners to create a strong model. Boosting focuses on iteratively improving the performance of the ensemble by giving more attention to misclassified instances or areas where the model performs poorly. In this chapter, we will explore two popular boosting algorithms: AdaBoost and Gradient Boosting.

16.2.1 AdaBoost (Adaptive Boosting)

AdaBoost is a boosting algorithm that iteratively trains a series of weak learners, giving more weight to misclassified instances at each iteration. The key steps in AdaBoost are as follows:

Weight Initialization: Assign equal weights to all instances in the training data.

Weak Learner Training: Train a weak learner (e.g., a decision tree with limited depth) on the weighted training data. The weak learner's goal is to perform better than random guessing.

Weight Update: Increase the weights of misclassified instances, making them more influential for the next weak learner. Decrease the weights of correctly classified instances, making them less influential.

Ensemble Construction: Combine the weak learners into an ensemble by assigning a weight to each weak learner based on its performance. The weight represents the learner's contribution to the final prediction.

Final Prediction: Predict the class labels or regression values by combining the predictions of all weak learners in the ensemble, weighted by their respective weights.

AdaBoost focuses on difficult instances that are misclassified by previous weak learners, allowing subsequent learners to improve performance in those areas. By iteratively updating instance weights and combining weak learners, AdaBoost creates a strong ensemble that achieves better predictive performance.

16.2.2 Gradient Boosting

Gradient Boosting is another boosting algorithm that builds an ensemble of weak learners by sequentially minimizing a loss function using gradient descent. Unlike AdaBoost, Gradient Boosting can handle a wide range of loss functions and is particularly effective for regression tasks. The key steps in Gradient Boosting are as follows:

Initialize the Ensemble: Initialize the ensemble by fitting an initial model (e.g., a decision tree) to the training data.

Residual Calculation: Calculate the residuals (the difference between the true values and the predicted values) for each instance in the training data.

Weak Learner Training: Train a weak learner on the residuals. The weak learner's goal is to predict the residuals and minimize the loss function.

Ensemble Update: Update the ensemble by adding the trained weak learner with a shrinkage factor (learning rate). The shrinkage factor controls the contribution of each weak learner to the final prediction.

Residual Update: Update the residuals by subtracting the predicted residuals from the previous step.

Iteration: Repeat steps 3 to 5 until a specified number of weak learners are trained or a convergence criterion is met.

Final Prediction: Predict the class labels or regression values by combining the predictions of all weak learners in the ensemble.

Gradient Boosting improves the ensemble's performance by iteratively reducing the residuals and fitting weak learners to the gradients of the loss function. It gradually learns to correct the mistakes made by previous weak learners and produces a powerful ensemble model.

16.2.3 Benefits of Boosting Algorithms

Boosting algorithms offer several benefits:

Improved Performance: Boosting can significantly improve the performance of the ensemble by combining multiple weak learners. It can achieve higher accuracy or lower loss compared to individual models.

Handling Complex Relationships: Boosting algorithms can capture complex relationships between features and the target variable by iteratively focusing on difficult instances or areas of the data.

Robustness: Boosting is robust to noise and outliers, as subsequent weak learners give more attention to misclassified instances.

Feature Importance: Boosting algorithms provide insights into feature importance. By analyzing the contribution of features across weak learners, we can identify the most relevant features for the prediction task.

Flexibility: Boosting algorithms can handle both classification and regression tasks, and they can be used with various weak learners, such as decision trees, neural networks, or support vector machines.

16.2.4 Considerations for Boosting Algorithms

When using boosting algorithms, consider the following:

Model Complexity: Boosting algorithms tend to increase model complexity with each iteration, which can lead to overfitting.

Regularization techniques such as shrinkage (learning rate) and early stopping can help mitigate overfitting.

Hyperparameter Tuning: Tuning hyperparameters is crucial for optimizing the performance of boosting algorithms. Key hyperparameters include the number of weak learners, learning rate, and the maximum depth of weak learners (e.g., decision trees).

Data Imbalance: Boosting algorithms may struggle with imbalanced datasets. Techniques such as class weighting, undersampling, or oversampling can help address class imbalance.

Computational Resources: Boosting algorithms can be computationally intensive, especially with large datasets and complex weak learners. Consider the available computational resources and scalability requirements when using boosting algorithms.

16.2.5 Conclusion

Boosting algorithms, such as AdaBoost and Gradient Boosting, are powerful ensembling techniques that combine multiple weak learners to create a strong ensemble model. By iteratively focusing on misclassified instances or residuals, these algorithms progressively improve performance and handle complex relationships in the data. Understanding the principles, benefits, and considerations of boosting algorithms allows for effective utilization of these techniques in machine learning tasks.

16.3 Stacking Models for Improved Performance

Model stacking, also known as stacked generalization, is an advanced ensembling technique that combines multiple individual models by training a meta-model to make predictions based on their outputs. Stacking leverages the diverse predictions and strengths of individual models to create a more accurate and robust ensemble. In this chapter, we will explore the concept of model stacking and its benefits.

16.3.1 Understanding Model Stacking

Model stacking involves multiple steps to create a stacked ensemble:

Base Model Training: Train a set of diverse individual models on the training data. These models can use different algorithms, architectures, or feature representations.

Base Model Predictions: Generate predictions on the validation data using the trained individual models.

Meta-Model Training: Use the predictions of the individual models as input features and the ground truth labels as target variables to train a meta-model. The meta-model learns to combine the predictions and make a final prediction.

Meta-Model Prediction: Apply the trained meta-model to the test data. The individual models generate predictions on the test data, which are then used as input to the meta-model to obtain the final prediction.

The meta-model learns to effectively combine the predictions of the individual models and adaptively assign weights to each model's contribution based on their performance and reliability.

16.3.2 Benefits of Model Stacking

Model stacking offers several benefits:

Improved Performance: Model stacking leverages the diversity and complementary strengths of individual models, leading to improved prediction accuracy compared to individual models or simple ensembling techniques.

Robustness: Stacked ensembles are often more robust to noise and outliers since they can learn to downweight the influence of less reliable models.

Flexibility: Model stacking allows for flexibility in selecting and combining different types of models. It can handle a wide range of algorithms and architectures, making it applicable to various machine learning tasks.

Adaptability: The meta-model in model stacking learns to adaptively combine the predictions of individual models. It can learn the optimal way of combining the models' outputs based on the characteristics of the data or task at hand.

16.3.3 Considerations for Model Stacking

When using model stacking, consider the following:

Diversity of Models: It is important to select diverse individual models for stacking. The models should capture different aspects of the data or use different algorithms/techniques. Diversity helps ensure that the ensemble benefits from the strengths of different models.

Performance Evaluation: Proper evaluation of individual models is crucial for model stacking. Use appropriate validation techniques, such as cross-validation, to assess the performance of each model and select the best models for stacking.

Model Complexity: Consider the complexity of individual models and their impact on the ensemble's performance and computational resources. Combining models of varying complexities can strike a balance between accuracy and efficiency.

Meta-Model Selection: The choice of the meta-model is important. Commonly used meta-models include linear models, neural networks, or gradient boosting machines. The selection depends on the specific task and the characteristics of the individual models.

16.3.4 Conclusion

Model stacking is a powerful ensembling technique that combines the predictions of multiple individual models by training a meta-model. By leveraging the diversity and strengths of individual models, stacking can significantly improve prediction accuracy and robustness. Consideration of model diversity, performance evaluation, model complexity, and meta-model selection allows for effective utilization of model stacking in machine learning tasks.

16.4 Voting Classifiers and Regressors

Voting classifiers and regressors are ensembling techniques that combine the predictions of multiple individual models by using a voting scheme. Voting ensembles are effective in improving prediction accuracy and reducing model bias. In this chapter, we will explore voting classifiers and regressors and how they can be used to create robust ensembles.

16.4.1 Voting Classifiers

Voting classifiers are used for classification tasks and combine the predictions of multiple individual models to make the final prediction. There are three common types of voting classifiers:

Majority Voting: Each model in the ensemble predicts the class label, and the class that receives the majority of votes is selected as the final prediction. This approach is suitable for classification tasks with a balanced class distribution.

Weighted Voting: Weighted voting assigns different weights to each model's prediction based on its performance or confidence level. The weighted predictions are combined, and the class with the highest weighted sum is chosen as the final prediction. Weighted voting allows more influential models to have a greater impact on the ensemble's decision.

Soft Voting: Soft voting is applicable when models provide probability estimates for each class. Each model's probability predictions are averaged, and the class with the highest average probability is selected as the final prediction. Soft voting can provide more nuanced and accurate predictions compared to majority voting.

Voting classifiers leverage the collective knowledge of multiple models, considering their individual predictions to make the final decision. They can improve the ensemble's overall accuracy and robustness.

16.4.2 Voting Regressors

Voting regressors are used for regression tasks and combine the predictions of multiple individual models to make the final regression estimate. Similar to voting classifiers, there are three types of voting regressors:

Average Voting: Each model in the ensemble predicts a regression value, and the final prediction is the average of these values. This approach is suitable when individual models are expected to have similar performance.

Weighted Voting: Weighted voting assigns different weights to each model's prediction based on its performance or confidence level. The weighted predictions are combined, and the final prediction is the weighted average of the individual predictions. Weighted voting allows more accurate models to have a greater influence on the ensemble's decision.

Median Voting: Median voting selects the median value of the individual model predictions as the final prediction. This approach is robust to outliers and can provide more reliable estimates.

Voting regressors leverage the diversity and strengths of individual models to create a more accurate regression estimate. By considering the collective knowledge of multiple models, voting regressors can reduce prediction errors and improve the robustness of the ensemble.

16.4.3 Benefits of Voting Classifiers and Regressors

Voting classifiers and regressors offer several benefits:

Improved Prediction Accuracy: Voting ensembles can achieve higher accuracy compared to individual models by leveraging the collective knowledge of multiple models.

Reduction of Model Bias: Voting ensembles can reduce model bias by considering the diverse perspectives and strengths of individual models.

Robustness: Voting ensembles are often more robust to outliers and noisy data compared to individual models, as the ensemble's decision is based on the majority or weighted consensus of multiple models.

Flexibility: Voting classifiers and regressors can combine models of different algorithms or architectures, allowing flexibility in model selection and adaptation to different data characteristics.

16.4.4 Considerations for Voting Classifiers and Regressors

When using voting classifiers and regressors, consider the following:

Model Diversity: It is important to select diverse individual models for voting ensembles. The models should capture different aspects of the data or use different algorithms/techniques. Diversity helps ensure that the ensemble benefits from the strengths of different models.

Performance Evaluation: Proper evaluation of individual models is crucial for voting ensembles. Use appropriate validation techniques, such as cross-validation, to assess the performance of each model and select the best models for the ensemble.

Weighting Strategies: Consider the weighting strategies for weighted voting. Weighting can be based on model performance metrics, such as accuracy or F1-score, or confidence levels derived from model probabilities or confidence intervals.

Interpretability: Voting ensembles may sacrifice some interpretability compared to individual models, as the final decision is based on the combination of multiple models' predictions. Consider the trade-off between interpretability and ensemble performance.

16.4.5 Conclusion

Voting classifiers and regressors are ensembling techniques that combine the predictions of multiple individual models using a voting scheme. By leveraging the collective knowledge and strengths of the models, these ensembles improve prediction accuracy and reduce model bias. Proper consideration of model diversity, performance evaluation, weighting strategies, and interpretability allows for effective utilization of voting classifiers and regressors in machine learning tasks.

Chapter 17: Handling Imbalanced Data

Imbalanced data refers to a situation in which the classes or categories in a dataset are not represented equally. Imbalanced data is a common challenge in machine learning, particularly in classification tasks, and can lead to biased models with poor performance. In this chapter, we will explore techniques and strategies for handling imbalanced data to ensure fair and accurate model training.

17.1 Understanding Imbalanced Data

Imbalanced data occurs when one class or category is significantly more prevalent than the others. For example, in a fraud detection task, the number of fraudulent transactions may be much smaller compared to the number of legitimate transactions. Imbalanced data poses challenges for machine learning models as they tend to be biased towards the majority class, leading to poor classification performance for the minority class.

17.2 Effects of Imbalanced Data

Imbalanced data can have several effects on model training and evaluation:

Bias: Models trained on imbalanced data are prone to being biased towards the majority class. They may have difficulty capturing patterns and making accurate predictions for the minority class.

Poor Generalization: Imbalanced data can lead to poor generalization to new and unseen data. Models may struggle to correctly classify minority class instances in real-world scenarios.

Evaluation Metrics: Traditional evaluation metrics like accuracy can be misleading in imbalanced data scenarios. A high accuracy may be achieved by simply predicting the majority class for all instances, masking the poor performance on the minority class.

17.3 Strategies for Handling Imbalanced Data

To address the challenges posed by imbalanced data, several strategies and techniques can be employed:

17.3.1 Data-Level Techniques

Data-level techniques involve manipulating the dataset itself to rebalance the class distribution. Some common techniques include:

Undersampling: Randomly removing instances from the majority class to match the number of instances in the minority class. This can help reduce the imbalance but may result in loss of information.

Oversampling: Creating additional synthetic instances for the minority class to increase its representation. Techniques like

SMOTE (Synthetic Minority Over-sampling Technique) generate synthetic instances based on the characteristics of existing minority class instances.

Hybrid Approaches: Combining undersampling and oversampling techniques to achieve a more balanced dataset. This approach aims to preserve the information in the majority class while increasing the representation of the minority class.

17.3.2 Algorithmic Techniques

Algorithmic techniques involve modifying the learning algorithm to handle imbalanced data effectively. Some common techniques include:

Cost-Sensitive Learning: Assigning different misclassification costs to different classes. By penalizing misclassifications of the minority class more heavily, the model is encouraged to prioritize its correct classification.

Ensemble Methods: Employing ensemble methods, such as bagging, boosting, or stacking, with modifications that give more weight or importance to the minority class. This can help the ensemble focus on correctly classifying the minority class instances.

Anomaly Detection: Treating the minority class as an anomaly and applying anomaly detection techniques to identify and classify instances that deviate from the majority class. This approach is particularly useful when the minority class represents rare events or outliers.

17.3.3 Evaluation Metrics

When dealing with imbalanced data, it is important to choose appropriate evaluation metrics that reflect the performance on both the majority and minority classes. Some commonly used metrics include:

Precision and Recall: Precision measures the proportion of correctly predicted positive instances among all instances predicted as positive. Recall measures the proportion of correctly predicted positive instances among all actual positive instances. Focusing on both precision and recall provides a balanced view of model performance.

F1-Score: The F1-score is the harmonic mean of precision and recall. It provides a single metric that balances the trade-off between precision and recall.

Area Under the Precision-Recall Curve (AUPRC): The AUPRC summarizes the trade-off between precision and recall across different classification thresholds. It is particularly useful when the class distribution is highly imbalanced.

17.4 Conclusion

Handling imbalanced data is crucial to ensure fair and accurate model training. By employing data-level techniques, algorithmic modifications, and appropriate evaluation metrics, the challenges posed by imbalanced data can be addressed effectively. Consideration of the specific characteristics of the dataset and the task at hand allows for the selection of the most suitable techniques. By doing so, models can be trained to provide fair and accurate predictions for all classes, improving the overall performance and reliability of the system.

17.1 Techniques for Dealing with Imbalanced Data

Dealing with imbalanced data is crucial in machine learning to ensure fair and accurate model training. Imbalanced data occurs when one class or category is significantly more prevalent than the others, which can lead to biased models and poor performance on minority classes. In this section, we will explore several techniques for handling imbalanced data and improving the performance of machine learning models.

17.1.1 Resampling Techniques

Resampling techniques are commonly used to address class imbalance by modifying the class distribution in the training data. There are two main resampling techniques:

Undersampling: Undersampling involves reducing the size of the majority class to match the number of instances in the minority class. This technique randomly removes instances from the majority class, which can help rebalance the class distribution.

However, undersampling may result in the loss of valuable information and could lead to underfitting.

Oversampling: Oversampling involves increasing the size of the minority class by creating synthetic instances. The synthetic instances can be generated by techniques like Synthetic Minority Over-sampling Technique (SMOTE), which creates new instances by interpolating between existing minority class instances. Oversampling helps to increase the representation of the minority class and mitigate the imbalance. However, oversampling may result in overfitting if not applied carefully.

A hybrid approach combining undersampling and oversampling techniques can also be used to achieve a balanced class distribution. It involves applying undersampling to the majority class and oversampling to the minority class simultaneously, ensuring a more balanced dataset.

17.1.2 Cost-Sensitive Learning

Cost-sensitive learning is an approach that assigns different misclassification costs to different classes during model training. By assigning higher misclassification costs to the minority class, the model is incentivized to focus more on correctly classifying instances of the minority class. This approach helps to address the imbalance and improve the model's performance on the minority class. Cost-sensitive learning can be implemented by modifying the loss function or adjusting the class weights in the learning algorithm.

17.1.3 Ensemble Methods

Ensemble methods can effectively handle imbalanced data by combining predictions from multiple models. Ensemble methods such as bagging, boosting, and stacking can be employed with modifications to give more weight or importance to the minority class. This allows the ensemble to focus on correctly classifying minority class instances and improve overall performance. Ensemble methods provide a robust solution for handling imbalanced data by leveraging the diversity of multiple models.

17.1.4 One-Class Classification

One-class classification is a technique used when the minority class is of particular interest, such as anomaly detection. In one-class classification, the focus is on modeling the minority class without considering the majority class. Techniques like Support Vector Machines (SVM) with a radial basis function kernel or autoencoders can be used to build models that can identify instances that deviate from the normal behavior of the minority class. One-class classification is useful when the minority class represents rare events or outliers.

17.1.5 Evaluation Metrics

When working with imbalanced data, it is essential to choose evaluation metrics that accurately reflect the performance of the model. Traditional metrics like accuracy may not be informative in imbalanced scenarios. Instead, metrics such as precision, recall, F1-score, and area under the precision-recall curve (AUPRC) are more appropriate.

Precision measures the proportion of correctly predicted positive instances among all instances predicted as positive. It indicates how well the model identifies the minority class instances correctly.

Recall (also known as sensitivity or true positive rate) measures the proportion of correctly predicted positive instances among all actual positive instances. It captures the model's ability to find the minority class instances.

F1-score is the harmonic mean of precision and recall. It provides a balanced measure of the model's performance on both precision and recall.

AUPRC summarizes the precision-recall trade-off across different classification thresholds and is particularly useful when class distributions are highly imbalanced.

Choosing the appropriate evaluation metrics helps in assessing the model's performance accurately and identifying areas where improvement is needed.

17.1.6 Conclusion

Dealing with imbalanced data is crucial for building fair and accurate machine learning models. Resampling techniques, cost-sensitive learning, ensemble methods, one-class classification, and appropriate evaluation metrics are effective approaches to address class imbalance and improve model performance. The choice of technique depends on the specific characteristics of the dataset, the task at hand, and the desired outcome. By applying these techniques, models can be trained to provide reliable and unbiased predictions for all classes, ensuring the success of machine learning projects in imbalanced data scenarios.

17.2 Oversampling (SMOTE, ADASYN)

Oversampling is a data-level technique used to address class imbalance by increasing the number of instances in the minority class. This approach helps to improve the representation of the minority class and mitigate the imbalance. In this section, we will focus on two popular oversampling techniques: SMOTE (Synthetic Minority Over-sampling Technique) and ADASYN (Adaptive Synthetic Sampling).

17.2.1 SMOTE (Synthetic Minority Over-sampling Technique)

SMOTE is a widely used oversampling technique that generates synthetic instances for the minority class by interpolating between existing minority class instances. The key steps in the SMOTE algorithm are as follows:

Identify Minority Class Instances: Identify the instances belonging to the minority class in the imbalanced dataset.

Select Nearest Neighbors: For each minority class instance, identify its k nearest neighbors in the feature space. The value of k is a hyperparameter that determines the level of oversampling.

Create Synthetic Instances: For each minority class instance, randomly select one of its k nearest neighbors. Generate a new synthetic instance by interpolating between the selected instance and the original instance. The interpolation is performed by selecting random points along the line segment connecting the two instances.

Repeat: Repeat steps 2 and 3 to create the desired number of synthetic instances.

SMOTE effectively increases the representation of the minority class by creating synthetic instances that capture the underlying characteristics of the minority class. It helps to balance the class distribution and improve the model's ability to learn the minority class patterns.

17.2.2 ADASYN (Adaptive Synthetic Sampling)

ADASYN is an extension of the SMOTE algorithm that introduces adaptivity to the oversampling process. ADASYN focuses on generating synthetic instances for those minority class instances that are more challenging to classify correctly. The key steps in the ADASYN algorithm are as follows:

Calculate Sample Proportions: Calculate the imbalance ratio of the dataset, which is the ratio of the number of majority class instances to the number of minority class instances.

Compute Sample Importance: Compute the importance of each minority class instance based on the difficulty of classification.

Instances that are misclassified more often are assigned higher importance.

Adjust Sample Importance: Adjust the importance scores based on the imbalance ratio. Instances from the minority class with higher importance are given higher weights to increase their chance of being selected for synthetic instance generation.

Generate Synthetic Instances: For each minority class instance, calculate the number of synthetic instances to be generated based on its importance score. Apply the SMOTE algorithm to generate synthetic instances for each selected minority class instance.

ADASYN adaptively adjusts the generation of synthetic instances based on the difficulty of classification for each instance. It focuses more on the minority class instances that are harder to classify correctly, resulting in a better representation of challenging instances in the oversampled data.

17.2.3 Considerations for Oversampling Techniques

When using oversampling techniques like SMOTE and ADASYN, it is important to consider the following:

Hyperparameter Selection: The selection of hyperparameters, such as the number of nearest neighbors (k) in SMOTE or the imbalance ratio threshold in ADASYN, can impact the performance of the oversampling technique. It is essential to experiment with different values to find the optimal configuration for the specific dataset and task.

Model Evaluation: When evaluating the performance of models trained on oversampled data, it is crucial to use appropriate evaluation metrics that consider the class imbalance, such as precision, recall, F1-score, or area under the precision-recall curve (AUPRC).

Risk of Overfitting: Oversampling techniques, if not applied carefully, can lead to overfitting, especially if synthetic instances are too similar to existing minority class instances. Regularization techniques and cross-validation can help mitigate the risk of overfitting.

Impact on Model Training Time: Oversampling techniques increase the number of instances in the dataset, which can impact the training time of machine learning models, particularly for computationally intensive algorithms. Consider the available computational resources and scalability requirements when using oversampling techniques.

17.2.4 Conclusion

Oversampling techniques, such as SMOTE and ADASYN, are effective approaches for addressing class imbalance by generating synthetic instances for the minority class. These techniques help to improve the representation of the minority class and mitigate the imbalance in the dataset. By applying SMOTE or ADASYN, machine learning models can be trained on more balanced data, leading to better performance on the minority class and reducing the bias introduced by the class imbalance.

17.3 Undersampling (Random Undersampling, Tomek Links)

Undersampling is a data-level technique used to address class imbalance by reducing the number of instances in the majority class. This approach aims to balance the class distribution by removing instances from the majority class, allowing the minority class to have a greater influence during model training. In this section, we will focus on two popular undersampling techniques: random undersampling and Tomek links.

17.3.1 Random Undersampling

Random undersampling is a straightforward technique where instances from the majority class are randomly selected and removed from the dataset until a desired class balance is achieved. The key steps in random undersampling are as follows:

Identify Majority Class Instances: Identify the instances belonging to the majority class in the imbalanced dataset.

Random Selection: Randomly select a subset of instances from the majority class equal to the number of instances in the minority class.

Create Balanced Dataset: Combine the selected instances from the majority class with the instances from the minority class to create a balanced dataset.

Random undersampling is a simple and quick technique to address class imbalance. However, it may result in the loss of valuable information, particularly if the majority class instances contain important patterns or represent important data points.

17.3.2 Tomek Links

Tomek links are pairs of instances from different classes that are close to each other. In imbalanced datasets, Tomek links can be used to identify and remove instances from the majority class that are near the minority class instances. The key steps in the Tomek links algorithm are as follows:

Identify Tomek Links: Identify pairs of instances from different classes that form a Tomek link. A Tomek link exists between two instances when there are no instances from other classes between them.

Remove Majority Class Instances: Remove the instances from the majority class that form Tomek links with the minority class instances.

Tomek links are useful for removing noisy and ambiguous instances from the majority class that are close to the minority class. By eliminating these instances, the decision boundary between classes can be better defined, improving the classification performance for the minority class.

17.3.3 Considerations for Undersampling Techniques

When using undersampling techniques like random undersampling and Tomek links, it is important to consider the following:

Data Loss: Undersampling techniques can result in the loss of information from the majority class. This loss may impact the model's ability to generalize and accurately classify instances from the majority class. Care should be taken to ensure that important patterns or data points are not removed.

Model Sensitivity: Undersampling techniques may lead to models being overly sensitive to the remaining instances in the majority class. Models trained on undersampled data may struggle to generalize to new and unseen data.

Evaluation Metrics: When evaluating the performance of models trained on undersampled data, it is important to use appropriate evaluation metrics that consider the class imbalance, such as precision, recall, F1-score, or area under the precision-recall curve (AUPRC).

Combined Techniques: Undersampling techniques can be combined with other approaches, such as oversampling or algorithmic modifications, to achieve better class balance and improve model performance.

17.3.4 Conclusion

Undersampling techniques, such as random undersampling and Tomek links, offer effective approaches for addressing class imbalance by reducing the number of instances in the majority class. These techniques help to balance the class distribution and increase the influence of the minority class during model training. However, it is important to consider the potential loss of information and the impact on model sensitivity. By using undersampling techniques appropriately and in combination with other approaches, machine learning models can achieve fair and accurate predictions for all classes in imbalanced datasets.

17.4 Ensemble Techniques for Imbalanced Data

Ensemble techniques are powerful approaches for handling imbalanced data as they combine multiple models to make predictions. Ensemble models can effectively address the challenges posed by class imbalance by leveraging the diversity and strengths of individual models. In this section, we will explore ensemble techniques specifically designed for imbalanced data.

17.4.1 Bagging

Bagging, short for bootstrap aggregating, is an ensemble technique that involves training multiple models on different subsets of the original dataset. Each model is trained on a randomly sampled subset of the data, allowing them to learn different aspects of the dataset. Bagging can be particularly useful for imbalanced data as it helps to reduce the impact of the majority class and improve the representation of the minority class.

In the context of imbalanced data, bagging can be applied as follows:

Generate Bootstrap Samples: Randomly sample subsets of the original dataset with replacement. The size of each subset should match the size of the minority class.

Train Base Models: Train individual models on each bootstrap sample. This can be done using any suitable algorithm, such as decision trees, support vector machines, or neural networks.

Aggregate Predictions: Combine the predictions of the individual models using majority voting (for classification tasks) or averaging (for regression tasks) to make the final ensemble prediction.

Bagging helps to address the bias towards the majority class by giving more weight to the predictions of the minority class instances. By combining the predictions of multiple models, bagging ensembles improve the overall performance and robustness of the model.

17.4.2 Boosting

Boosting is another ensemble technique that sequentially trains models, with each subsequent model giving more attention to misclassified instances. Boosting can be effective in handling imbalanced data by focusing on improving the performance of the minority class.

Key boosting algorithms suitable for imbalanced data include:

AdaBoost (Adaptive Boosting): AdaBoost assigns higher weights to misclassified instances, allowing subsequent models to focus on correcting these mistakes. It iteratively trains weak models and adjusts the weights of the instances to improve the ensemble's performance.

Gradient Boosting: Gradient boosting builds models in a stage-wise manner by minimizing a loss function using gradient descent. It trains subsequent models to correct the errors made by previous models, with a particular focus on misclassified instances.

Boosting algorithms help to improve the performance of the minority class by iteratively adjusting the models' focus on challenging instances. By combining the predictions of multiple models, boosting ensembles provide robust and accurate predictions for imbalanced datasets.

17.4.3 Stacking

Stacking, also known as stacked generalization, is an ensemble technique that combines multiple models using a meta-model. In stacking, the predictions of individual models serve as input features for the meta-model, which learns to make the final prediction. Stacking can be effective for imbalanced data as it allows models with different strengths and weaknesses to complement each other.

The steps involved in stacking are as follows:

Train Base Models: Train multiple models using different algorithms or configurations on the original imbalanced dataset. Each model produces predictions for the target variable.

Create Stacking Dataset: Combine the predictions of the base models with the original features of the dataset, creating a new dataset where the predictions serve as additional features.

Train Meta-Model: Train a meta-model (often a simple model like logistic regression or decision tree) on the stacking dataset. The meta-model learns to make the final prediction based on the base models' predictions.

Stacking ensembles leverage the diverse predictions of individual models to create a more accurate and robust final prediction. By combining models with different strengths and weaknesses, stacking can effectively handle imbalanced data and improve overall model performance.

17.4.4 Conclusion

Ensemble techniques, such as bagging, boosting, and stacking, are powerful tools for addressing class imbalance in machine learning. These techniques leverage the diversity and strengths of individual models to improve the representation of the minority class and reduce the bias towards the majority class. By combining predictions from multiple models, ensemble techniques provide robust and accurate predictions for imbalanced datasets.

Chapter 18: Debugging and Troubleshooting in Machine Learning

Machine learning models are complex systems that require careful development and debugging to ensure optimal performance. In this chapter, we will explore various techniques and strategies for debugging and troubleshooting common issues that arise during the development and deployment of machine learning models.

18.1 Understanding the Data

Data Inspection: Start by inspecting the input data to identify any irregularities, missing values, or outliers. Visualize and summarize the data to gain insights into its distribution, patterns, and potential issues.

Data Preprocessing: Check the preprocessing steps applied to the data, such as scaling, normalization, or encoding. Ensure that the preprocessing steps are appropriate for the data and consistent across training and test datasets.

Data Splitting: Verify that the data splitting into training, validation, and test sets is done correctly and that the data distribution is preserved across the splits. Improper data splitting can lead to biased evaluation and unreliable model performance.

18.2 Model Development

Model Architecture: Check the model architecture, layers, and activation functions. Ensure that the model design matches the problem at hand and that the layers are connected correctly.

Hyperparameters: Review the hyperparameters used for model training, such as learning rate, batch size, and regularization parameters. Experiment with different values to find the optimal configuration.

Loss Function and Metrics: Examine the choice of loss function and evaluation metrics. Ensure that they align with the problem type (classification, regression, etc.) and the specific goals of the project.

Overfitting and Underfitting: Monitor the model's performance on the training and validation sets. Look for signs of overfitting (excessive training performance but poor generalization) or underfitting (poor performance on both training and validation sets).

18.3 Training Process

Training Pipeline: Inspect the training pipeline to ensure that the data is being fed correctly to the model during the training process. Check for any issues with data loading, augmentation, or batching.

Loss Convergence: Analyze the loss curve during training. Ensure that the loss decreases consistently and that the model is converging. If the loss does not converge, consider adjusting the learning rate or model architecture.

Training Time: Monitor the training time and resource usage. If the training process is taking excessively long or utilizing too much memory, consider optimizing the code or using hardware acceleration techniques.

18.4 Evaluation and Performance

Evaluation Metrics: Choose appropriate evaluation metrics based on the problem type and goals. Ensure that the metrics align with the project requirements and that they provide meaningful insights into the model's performance.

Bias and Fairness: Investigate potential biases in the model's predictions. Analyze the model's behavior across different demographic groups and evaluate fairness metrics to ensure equitable performance.

Error Analysis: Perform a detailed error analysis to understand the types of errors the model is making. Identify patterns and recurring issues, such as misclassified instances or false positives/negatives, and use this information to improve the model.

18.5 Deployment and Monitoring

Model Deployment: Pay attention to the deployment process, including model serialization, API integration, and infrastructure setup. Ensure that the deployed model matches the trained model and that all dependencies are correctly managed.

Monitoring: Implement a monitoring system to track the model's performance in production. Monitor inputs, outputs, latency, and other relevant metrics to detect any anomalies or degradation in performance.

Error Handling: Prepare a robust error handling system that gracefully handles exceptions, missing data, or unexpected inputs. Include proper logging and error reporting mechanisms to facilitate troubleshooting.

18.6 Debugging Tools and Techniques

Logging and Debugging Statements: Incorporate logging statements throughout the code to capture relevant information during training and inference. Debugging statements can help identify issues and track the flow of execution.

Visualization and Interpretability: Utilize visualization techniques to gain insights into the model's behavior and decision-making process. Techniques such as feature importance analysis, saliency maps, or activation visualization can aid in identifying model issues.

Error Debugging: When encountering errors or unexpected behavior, use debugging tools like breakpoints, step-by-step execution, and variable inspection to identify the source of the problem. Use error messages and stack traces to pinpoint the problematic code.

18.7 Collaborative Debugging

Code Reviews: Conduct regular code reviews with team members to catch potential issues, ensure best practices, and gain fresh perspectives on the codebase.

Pair Programming: Collaborate with colleagues during debugging sessions by working together on a specific issue. Sharing ideas and knowledge can lead to quicker problem resolution.

Online Communities and Forums: Engage with online communities and forums dedicated to machine learning and data science. Seek advice, ask questions, and learn from the experiences of others who have faced similar challenges.

18.8 Documentation and Version Control

Documentation: Maintain clear and up-to-date documentation of the model development process, including code documentation, model architecture, hyperparameters, and any troubleshooting steps taken. Proper documentation facilitates understanding and future debugging.

Version Control: Use version control systems like Git to track changes to the codebase. This enables easy rollbacks, collaboration, and traceability of changes made during debugging and troubleshooting.

18.9 Conclusion

Debugging and troubleshooting are integral parts of the machine learning development process. By following the techniques and strategies outlined in this chapter, you can effectively identify and address issues that arise during data preparation, model development, training, evaluation, deployment, and monitoring. Through systematic debugging, collaboration, and proper documentation, you can ensure the reliability, performance, and stability of your machine learning models.

18.1 Identifying and Addressing Common Errors

During the development and deployment of machine learning models, it is common to encounter various errors that can hinder the progress and performance of the system. In this section, we will discuss some common errors that occur in machine learning and provide strategies for identifying and addressing them.

18.1.1 Data Errors

Data Formatting Errors: Check if the data is in the correct format expected by the model. Ensure that the input features are of the right data type, shape, and range.

Missing Data: Identify if there are any missing values in the dataset. Decide on an appropriate strategy for handling missing data, such as imputation or removing instances with missing values.

Data Leakage: Ensure that there is no data leakage, where information from the test set or future data is inadvertently included in the training process. Data leakage can lead to over-optimistic performance metrics and poor generalization.

Data Imbalance: Identify if the dataset suffers from class imbalance, where one class dominates the others. Apply appropriate techniques, such as oversampling or undersampling, to address class imbalance and improve model performance.

18.1.2 Model Errors

Model Architecture Errors: Verify if the model architecture is correctly defined, with appropriate layers, connections, and activation functions. Check if the input and output dimensions match the data and task requirements.

Hyperparameter Errors: Review the hyperparameters used during model training. Ensure that the learning rate, batch size, regularization parameters, and other hyperparameters are set to appropriate values for the problem at hand. Experiment with different values to find the optimal configuration.

Overfitting and Underfitting: Monitor the model's performance on the training and validation sets. If the model shows high training performance but poor generalization, it might be overfitting. If the model performs poorly on both training and validation sets, it might be underfitting. Adjust the model complexity, regularization techniques, or dataset size to mitigate overfitting or underfitting.

Gradient Vanishing/Exploding: If the model fails to converge during training or exhibits slow convergence, it could be due to gradient vanishing or exploding. Consider using techniques like weight initialization, gradient clipping, or different activation functions to address these issues.

18.1.3 Training and Evaluation Errors

Training Pipeline Errors: Review the code responsible for data loading, preprocessing, augmentation, and batching. Ensure that the data is correctly fed to the model during the training process.

Incorrect Loss Function or Metrics: Check if the chosen loss function and evaluation metrics align with the problem type and objectives. Select appropriate loss functions and evaluation metrics based on the specific task, such as categorical cross-entropy for classification or mean squared error for regression.

Improper Training/Validation Split: Verify that the dataset is properly split into training and validation sets. A common error is to use the entire dataset for training, leading to over-optimistic performance evaluation. Ensure that the validation set is representative of the test set or future data.

Incorrect Evaluation Procedure: Double-check the evaluation procedure to ensure consistency and correctness. Ensure that the evaluation metrics are calculated on the correct dataset splits and that any preprocessing or normalization is applied consistently during evaluation.

18.1.4 Deployment and Runtime Errors

Model Serialization/Deserialization: If errors occur during model serialization or deserialization, ensure that the model is correctly saved and loaded. Check for any version mismatches or dependencies that might affect the model's serialization process.

Input Data Formatting: Verify that the input data is correctly formatted and matches the expected input format of the deployed model. Ensure that the input features are scaled, normalized, or preprocessed appropriately before making predictions.

Infrastructure or Dependency Issues: Check for any infrastructure or dependency-related errors during model deployment. Ensure that the necessary libraries, frameworks, and dependencies are installed and configured correctly in the deployment environment.

Input Data Quality: Address any issues related to the quality or integrity of the input data during runtime. Implement error handling mechanisms to handle unexpected or invalid input data gracefully.

18.1.5 Debugging Strategies

Error Messages and Stack Traces: Pay attention to error messages and stack traces generated during runtime. They provide valuable information about the source of the error and can help narrow down the issue.

Debugging Statements and Logging: Incorporate debugging statements and logging throughout the codebase to capture relevant information during runtime. Print or log intermediate results, variable values, and any error-related information to aid in debugging.

Divide and Conquer: If faced with a complex issue, divide the problem into smaller parts and debug each component separately. This approach helps to isolate the source of the error and identify specific areas that need attention.

Test Cases and Unit Testing: Implement test cases and unit tests to validate the functionality of individual components or modules. Run these tests regularly to catch any errors or unexpected behaviors early on.

Collaboration and Code Reviews: Engage in collaboration with colleagues, seek help from online communities, or perform code reviews to gain fresh perspectives and insights into the codebase. Another person's viewpoint can often reveal issues that might have been overlooked.

18.1.6 Conclusion

Identifying and addressing common errors is an essential part of the machine learning development process. By understanding the potential sources of errors, reviewing data quality, checking model architecture and hyperparameters, ensuring proper training and evaluation procedures, and debugging effectively, you can enhance the reliability and performance of your machine learning models. Remember to leverage error messages, use debugging techniques, and seek collaboration when needed to resolve issues efficiently.

18.2 Debugging Model Performance Issues

When developing machine learning models, it's common to encounter performance issues that affect the model's accuracy, convergence, or generalization. In this section, we will discuss strategies for debugging and addressing model performance issues.

18.2.1 Underperforming Model

Insufficient Model Capacity: If the model is underperforming, it may lack the capacity to capture the complexity of the underlying data patterns. Consider increasing the model's capacity by adding more layers, neurons, or using a more complex architecture.

Incorrect Hyperparameters: Review the hyperparameters used during model training. Ensure that the learning rate, regularization parameters, batch size, and other hyperparameters are properly tuned. Experiment with different values to find the optimal configuration.

Insufficient Training Data: If the model is not learning well, it may not have enough diverse training data to capture the underlying patterns. Consider acquiring more labeled data or applying data augmentation techniques to increase the diversity of the training set.

Poor Data Quality: Check the quality of the input data. Look for issues such as mislabeled data, outliers, or inconsistent data formatting. Clean the data, remove outliers, and ensure proper preprocessing steps are applied to improve the data quality.

18.2.2 Overfitting

Model Complexity: Overfitting occurs when the model becomes too complex and starts to memorize the training data instead of generalizing from it. Reduce the model's complexity by decreasing the number of layers, neurons, or using regularization techniques such as L1 or L2 regularization.

Regularization Techniques: Apply regularization techniques like L1 or L2 regularization, dropout, or early stopping to prevent overfitting. These techniques help control the model's complexity and reduce the impact of noisy or irrelevant features.

Data Augmentation: Augment the training data by applying transformations such as rotation, scaling, or flipping to increase the diversity of the training examples. Data augmentation can help prevent overfitting by providing the model with more variations of the same data.

Cross-Validation: Use cross-validation to evaluate the model's performance on multiple folds of the data. If the model consistently overfits across different folds, it indicates a generalization issue. Adjust the model architecture, regularization techniques, or training strategy accordingly.

18.2.3 Convergence Issues

Learning Rate: Adjust the learning rate to control the convergence speed. If the learning rate is too high, the model may fail to converge. If it is too low, the model may converge slowly. Experiment with different learning rates to find an appropriate value.

Learning Rate Scheduling: Implement learning rate scheduling techniques such as reducing the learning rate over time (e.g., using learning rate decay or cyclical learning rates). These techniques can help the model converge more effectively.

Batch Size: Modify the batch size used during training. A smaller batch size allows the model to update its parameters more frequently, which can improve convergence. However, very small batch sizes can introduce noise in the gradient estimation. Experiment with different batch sizes to find the right balance.

Weight Initialization: Poor weight initialization can lead to convergence issues. Ensure that the model's weights are initialized properly, using techniques such as Xavier/Glorot initialization or He initialization, depending on the activation function.

18.2.4 Generalization Issues

Model Complexity: Simplify the model architecture if it is too complex. A complex model may memorize the training data without learning generalizable patterns. Reduce the number of layers, neurons, or parameters to encourage better generalization.

Regularization: Regularization techniques such as L1 or L2 regularization, dropout, or early stopping can help improve model generalization. These techniques prevent the model from overfitting to the training data and promote better generalization to unseen examples.

Dataset Diversity: Ensure that the training dataset represents the real-world distribution and includes diverse examples. If the training data is not representative, the model may struggle to generalize to new examples. Collect more diverse data or employ data augmentation techniques to increase dataset diversity.

Hyperparameter Tuning: Fine-tune the model's hyperparameters to find the best configuration for generalization. Experiment with different hyperparameter values, such as learning rate, regularization strength, or dropout rate, and use techniques like grid search or random search to find the optimal combination.

18.2.5 Conclusion

Debugging model performance issues is a critical part of the machine learning development process. By understanding the potential causes of underperformance, overfitting, convergence issues, and generalization problems, you can take appropriate actions to address them. Experimentation, careful parameter tuning, regularization techniques, and data quality control are key steps in improving the performance and generalization ability of your machine learning models.

18.3 Addressing Overfitting and Underfitting

Overfitting and underfitting are common challenges in machine learning that affect the model's ability to generalize well to unseen data. In this section, we will discuss strategies for addressing overfitting and underfitting to improve the performance and generalization of machine learning models.

18.3.1 Overfitting

Overfitting occurs when the model performs well on the training data but fails to generalize to new, unseen data. Here are some strategies to address overfitting:

Increase Training Data: Collect more training data to provide the model with a larger and more diverse set of examples. With more data, the model can learn better representations and reduce the chances of overfitting.

Data Augmentation: Apply data augmentation techniques to artificially increase the size of the training set. Augmentation techniques such as rotation, scaling, flipping, or adding noise can introduce variations to the training data and improve the model's ability to generalize.

Regularization Techniques: Regularization techniques help prevent overfitting by adding a penalty term to the loss function. Two common regularization techniques are L1 regularization (Lasso) and L2 regularization (Ridge). Regularization encourages the model to learn simpler and more generalizable patterns.

Dropout: Implement dropout regularization, which randomly drops out a fraction of neurons during training. This technique introduces redundancy in the network and helps prevent over-reliance on specific neurons, leading to better generalization.

Early Stopping: Monitor the model's performance on a validation set during training. If the validation loss starts to increase or accuracy stagnates, stop the training early to prevent further overfitting. Early stopping allows the model to generalize better by finding the optimal point before overfitting occurs.

Model Simplification: Reduce the complexity of the model architecture by decreasing the number of layers, neurons, or parameters. Simpler models tend to generalize better as they are less prone to overfitting.

18.3.2 Underfitting

Underfitting occurs when the model fails to capture the underlying patterns in the training data. Here are some strategies to address underfitting:

Increase Model Capacity: If the model is too simple and lacks the capacity to capture complex patterns, increase its capacity by adding more layers, neurons, or parameters. A more complex model can better represent intricate relationships in the data.

Feature Engineering: Analyze the input features and consider engineering new features that may better capture the underlying patterns in the data. Feature engineering involves transforming or combining existing features to provide more meaningful information to the model.

Adjust Model Complexity: Experiment with different model architectures, such as increasing or decreasing the number of layers or changing activation functions. Find the right balance between model complexity and simplicity to achieve better performance.

Hyperparameter Tuning: Fine-tune the model's hyperparameters, such as learning rate, regularization strength, or batch size, to find the optimal combination. Use techniques like grid search or random search to explore the hyperparameter space efficiently.

Ensemble Learning: Combine multiple models to create an ensemble that collectively performs better than individual models. Ensemble techniques like bagging or boosting can help improve model performance and generalization.

Cross-Validation: Use cross-validation to evaluate the model's performance on multiple folds of the data. If the model consistently underfits across different folds, consider increasing the model's complexity or revisiting the data preprocessing steps.

18.3.3 Conclusion

Addressing overfitting and underfitting is crucial for building machine learning models that can generalize well to new data. By employing techniques such as increasing training data, applying data augmentation, using regularization, adjusting model complexity, and fine-tuning hyperparameters, you can mitigate the effects of overfitting and underfitting. It is important to strike a balance between model complexity and simplicity to achieve optimal performance and generalization.

18.4 Handling Data Leakage

Data leakage is a common issue in machine learning where information from the test set or future data unintentionally leaks into the training process, leading to overly optimistic performance evaluations and unreliable models. In this section, we will discuss strategies to handle data leakage and ensure the integrity of the machine learning pipeline.

18.4.1 Identifying Data Leakage

Review Data Sources: Examine the source of the data and ensure that the data used for training, validation, and testing comes from separate and independent sources. If data from the future or test set is inadvertently included in the training data, it can lead to data leakage.

Understand Feature Engineering: Investigate the feature engineering process and check if any features are derived using information that would not be available at the time of prediction. For example, using future information to create features that rely on future events can introduce data leakage.

Time-based Data Leakage: Pay attention to time-based data leakage, where information from the future is leaked into the training process. Ensure that the training data only includes information that would have been available at the time of prediction.

Domain Knowledge: Leverage domain knowledge and subject matter expertise to identify potential sources of data leakage. Understand the problem domain and the context in which the data is collected to detect any potential leaks.

18.4.2 Strategies to Handle Data Leakage

Proper Data Splitting: Ensure that the data splitting is done correctly, separating the data into distinct training, validation, and test sets. The test set should be kept completely separate until the final evaluation stage to prevent leakage.

Feature Engineering Awareness: Be cautious when engineering features and avoid using information that would not be available at the time of prediction. Features should be derived solely from the training data and not contain any future or test set information.

Time-based Validation: For time series data or temporal problems, use time-based validation strategies such as forward-chaining or rolling window validation. This approach ensures that the model is trained on past data and evaluated on future data.

Cross-Validation Considerations: If using cross-validation, ensure that each fold represents an independent subset of the data. Avoid leaking information across folds by performing feature engineering and preprocessing steps within each fold independently.

Feature Selection: Perform feature selection techniques within the training set only. If feature selection is based on information from the validation or test set, it can lead to data leakage. Use techniques like recursive feature elimination with cross-validation (RFECV) to select features properly.

Error Analysis: Conduct detailed error analysis to identify instances where data leakage might have occurred. Analyze model predictions on specific instances and evaluate if the predictions align with the expected behavior given the information available at prediction time.

18.4.3 Conclusion

Handling data leakage is crucial for developing reliable and trustworthy machine learning models. By understanding the sources of data leakage, properly splitting the data, being cautious during feature engineering, and following appropriate validation and feature selection techniques, you can mitigate the risk of data leakage and ensure the integrity of your machine learning pipeline.

Chapter 19: Continuous Learning and Model Maintenance

19.1 The Need for Continuous Learning and Model Maintenance

Machine learning models are not static entities but require continuous learning and maintenance to stay relevant and perform at their best. In this chapter, we will explore the importance of continuous learning and model maintenance, along with strategies and best practices for keeping your models up-to-date.

19.2 Monitoring Model Performance

Performance Metrics: Establish a set of performance metrics to monitor the model's performance over time. Track metrics such as accuracy, precision, recall, F1-score, or area under the curve (AUC) to gauge the model's effectiveness.

Data Drift Detection: Monitor data drift, which refers to changes in the distribution or characteristics of the input data. Implement techniques to detect data drift and assess its impact on the model's performance. If significant drift is detected, consider retraining the model or applying domain adaptation techniques.

Model Confidence: Monitor the model's confidence or uncertainty estimates. High uncertainty in predictions may indicate instances where the model lacks sufficient knowledge or encounters unfamiliar data. Use techniques like confidence thresholds or calibration methods to identify and handle uncertain predictions appropriately.

19.3 Retraining and Updating Models

Incremental Learning: Implement incremental learning techniques that allow the model to learn from new data without discarding previously acquired knowledge. Techniques such as online learning, transfer learning, or active learning can be used to update the model with new information.

Retraining Schedule: Determine the optimal retraining schedule based on the specific use case and the rate of data change. Regularly retrain the model to adapt to evolving patterns and ensure that it remains effective over time.

Data Collection and Labeling: Continuously collect new data and ensure that it is properly labeled. The availability of fresh and relevant data is essential for updating and retraining the model.

Retraining Pipeline: Establish a robust pipeline for model retraining. This includes data preprocessing, feature engineering, model training, and evaluation. Automate this process as much as possible to streamline the update and maintenance workflow.

19.4 Managing Model Versions and Deployment

Version Control: Utilize version control systems to manage different versions of your model. This allows for easy comparison, rollback, and collaboration when making changes or updates to the model.

A/B Testing: Implement A/B testing to compare the performance of different model versions or strategies. This helps in evaluating the impact of changes before deploying them to production and allows for data-driven decision-making.

Deployment Infrastructure: Maintain a robust deployment infrastructure that supports seamless updates and rollbacks. Implement mechanisms for easy deployment, scaling, and monitoring of the updated models.

Backward Compatibility: Consider backward compatibility when making updates to the model. Ensure that the updated model can seamlessly integrate with existing systems and processes without causing disruptions.

19.5 Model Documentation and Knowledge Transfer

Documentation: Maintain comprehensive documentation of the model, including its architecture, hyperparameters, data preprocessing steps, and any specific considerations or assumptions made during its development. This documentation ensures that knowledge is preserved and can be transferred to other team members.

Knowledge Sharing: Foster a culture of knowledge sharing within the team. Conduct regular knowledge-sharing sessions, code reviews, or team discussions to transfer knowledge and best practices related to model maintenance.

Collaboration and Communication: Establish effective communication channels within the team to facilitate collaboration and discussion regarding model updates, improvements, and potential issues.

19.6 Ethical and Legal Considerations

Privacy and Data Protection: Ensure compliance with privacy regulations and protect sensitive user information. Take necessary precautions to anonymize or encrypt data when required.

Bias and Fairness: Continuously monitor for biases in the model's predictions and take steps to mitigate any unfair or discriminatory outcomes. Regularly assess the model's fairness metrics and make adjustments if necessary.

Model Governance: Establish a framework for model governance, including regular audits, risk assessments, and adherence to ethical guidelines. Monitor the impact and consequences of the model's predictions on individuals or groups.

19.7 Conclusion

Continuous learning and model maintenance are critical for keeping machine learning models relevant, accurate, and reliable over time. By monitoring model performance, retraining and updating models, managing versions and deployments, documenting knowledge, and considering ethical and legal considerations, you can ensure that your models remain effective and aligned with evolving needs and requirements.

19.1 Importance of Continuous Learning

In the rapidly evolving field of machine learning, continuous learning is essential to ensure that models remain effective, accurate, and relevant over time. The importance of continuous learning can be understood from the following perspectives:

Adaptation to Changing Data: The data on which machine learning models are trained can change over time. New patterns, trends, and anomalies may emerge, requiring the model to adapt and learn from the updated data. Continuous learning enables models to stay up-to-date and make accurate predictions in changing environments.

Evolving Business Requirements: Business requirements and objectives may change over time. Models need to be continuously updated to align with these changing requirements. Continuous learning allows models to evolve and address new challenges, ensuring they continue to provide valuable insights and support business decision-making.

Improved Performance: Continuous learning helps improve model performance by leveraging new data and insights. By incorporating additional labeled or unlabeled data, models can learn from a larger and more diverse dataset, potentially leading to better accuracy, precision, and recall.

Detecting Concept Drift: Concept drift occurs when the statistical properties of the data change over time. Continuous learning enables the detection of concept drift and allows models to adapt to these changes. By monitoring data distribution and performance metrics, models can identify when their predictions are becoming less accurate and take corrective actions.

Keeping Pace with Technology Advancements: The field of machine learning is constantly evolving, with new algorithms, techniques, and tools emerging regularly. Continuous learning enables model developers to stay updated with the latest advancements and integrate them into their models, improving their performance and capabilities.

Rapid Feedback Loop: Continuous learning facilitates a rapid feedback loop between model development and real-world deployment. By continuously monitoring model performance, developers can identify issues, make necessary adjustments, and quickly iterate on the model, leading to continuous improvement.

Scalability and Efficiency: Continuous learning allows models to handle increasing data volumes efficiently. By incrementally updating models with new data, it becomes feasible to scale the learning process without retraining the entire model from scratch.

Competitive Advantage: In a competitive landscape, organizations that embrace continuous learning gain a competitive advantage. By continuously improving their models, they can deliver better products, services, and user experiences, leading to customer satisfaction and loyalty.

Risk Management and Compliance: Continuous learning enables models to adapt to changing regulations, compliance requirements, and ethical considerations. It helps organizations mitigate risks associated with outdated models and ensures compliance with evolving legal and ethical standards.

Lifelong Learning: Continuous learning aligns with the concept of lifelong learning in the field of artificial intelligence. It promotes the idea that models should continuously acquire knowledge and improve their performance over their entire lifespan, mirroring the way humans learn and adapt to new information.

In summary, continuous learning is crucial for maintaining model performance, adapting to changing data and business requirements, leveraging technological advancements, and staying competitive in the field of machine learning. By embracing continuous learning, organizations can ensure that their models remain effective, reliable, and aligned with the evolving needs of their stakeholders.

19.2 Updating Models with New Data

One of the key aspects of continuous learning is updating machine learning models with new data to ensure their accuracy and relevance. In this section, we will discuss strategies for effectively updating models with new data.

Collecting New Data: Continuously collect new data that is relevant to the problem your model is solving. This can be done through various means such as user interactions, sensors, external sources, or crowdsourcing. Ensure that the new data represents the current distribution and covers a wide range of scenarios.

Data Preprocessing: Preprocess the new data using the same preprocessing steps applied during the initial model training. This includes handling missing values, scaling features, encoding categorical variables, and performing any necessary data transformations. Consistency in preprocessing ensures that the new data is compatible with the existing model.

Retraining on New Data: Depending on the amount of new data and the computational resources available, you may choose to retrain the entire model or update specific parts of it. Retraining the entire model involves using the new data along with the existing training data to train a new model from scratch. Alternatively, you can use the new data to fine-tune specific layers or parameters of the existing model, a process known as transfer learning or incremental learning.

Incremental Learning: Incremental learning techniques enable models to learn from new data without discarding previously acquired knowledge. This approach is useful when the new data arrives in a continuous stream or when computational resources are limited. Incremental learning can be achieved through techniques such as online learning, where the model updates its parameters as new data arrives, or by using memory-based approaches like reservoir sampling to store and learn from a subset of the new data.

Model Evaluation and Validation: After updating the model with new data, it is essential to evaluate its performance to ensure that the updates have improved its accuracy and generalization. Use appropriate evaluation metrics and validation techniques, such as cross-validation or holdout sets, to assess the model's performance on the new data. This step helps in identifying potential issues and ensuring that the updated model meets the desired performance criteria.

Monitoring Model Performance: Continuously monitor the performance of the updated model using metrics and validation techniques. Track its accuracy, precision, recall, or any other relevant performance measures over time. Monitoring helps identify performance degradation, concept drift, or other issues that may arise with the updated model.

Feedback Loop: Establish a feedback loop between the model update process and the real-world application. Gather feedback from users or domain experts to understand the model's performance in real-world scenarios. This feedback can help identify areas for improvement and guide further updates to the model.

Documentation and Version Control: Maintain documentation of the updates made to the model, including the data used, preprocessing steps, and the rationale behind the updates. Proper version control ensures that you can track the changes made to the model and revert to previous versions if necessary.

Updating models with new data is an ongoing process that requires careful consideration and monitoring. By collecting new data, preprocessing it consistently, retraining or fine-tuning the model, evaluating performance, and establishing a feedback loop, you can ensure that your models remain up-to-date and effective in making accurate predictions.

19.3 Retraining and Reevaluation Strategies

When updating machine learning models with new data, it is important to employ effective retraining and reevaluation strategies. In this section, we will discuss some strategies to ensure that models are appropriately retrained and reevaluated.

Retraining Schedule: Determine the optimal schedule for retraining the model based on the rate of data change and the specific problem domain. If the data changes frequently or if there are significant shifts in the underlying patterns, more frequent retraining may be necessary. However, if the data changes gradually or the problem is relatively stable, less frequent retraining may suffice.

Incremental Learning: Consider employing incremental learning techniques to update the model with new data. Incremental learning allows the model to learn from new examples without discarding the knowledge acquired from the previous data. This approach is particularly useful when computational resources are limited or when new data arrives in a continuous stream.

Transfer Learning: If the new data is related to the original task or domain, explore the possibility of using transfer learning. Transfer learning leverages the knowledge gained from pretraining on a related task or a larger dataset and fine-tunes the model using the new data. This approach can speed up the learning process and require less data for training.

Model Freezing and Fine-tuning: In some cases, it may be beneficial to freeze certain layers or parameters of the model while updating others. By freezing lower-level layers responsible for low-level feature extraction, you can preserve previously learned representations, while updating higher-level layers to adapt to the new data. This technique can save computational resources and mitigate catastrophic forgetting.

Evaluation Metrics: Use appropriate evaluation metrics to assess the performance of the updated model. Consider metrics such as accuracy, precision, recall, F1-score, or area under the curve (AUC), depending on the problem at hand. Compare the performance of the updated model with the previous version to gauge the impact of the updates.

Validation Techniques: Use validation techniques such as holdout sets, cross-validation, or time-based validation to evaluate the performance of the updated model. These techniques help assess how well the updated model generalizes to new, unseen data. Ensure that the validation set is representative of the data distribution and is separate from the training and testing data.

Concept Drift Detection: Continuously monitor for concept drift, which refers to changes in the data distribution over time. Employ concept drift detection techniques to identify shifts in the underlying patterns or relationships between the input features and the target variable. If concept drift is detected, consider retraining the model or employing techniques to adapt to the changing data distribution.

User Feedback and Domain Expertise: Solicit feedback from users or domain experts who interact with the model in real-world scenarios. Their feedback can provide valuable insights into the model's performance and help identify areas for improvement. Incorporating user feedback and domain expertise in the retraining process can lead to more effective updates.

Documentation and Version Control: Maintain detailed documentation of the retraining process, including the data used, preprocessing steps, hyperparameters, and any changes made to the model architecture. Use version control systems to track the different versions of the model, allowing for easy comparison and rollback if needed.

Monitoring and Alerting: Implement a system for monitoring the performance of the updated model in real-time. Set up alerts or notifications to flag any significant changes in performance, such as a drop in accuracy or an increase in error rates. Prompt monitoring helps identify issues early and enables timely interventions.

By employing these retraining and reevaluation strategies, you can ensure that updated models effectively leverage new data and maintain their accuracy and relevance over time.

19.4 Model Versioning and Documentation

When updating and maintaining machine learning models, it is crucial to establish effective model versioning and documentation practices. These practices help track the changes made to the models, ensure reproducibility, and facilitate collaboration. In this section, we will discuss strategies for model versioning and documentation.

Version Control System: Utilize a version control system, such as Git, to track and manage different versions of your models. Version control allows you to keep a history of changes, compare different versions, and easily revert to previous versions if needed. It also enables collaboration among team members and provides a centralized repository for the models.

Semantic Versioning: Adopt a semantic versioning scheme to label your models. Semantic versioning consists of three numbers: MAJOR.MINOR.PATCH. Increase the MAJOR version when making incompatible changes, the MINOR version for backward-compatible additions or enhancements, and the PATCH version for backward-compatible bug fixes.

Model Metadata: Create comprehensive metadata for each model version. Include information such as the model's architecture, hyperparameters, training data, and any specific considerations or assumptions made during its development. This metadata serves as a reference and provides valuable context for future use and understanding.

Documentation: Maintain detailed documentation for each model version. Document the purpose of the model, its inputs and outputs, the underlying algorithms, and any limitations or assumptions. Include information on the training process, including the data preprocessing steps, hyperparameter settings, and model evaluation metrics.

Experiment Tracking: Use an experiment tracking tool to record the experiments conducted during model development. These tools capture information such as the code, data, hyperparameters, and evaluation metrics for each experiment. They provide a comprehensive record of the experiments conducted, facilitating reproducibility and troubleshooting.

Model Deployment Documentation: Document the steps required to deploy the model into a production environment. Include information about the required dependencies, deployment scripts, and any configuration settings. This documentation ensures that the deployment process is well-documented and can be replicated easily.

Change Logs: Maintain a change log that records the modifications made to each model version. Include a summary of the changes, the reasons behind them, and any potential impacts on model performance or behavior. Change logs help track the evolution of the models and provide transparency on updates and improvements.

Collaboration and Communication: Establish effective communication channels within the team to facilitate collaboration and knowledge sharing. Conduct regular code reviews, team discussions, or knowledge-sharing sessions to ensure that all team members are aware of model updates, changes, and documentation.

Accessibility and Organization: Ensure that the model versions and their associated documentation are easily accessible and well-organized. Use consistent naming conventions and directory structures to maintain a clear and structured repository of models. This makes it easier for team members to locate and understand different versions of the models.

Archiving and Backup: Regularly back up the models, documentation, and associated metadata to prevent loss of critical information. Establish an archiving process to store previous versions of the models securely. This ensures that historical versions are retained and can be referred to if needed.

By implementing robust model versioning and documentation practices, you can track the changes made to the models, maintain reproducibility, facilitate collaboration, and ensure that models can be effectively updated and maintained over time.

Chapter 20: Future Trends in Machine Learning

Machine learning is a rapidly evolving field that continuously presents new opportunities and challenges. In this final chapter, we will explore some of the future trends and advancements that are shaping the landscape of machine learning.

Deep Learning Advancements: Deep learning has revolutionized the field of machine learning with its ability to learn hierarchical representations from raw data. Future advancements in deep learning will focus on improving model architectures, training algorithms, and regularization techniques. We can expect more efficient and effective deep learning models that can handle even larger and more complex datasets.

Explainable AI: As machine learning models become more prevalent in critical decision-making processes, there is an increasing demand for explainable AI. Future research will focus on developing techniques and methods to interpret and explain the decisions made by complex models, providing transparency and building trust with users and stakeholders.

Federated Learning: Federated learning is an emerging approach that enables training machine learning models on decentralized data sources while preserving data privacy. It allows models to be trained collaboratively across multiple devices or organizations without sharing the raw data. This technique will gain prominence in scenarios where data privacy and security are paramount.

AutoML and Automated Model Deployment: AutoML (Automated Machine Learning) aims to automate the process of building, training, and deploying machine learning models. Future advancements in AutoML will simplify the machine learning workflow, making it accessible to a wider audience and reducing the need for expert knowledge. Automated model deployment techniques will also facilitate seamless integration of models into production systems.

Reinforcement Learning Breakthroughs: Reinforcement learning has shown promise in solving complex decision-making problems. Future research will focus on addressing challenges such as sample inefficiency, exploration-exploitation trade-offs, and generalization to complex real-world environments. We can expect breakthroughs in reinforcement learning algorithms and applications in areas such as robotics, healthcare, and autonomous systems.

Quantum Machine Learning: Quantum computing has the potential to revolutionize machine learning by solving computationally intensive problems more efficiently. Quantum machine learning algorithms and models will be developed to harness the power of quantum computing, enabling faster optimization, enhanced pattern recognition, and improved data analysis.

Transfer Learning for Small Data: Transfer learning has proven to be effective in leveraging pre-trained models for new tasks. Future research will focus on transfer learning techniques that can adapt to small data scenarios, where labeled data is limited. This will enable the application of machine learning in domains with scarce data availability.

Ethical and Fair AI: With the increasing impact of machine learning on society, there is a growing emphasis on ethical and fair AI. Future developments will focus on addressing biases, ensuring fairness, and reducing the potential negative impact of AI on vulnerable populations. The integration of ethics into the design, development, and deployment of machine learning models will be a key area of focus.

Edge Computing and IoT: The proliferation of Internet of Things (IoT) devices generates massive amounts of data that can be leveraged for machine learning. Edge computing, which enables data processing and model deployment closer to the data source, will play a significant role in real-time analysis and decision-making. Machine learning models will be optimized for resource-constrained edge devices, allowing for intelligent processing at the edge.

Human-AI Collaboration: Future machine learning systems will focus on enabling seamless collaboration between humans and AI. This includes interactive machine learning techniques that allow users to actively participate in the learning process, as well as AI systems that can effectively understand and respond to human input, leading to more intuitive and user-friendly experiences.

These are just a few of the many exciting future trends in machine learning. As the field continues to evolve, we can expect groundbreaking advancements that will shape the way we interact with technology, make decisions, and solve complex problems.

20.1 Emerging Technologies and Advancements

The field of machine learning is continuously evolving, and several emerging technologies and advancements are shaping its future. In this section, we will explore some of these technologies and their potential impact on machine learning.

Generative Adversarial Networks (GANs): GANs have gained significant attention for their ability to generate realistic synthetic data. This technology has applications in various domains, including image synthesis, text generation, and data augmentation. Future advancements in GANs will focus on improving stability, convergence, and the generation of high-quality and diverse samples.

Graph Neural Networks (GNNs): GNNs are specialized neural networks designed to model and process structured data represented as graphs. GNNs have shown great promise in areas such as social network analysis, recommendation systems, and drug discovery. Future advancements in GNNs will focus on enhancing their capabilities, scalability, and interpretability.

Reinforcement Learning in Real-World Applications: Reinforcement learning has demonstrated success in game-playing scenarios and simulated environments. Future advancements will focus on applying reinforcement learning to real-world applications, such as robotics, autonomous vehicles, and industrial automation. Overcoming challenges like sample efficiency, safety, and scalability will be key areas of research.

Quantum Machine Learning: Quantum computing has the potential to revolutionize machine learning by enabling faster computations and solving complex optimization problems more efficiently. Quantum machine learning algorithms are being developed to leverage the power of quantum computing for tasks like optimization, recommendation systems, and data analysis. Future advancements will focus on developing more robust quantum algorithms and hardware.

Edge Computing and Federated Learning: The proliferation of edge devices and IoT systems generates vast amounts of data that can be leveraged for machine learning. Edge computing allows for local data processing and model deployment on edge devices, reducing latency and enhancing privacy. Federated learning enables model training on distributed data without centralizing it, maintaining privacy and data security. Future advancements will focus on optimizing edge computing and federated learning techniques for resource-constrained devices and improving the efficiency of distributed learning.

Automated Machine Learning (AutoML): AutoML aims to automate the end-to-end process of machine learning, including model selection, hyperparameter optimization, and feature engineering. Future advancements in AutoML will focus on developing more advanced algorithms and tools that can handle complex tasks, domain-specific constraints, and large-scale datasets. AutoML will make machine learning accessible to non-experts and streamline the development and deployment of models.

Explainable AI (XAI): The interpretability and explainability of machine learning models have gained significant attention due to their impact on trust, accountability, and ethical considerations.

Future advancements in XAI will focus on developing techniques and frameworks to provide meaningful explanations for model decisions, enabling stakeholders to understand and trust the outputs of AI systems.

Meta-Learning: Meta-learning, or learning to learn, focuses on developing algorithms that can quickly adapt to new tasks and domains with limited data. Meta-learning allows models to leverage prior knowledge and experience to facilitate faster learning and better generalization. Future advancements in meta-learning will focus on improving sample efficiency, transferability, and scalability across a wide range of tasks.

Synthetic Data Generation: Generating synthetic data that closely resembles real data is an emerging area of research. Synthetic data generation techniques have the potential to address data privacy concerns, overcome data scarcity, and enhance data augmentation. Future advancements will focus on developing more sophisticated generative models that can capture the complexity and diversity of real-world data.

Ethical Considerations and Responsible AI: As machine learning becomes increasingly integrated into society, ethical considerations and responsible AI practices are gaining prominence. Future advancements will focus on developing frameworks, guidelines, and regulations to ensure fairness, transparency, and accountability in machine learning systems. Responsible AI practices will aim to mitigate bias, address social and cultural impact, and ensure that machine learning benefits all segments of society.

These emerging technologies and advancements in machine learning have the potential to transform various industries and drive innovation. By staying informed about these developments, researchers and practitioners can adapt their approaches and leverage these technologies to tackle complex problems and create positive societal impact.

20.2 Interdisciplinary Fields (AI, ML, and Robotics)

Machine learning is closely intertwined with other interdisciplinary fields, such as Artificial Intelligence (AI) and Robotics. The convergence of these fields has the potential to bring about transformative advancements and shape the future of technology. In this section, we will explore the relationship between AI, ML, and Robotics and their impact on various domains.

Artificial Intelligence (AI): AI is a broader field encompassing the study of intelligent agents and systems that can perceive, reason, learn, and make decisions. Machine learning is a subset of AI that focuses on algorithms and models that enable systems to learn from data. AI techniques, including machine learning, play a crucial role in enabling intelligent behavior in systems and facilitating human-like decision-making.

Robotics: Robotics combines AI, ML, and other disciplines to design and develop intelligent machines that can interact with the physical world. Robotics integrates perception, cognition, and control to enable robots to perform tasks autonomously or in collaboration with humans. ML algorithms and techniques are used in robotics to enhance perception, motion planning, control, and decision-making capabilities.

Reinforcement Learning in Robotics: Reinforcement learning is particularly relevant to robotics, as it enables robots to learn through trial and error and improve their behavior based on feedback from the environment. Reinforcement learning can be used to train robots to perform complex tasks, such as grasping objects, navigation, manipulation, and even advanced tasks like playing sports or assisting in healthcare settings.

Human-Robot Interaction: ML techniques are employed in human-robot interaction to enable robots to understand and respond to human behavior and intent. This includes natural language processing for communication, computer vision for human gesture recognition, and sentiment analysis for emotion detection. ML algorithms help robots adapt to human preferences and provide personalized assistance.

Autonomous Systems: The integration of AI, ML, and Robotics has led to the development of autonomous systems that can operate independently and make decisions without human intervention. Autonomous vehicles, drones, and smart home systems are examples of autonomous systems that leverage ML algorithms for perception, decision-making, and control. These systems have significant implications for transportation, healthcare, and other industries.

Cognitive Robotics: Cognitive robotics aims to build robots that possess cognitive abilities similar to human intelligence. ML techniques are used to enable robots to perceive, reason, learn, and plan in complex and uncertain environments. Cognitive robotics research focuses on understanding human cognition and translating those principles into algorithms and models for intelligent machines.

Ethical Considerations: The interdisciplinary nature of AI, ML, and Robotics raises important ethical considerations. As these technologies become more pervasive, it is crucial to address issues related to bias, privacy, transparency, and accountability. Ethical guidelines and frameworks are being developed to ensure that these technologies are used responsibly and align with societal values.

Synergies and Collaboration: The intersection of AI, ML, and Robotics fosters synergies and collaboration among researchers and practitioners from different fields. Collaboration between AI researchers, ML experts, and roboticists enables the exchange of knowledge, ideas, and best practices. It drives innovation and accelerates progress in developing intelligent systems and advanced robotics applications.

The close integration of AI, ML, and Robotics creates opportunities for advancements in diverse domains, such as healthcare, manufacturing, transportation, and entertainment. As these fields continue to converge, we can expect breakthroughs in intelligent systems, human-robot collaboration, and autonomous technologies that will shape the future of technology and society.

20.3 Ethical and Social Implications

As machine learning continues to advance and become integrated into various aspects of our lives, it is crucial to consider the ethical and social implications that arise from its use. In this section, we will explore some of these implications and discuss the importance of addressing them.

Bias and Fairness: Machine learning models can inadvertently perpetuate biases present in the data they are trained on, leading to unfair outcomes and discrimination. It is important to address bias in data collection, preprocessing, and model training to ensure fairness and prevent unintended harm to individuals or groups. Techniques such as bias detection, debiasing, and fairness-aware learning are being developed to mitigate bias and promote fairness in machine learning.

Privacy and Data Protection: Machine learning often relies on vast amounts of data, raising concerns about privacy and data protection. It is essential to handle data in a way that respects individual privacy rights and complies with relevant regulations. Techniques such as federated learning, secure multi-party computation, and differential privacy are being developed to enable privacy-preserving machine learning without compromising the utility of the models.

Transparency and Explainability: The black-box nature of some machine learning models can make it challenging to understand and explain their decision-making process. This lack of transparency can erode trust and hinder accountability. Efforts are being made to develop explainable AI techniques that provide interpretable explanations for model predictions, enabling users to understand the reasoning behind decisions made by the models.

Social Impact and Job Displacement: The widespread adoption of machine learning and automation technologies has the potential to impact the workforce and job markets. While these technologies can improve efficiency and productivity, they may also lead to job displacement and socioeconomic inequalities. It is crucial to consider the social implications and develop strategies for reskilling and upskilling workers to adapt to the changing job landscape.

Ethical Frameworks and Guidelines: The development and use of machine learning should be guided by ethical frameworks and guidelines. These frameworks can provide principles and guidelines to ensure responsible and ethical use of machine learning technologies. Organizations and researchers are working towards establishing ethical standards that promote transparency, accountability, and the protection of individual rights and well-being.

Human-AI Collaboration: As machine learning becomes more pervasive, it is important to consider the role of humans in the decision-making process. Human-AI collaboration models should be designed to leverage the strengths of both humans and machines, taking into account human values, preferences, and ethical considerations. Collaboration between humans and AI systems can lead to more informed and responsible decision-making.

Accountability and Governance: There is a need for clear accountability and governance frameworks to ensure that the development, deployment, and use of machine learning models are carried out responsibly. This includes mechanisms for auditing and monitoring the performance and impact of the models, as well as legal and regulatory frameworks that address potential risks and harms.

Cultural and Ethical Sensitivity: Machine learning models can be influenced by cultural biases present in the data and the algorithms used. It is crucial to develop culturally sensitive and context-aware models that respect diverse perspectives and avoid reinforcing stereotypes or discriminatory practices. Ensuring cultural and ethical sensitivity in machine learning requires diverse and inclusive representation in the development and evaluation processes.

By actively addressing the ethical and social implications of machine learning, we can maximize its potential benefits while mitigating risks and harms. Collaboration among researchers, policymakers, and stakeholders is essential to create a responsible and ethical framework for the development, deployment, and use of machine learning technologies.

20.4 Opportunities and Challenges in Machine Learning

Machine learning offers immense opportunities across various industries and domains. However, it also comes with its own set of challenges. In this section, we will explore the opportunities and challenges that lie ahead in the field of machine learning.

Opportunities:

Enhanced Decision-Making: Machine learning enables organizations to make data-driven decisions by extracting insights and patterns from large volumes of data. It empowers businesses to gain a competitive edge, optimize processes, and improve customer experiences.

Automation and Efficiency: Machine learning automates repetitive tasks, reducing human effort and improving operational efficiency. It enables organizations to automate complex processes, optimize resource allocation, and streamline workflows, leading to cost savings and productivity gains.

Personalized Experiences: Machine learning allows organizations to personalize products, services, and recommendations based on individual preferences and behavior. This leads to enhanced customer experiences, increased engagement, and improved customer satisfaction.

Healthcare and Medicine: Machine learning has the potential to revolutionize healthcare by enabling early disease detection, personalized treatment plans, and improved patient outcomes. ML algorithms can analyze medical records, genetic data, and imaging to assist in diagnosis and treatment decisions.

Natural Language Processing: Advances in natural language processing (NLP) enable machines to understand and generate human language, opening doors for applications such as chatbots, voice assistants, sentiment analysis, and machine translation. NLP facilitates human-machine interaction and enhances user experiences.

Challenges:

Data Quality and Availability: Machine learning heavily relies on high-quality data. However, ensuring data quality, availability, and accessibility remains a challenge. Data may be incomplete, biased, or of low quality, leading to suboptimal model performance. Collecting and curating large-scale, labeled datasets can be time-consuming and expensive.

Interpretability and Explainability: Many machine learning models, especially deep learning models, are often considered black boxes, making it difficult to interpret their decision-making process. Explainable AI techniques are needed to provide insights into model predictions and explain the rationale behind them.

Algorithmic Bias and Fairness: Machine learning models can inadvertently amplify biases present in the data, leading to unfair outcomes and discrimination. Addressing algorithmic bias and ensuring fairness in machine learning models is a critical challenge that requires careful consideration and mitigation strategies.

Ethical Considerations: As machine learning models become more pervasive, ethical considerations become increasingly important. It is crucial to address issues related to privacy, data protection, accountability, and societal impact. Developing ethical frameworks and guidelines is necessary to guide responsible and ethical use of machine learning.

Scalability and Efficiency: As datasets and computational requirements grow, scalability and efficiency become crucial. Training large-scale models and deploying them in real-time, resource-constrained environments pose challenges. Developing scalable algorithms, leveraging distributed computing, and optimizing model architectures are areas of focus.

Continuous Learning and Adaptability: Machine learning models need to continuously adapt to new data and evolving environments. Developing techniques for continuous learning, model updating, and adaptation to concept drift is important to maintain model performance over time.

Human-Machine Collaboration: Balancing the roles of humans and machines in decision-making processes is an ongoing challenge. Designing effective human-machine collaboration systems that leverage the strengths of both humans and machines while ensuring transparency and accountability is crucial.

Navigating these challenges and capitalizing on the opportunities in machine learning requires interdisciplinary collaboration, continuous learning, and adherence to ethical principles. As the field evolves, addressing these challenges will lead to more responsible, fair, and impactful use of machine learning technologies.

Congratulations on completing this comprehensive guide to machine learning! We hope it has provided you with valuable insights and guidance for your journey in the field of Machine Learning. Good luck with your future endeavors!

Disclaimer & Copyright

 First Printing, 2023

www.ingramcontent.com/pod-product-compliance
Lightning Source LLC
LaVergne TN
LVHW080006210926
848481LV00011B/2958